MW00915029

The Comedian vs Cancer

The Show Must Go On

a memoir

DANIEL STOLFI

The Comedian vs Cancer
Copyright © 2022 by Daniel Stolfi

All rights reserved. No part of this publication may be
reproduced, distributed, or transmitted in any form or by
any means, including photocopying, recording, or other
electronic or mechanical methods, without the prior
written permission of the author, except in the case of
brief quotations embodied in critical reviews and certain
other non-commercial uses permitted by copyright law.

Tellwell Talent
www.tellwell.ca

ISBN
978-0-2288-6328-1 (Hardcover)
978-0-2288-6327-4 (Paperback)
978-0-2288-6329-8 (eBook)

For Etta Rose.

"I love you like the moons of Jupiter."

Contents

ACT III

A Note from the Author

I didn't intend to write a memoir about my cancer experience. I initially just wanted to write about what I was going through in real time, in a Word document, so I could maybe look back on it one day whenever I needed a reminder that life isn't so bad. This Word document sat at about 70 pages for several months because I was so physically ill that I couldn't find the strength or mental fortitude to actually sit down in a chair at a computer and write anymore. So it stayed a Word document, tucked away in a file on my parents' desktop computer for a couple of years. I did, however, keep a journal, which I wrote in almost every night while lying in bed. This was much more comfortable than sitting in my parents' computer room staring at a white screen and blinking black curser. My parents still have a computer room. True story.

I knew I wanted to revisit the document at some point post-treatment, but I was so consumed in the work I was doing on my solo show and getting my acting career up and running again, that it slipped to the bottom of the "To Do" pile. As I shared my story on stage, I realized that there was only so much I could share in a one-hour live show that could never fully encompass the scope of what it was truly like to face cancer for two years. But the Word document continued to sit unchanged on my parents' computer, collecting digital dust. I began to think that maybe this document wasn't meant to be anything other than a project that forever stayed at the bottom of the "To Do" pile.

In February of 2011, however, with just two hundred bucks in my pocket, I took a bus to New York City to attend a two-week intensive comedy workshop with the Upright Citizens Brigade, a world-famous improvisation company where some of the best and brightest comedians honed their skills to maybe one day be on *Saturday Night Live*. My days started at 8 a.m., where I threw myself into improvisation exercises and scenes with a variety of like-minded comedians until noon. In the evenings, I would perform stand-up comedy wherever I could get a spot, at the glut of open-mic nights around Manhattan. I rented an Airbnb deep in Brooklyn at the cheapest price I could afford, and with just $200 to get me through two weeks, travelling in and out of Manhattan was a once-a-day kind of deal. As a result, I had five hours to kill every day, in the middle of the day, in the dead of winter, in the heart of New York City. So, I went to the only place I could think of to spend five hours that was warm, quiet and free: The New York City Public Library. There, I would sit in the Rose Main Reading Room at a wooden desk, with my laptop open, typing madly about my cancer experience, while listening to rap music by Tupac and Snoop Dogg through my generic-brand earphones. I did this every day for the entirety of my two-week stay. The memories and details of my cancer experience were still so fresh in my mind that the words just flew out of me. After my trip, I knew I had to keep working on this memoir and look into what needed to be done to get it published.

Over the years I chipped away at it, asking friends to read it and offer notes. I approached literary professionals to get advice on how to get it published. I took a number of memoir-writing workshops to help write and rewrite. I approached ten literary agents, with query letters and 30-page "chapter by chapter" breakdowns, most of whom turned me down with a polite generic rejection letter. Two agents, however, were more detailed in their response and let me know that the material was "too close to them" and that a memoir is "very hard to sell" so they weren't interested. I became discouraged and let the memoir sit for a while in a much larger Word document, now on my laptop computer.

Then, an interesting thing happened. A global pandemic. You may have heard about it or been on the planet when it all went down, but it was a shot in the arm, a reminder that once again, life can change in an instant. A reminder to do the things you love while you still can. I shared my story on stage for a few reasons and they are the same reasons I chose to self-publish this book:

1. There came a point in my treatment where I knew death was very much a possibility. If I didn't get on stage again to share my story, I would have regretted it. I just wanted to perform one more time. What

happened after that would be considered gravy. As for this memoir, I would hate to have this story just sit in a Word document as I grow old, and one day be sitting on my deathbed thinking *I wish I had published that memoir!*

2. I was told "no" by a lot of people. A lot. And this scared me. I began to feel that this story wasn't worth telling because "professionals" told me so. Now, I'm using that as motivation. When I initially told people I wanted to perform a comedic one-person show about cancer, they looked at me like I was crazy. "You can't make cancer funny." "Someone else has already done a show about cancer." "No one wants to watch a show about cancer." It went on and on. Don't let someone else crush your vision just because they can't see it as clearly as you do. The noes scared me. But I can no longer let them.

3. And this is the biggest reason. As I got older and further removed from my cancer experience, I learned of more and more close friends, family and cancer community brothers and sisters beginning their cancer journeys. It seems that every month, I hear about another friend, colleague or family member being diagnosed, or worse, another friend, colleague or family member losing their lives to the illness. Maybe my story can help someone out there who needs it. Even if it helps one person, I know it will have made a difference.

I hope you enjoy this memoir. I write this for the survivors, the ones we've lost and the ones we love. Thank you for saying "yes" and taking a chance on this book.

ACT I

Cheating Death

"**I**'m gonna go for a sprint!" I shouted in a drunken slur.

"You're such an idiot, Stolfi!" my friend called back.

I took off down the busy Toronto sidewalk as fast as I could, past the piles of cardboard boxes and overflowed garbage bins lining Bloor Street. I was really picking up steam, pumping my arms and legs, while my cheap black Italian Guido dress shoes propelled me forward as they hit the concrete sidewalk. Cheap black Italian Guido dress shoes were all the rage in 2007 for any single, 25-year-old Italian living in the big city. I hit a patch of black ice. The thin layer of frozen water, camouflaging itself as pavement, hurled me forward and onto the ground. The city streetlights appeared to bend—orange and yellow streaks of light flashing before me—as gravity took control of my body in flight. "Brace!" my brain screamed, as my intoxicated instincts kicked in. I turned my body, seemingly weightless now, letting my right shoulder cushion the bulk of my upper torso as it crashed down to the ground. Alas, the speed I was running, mixed with my weight crashing into the cold pedestrian walkway equalled something I like to call "Einstein's Theory of Drunken Stupidity."

As soon as I hit the pavement, I heard two things. The first was the thud of my body hitting the ground, my shoulder acting as a bass drum, and the pavement, the drummer. The second was the sounds of "ooohs" and "ahhhs" from onlookers sitting on the cement steps of an ice-cream shop. I quickly got to my feet and immediately felt a sharp stinging pain in my right shoulder. I was sure I had popped it out of place, but the adrenalin from running and the fact that I was drunk numbed the pain enough for me to simultaneously laugh and cry as I hobbled past the hipsters on the steps. Embarrassed, I rejoined my friends.

"Get in the cab, would ya?" my friend Matt ordered.

"Guys, I think I dislocated my shoulder," I mumbled.

"Sure, buddy. You can move it, can't you? You probably just bruised it, ya pussy."

The cab moved slowly in the 2 a.m. post-bar gridlock traffic. Destination: Matt's apartment. The night was just starting. The pain, however, was telling me to maybe rethink my decision to keep the party going, as it shot through my entire body almost sobering me up instantly. As the taxi crept along the snow-covered streets, each speed bump and pothole sent a jolt of pain through my shoulder.

We entered Matt's apartment and he began to closely examine my ailment like the "never went to medical school" doctor that he was.

"Try to move your arm," he instructed.

As I attempted to comply with his rather simple request, my pain receptors kicked into high gear and sent an urgent message to my brain, commanding it to deliver a thunderstorm of electricity into my feeble joint. I grunted like a caveman, resorting to primal vocabulary to describe my discomfort while maintaining a tough and manly exterior in front of my friend. Ignoring my apelike grunts, Matt lifted my arm further still, straight out to my side, now parallel to the floor. "Ah, FUCK!" I yelled, through gritted teeth.

"Oh relax," his girlfriend called out. "It's not dislocated. If you can move it, then it's not dislocated."

Unqualified friend's girlfriend knows best, I thought. I was in too much pain to stay there and argue about the correct diagnosis. I decided it was best to head back to my place for the night. "Just shake it off, man," Matt prescribed as I slipped out the apartment door. My friends give such good advice.

I arrived at my apartment and made my way to the bathroom to assess the damage in the mirror. Maybe seeing it would give me a better understanding of how bad this really was. Taking off my shirt was almost impossible. I couldn't lift my injured arm over my head without an incredible amount of pain so I kept it tucked tightly to my side. Thankfully, I was wearing a button-up shirt. After undoing a few buttons, I was able to slip it off over my left shoulder. I then hung my torso down toward the washroom's white tiled floor to shake my right arm loose. I returned to an upright position and stood face to face with my reflection in the bathroom mirror. My right collarbone looked to be pushing my skin upward and outward, as if bursting through the flesh. *Remember when Lady Gaga had those weird shoulder implants, like spikes shooting up from underneath*

*her skin? Or when that tag-team wrestling duo "The Legion of Doom"
wore those spiky shoulder pads . . .?* These references may be of no
significance to you, but regardless, it looked like that.

I'm deformed! I thought in horror. *I'm going to puke.* My olive
complexion drained from my face, leaving me with a gaunt
and ghostly appearance. I started to feel faint, as the blood in
my body seemed to boil from within. I was dizzy, the room
was spinning, my face in the mirror blurred and I began to
fall to the washroom floor. "Brace!" my brain screamed for
the second time in an hour. My left hand gripped the white
porcelain sink as my knees began to buckle. It was no use; my
hands were limp and gravity was in control of my destiny now.
My chin struck the sink with a thundering crack. A vicious
shockwave travelled through my head, rattling my teeth as it
proceeded to my brain. Blackout.

I woke up what seemed to be a few minutes later but could
have been several minutes. I had no way of knowing. Large spots
of blood were splattered on the white cookie-cutter bathroom
tiles found in many old Toronto apartment buildings built in
the '60s. The cold floor gave my body a feeling of comfort. I
immediately thought of my roommate and best friend, Stefan.
Is he home? I heard him snoring through the door, fast asleep,
no idea what was transpiring in the washroom. Being the nice
guy that I am, I didn't want to bother him. I rationalized to
myself, *This is my mess and I am going to have to get myself out of it.*
I staggered to my feet, hoisting myself up with my left hand,
now slightly more capable than before, and steadied my weight
on the sink. I took a look in the mirror one more time, now

to assess the damage done to my face. I was still ghostly white with sunken glossed-over eyes, but this time my ugly mug had an extra feature. A quarter-sized section of my chin had burst open and thick chunks of skin were now protruding from the wound. The blood oozed out slowly, dripping periodically into the sink basin. I quickly rinsed my face with cold water and took a deep breath, attempting to calm myself and find focus. My head was ringing and my jaw was aching. I looked down at the spots of blood on the floor and made note that I would clean them up in the morning, before Stefan woke up. Like I said, it was my mess.

I turned off the bathroom lights, staggered into my room across the hall and fell into bed. My jaw was screaming, my teeth were clenched and my head was pounding. The shoulder, still throbbing, now took second fiddle to the chin but still acted as a reminder that sprinting down an icy sidewalk, drunk, at two in the morning, is never a good idea. I lay on my back and closed my eyes. Blackout.

I woke in the morning to a vicious headache and a horrible pain in my right shoulder. I attempted to call out to Stefan, but when I opened my mouth to speak, I felt a sudden stinging shock force my jaw shut. The only audible noise I could make was a clenched jawed murmur for help. "Herp!" I called out like the Tin Man needing his oilcan.

No response. I rolled onto my good shoulder and shimmied out of bed and onto my feet, dizzy. The parquet floors were dancing beneath my feet as I wobbled toward the bathroom. I saw the drops of blood, now a rusty brown, on the white tiled floor. I grabbed some toilet paper with my good hand and dampened it with warm water. I wiped up the drops, caked on and stubborn to remove, with as much vigour as I could muster. I felt like I was cleaning up after a crime scene. *I must hide all evidence of this happening!* The only crime committed here was another night of complete drunken idiocy.

I got back up to my feet and took another look in the mirror. My chin looked like it had taken a shot from a rifle, while my collarbone still looked like it was ready to break free from my body. I wanted to touch the wound, dark black and seemingly deeper and wider than what I remembered. I'm not good with the sight of blood, especially my own. It makes me nauseous. I was an absolute mess, and I still felt drunk.

I slipped my pants off, stepped into the bathtub and turned on the shower. The warm water felt nice on my back as I stood facing away from the steady stream of flowing water. I stood there for a moment and tried to reflect on what had happened, what *was* happening. Suddenly, weakness swept through my body from my head down to my feet, and with nothing to hold on to but a slippery tiled bathroom wall, I collapsed in the tub. The back of my head cracked down on the metal bathtub drain, just missing the thick stainless steel faucet.

Blackout.

My eyes opened quickly and I gasped for air. *Am I drowning?* The water was crashing down on me, relentless and unforgiving, seemingly punishing me for being such an idiot. I called out desperately for help, ignoring the shooting pain in my jaw, as I suddenly realized I could drown. "Stefan!" I shouted. I heard a knock on the door followed by a familiar voice coming from the other side.

"Are you okay?" Stefan called out in his subtle Bulgarian accent.

"No," I responded.

"Do you want me to come in?"

I pondered this for a moment. *Do I want him to come in? Do I want him to see me lying naked in the bathtub while water crashes down on my ripped-up face and beaten body with bloody rags of toilet paper in and around the garbage bin?*

"No! I'll be okay." I managed to shimmy away from the water and was surprised to find myself lying in a rather comfortable position. My left leg dangled precariously over the edge of the tub as the cool air gently chilled my wet skin. My face was now out of the shower's relentless downpour, settling my mind. I was not drowning. The water felt soothing again as it poured down onto my body. I lay there for a moment and reflected on what was happening (I like to reflect). *This is the lowest point in my entire life*, I thought. *I did this to myself and I have no one to lean on and no one to blame but me. I am a pathetic mess.*

I threw both of my legs over the basin's ledge and pressed my back up against the opposite wall. I thrust my hips forward, tossing my junk skyward in all its sloppy glory and pushed off the bottom of the tub with my good hand, hoisting myself over the edge and onto my feet. I towelled myself off gingerly, hobbled to my room and plunked myself down on my bed.

"You want me to make you breakfast?" Stefan asked, taking in my crumpled form atop my red duvet cover.

"I fucked up," I mumbled.

"You need to go to the hospital, man. Call Niheer. He has a car."

Stefan made me a sausage and egg breakfast and brought it to me in bed. Breakfast in bed by my Bulgarian roommate was almost as romantic as it sounds. "Tanks, man," I said through gritted teeth. I couldn't move my jaw to physically chew the food, so I sucked on the scrambled eggs and swallowed them like a dolphin throws back sardines at MarineLand. I called Niheer, another one of my best buddies.

"I fucked up." My voice cracked before I welled up and a wave of emotion flooded through my body. Tears streamed down my face as I began to sob. I was officially scared. "I fucked up, man. I need your help."

"What happened?"

"Can you drive me to the hospital?"

"Of course, man. I just need to get my shit together and I'll head over. Just give me a couple of minutes." I have great friends.

Niheer arrived in ten minutes and took me straight to Toronto East General Hospital. I was seen straight away. My shoulder was X-rayed and my busted chin stitched up. "Your stitches are in the shape of a star," the doctor said. "You mentioned you were an actor, right?"

"Yeah," I grunted.

"You're gonna be a star. Must be a sign." He laughed.

I smiled . . . painfully.

My mother happened to be in Toronto that day. I needed

my mom. I called her to let her know I was at the hospital. When she entered the room, I tried not to cry but instead laugh it off.

"Can I see your shoulder?" she asked. I was reluctant to show her because I had secretly gotten a tattoo when I was 18 on my upper back just behind the busted shoulder. For some reason, I thought she could still get me in trouble. Truth is, I didn't want to disappoint her. No one in my family had a tattoo. I was the rebel.

"Uh, just so you know, I have a tattoo!" I blurted out before lowering my blue hospital gown to let her take a peek.

"Oh, I don't care! What does it say?" she asked curiously.

"Commedia e Tragedia," I said sheepishly. Italian for "comedy and tragedy," written in cursive. It was an ode to my theatre roots and apparently the perfect tattoo to describe my life and what was about to come.

"I love it!" she declared.

"Thanks, Ma."

~

To this day, I always wonder if this was the moment that the cells in my body got so shook up that they didn't know what to do. They didn't know how to do their job. Heal my wounds and then die. Was it just coincidence? Was life trying to tell me to slow down? I didn't know it at the time, but this was the moment that began the most challenging and ruthless period of my life. At the age of 25 my life was about to change forever. I didn't think it could get worse than this . . . but then it did.

Warning Signs

February 15th, 2008, roughly two months after the shoulder incident, Stefan shuffled his way out of his cramped bedroom, wearing his brown furry torn-up slippers and dirty grey sweatpants. "Yo, can I have the apartment tonight? My girl is coming over for Valentine's Day."

He was a day late, but who was counting?

We lived in a dodgy eight-storey apartment complex in the east end of Toronto. It was a two-bedroom with parquet floors and a tiny kitchen. A touch of mould created a border around the windowpanes. But at $500 a month we weren't complaining about any possible health risk. After all, we were a couple of 25-year-old guys pursuing our dreams in the big city.

He wanted me out of the apartment for the night so he could, *I assume*, make sweet love to his girlfriend on the day after the most romantic day of the year.

"Yeah, no problem bro," I assured him. "I'll just shoot up to Ni's for the night."

"Cool. Thanks, man."

I called Niheer, who lived uptown with our mutual friend, Chris, and made plans to head over to their condo. Their place had amenities our shithole of an apartment could only dream of. They lived in an area of Toronto that is coined "Young and Eligible." All the people who live in these condo complexes are young, single, nine-to-five work types, who live for the weekends and party hard. The condo was swank, clean, and came with a party room, workout facilities, rooftop view of the city and most importantly a swimming pool. I tossed my lime-green trunks into my trusty knapsack and was on my way.

I exited my building. The cold February air punched me in the face like a swift jab from a seasoned boxer. I took a deep breath. The tiny hairs in my nose tingled as they quickly froze. I felt this strange energy surge throughout my entire body. It was a familiar ill feeling; one I had felt before with past bouts of the flu. This time, however, it felt unlike any other flu-like symptoms I had experienced before. This time, it felt different. The ill feeling was deeper, almost in my bones.

The snow was piled high on the sidewalks, so much so that people were actually walking on the street. The deep tire grooves left by the few cars that were slowly crawling down the street were a better bet for pedestrian travel. This was an unusual amount of snow for Toronto. As I approached the road, my eyes caught something in the distance that piqued my interest. Footprints and thin grooves in the snow led to what looked to be several large black garbage bags on the sidewalk. I cautiously followed the tracks. The bags of trash slowly turned into something more familiar, now appearing red and fuzzy. *Is that a jacket?* my mind pondered. A small white cart, once camouflaged by the snow, came into focus as well.

It appeared to be perched up against the red heap, the black wheels poking out of the snow. As I got closer, it became very apparent that this red furry bag of garbage wasn't garbage at all, but a person! *They aren't moving. Are they dead? How long have they been here? They could be frozen to death!* All of these things raced through my mind. I quickly rushed to their side. "Are you all right?" I asked calmly.

"Help!" an old woman's voice cried out meekly. "My back!" she continued. *She's alive!* "Please. Pick me up!" she called out. I couldn't believe this was happening.

"I don't want to hurt your back, so I'm going to lift lightly," I warned her.

"Just yank me up. I have a brace on. You can't hurt me." She was face down, her voice barely audible, her hands naked. I spotted her gloves a few feet away. I had no idea how long she had been lying there. *Am I dreaming?*

"Are you sure?" I asked one last time, as I reached my arms down toward her mid-section, preparing myself to hoist her up. I felt a jolt of pain in my shoulder, a sudden reminder of my fall just a couple of months ago. *Nope, definitely not dreaming.*

"Yes! Please, just yank me up!" she insisted. I reached my good arm under her stomach and pulled her up with all my strength, my bad arm acting as support, like the guiding hand when shooting a basketball. I brought her to her feet. She grabbed on to the cart and steadied herself. She stood all of four-and-a-half feet tall. I reached for her gloves and helped her place them on her cold red hands. Her grey curly hair was covered in snow. I brushed it off gently. "Are you okay?" I asked.

"You are an angel!" she cried out. Her thick English accent came through. Her face buried in the snow had muffled it out just moments ago. "An angel!"

"Oh, I don't know about that," I replied.

"An angel sent from heaven." I brushed the snow off her red felt coat.

"You shouldn't be out here. It's dangerous. Where is your home?" I asked. She motioned back to an apartment building just past mine. "I'm going to take you back home, okay?"

"What is your name, angel?" she asked.

"Daniel. And you?"

"Jane. Jane Benson," she said as if it should ring a bell, leaving a slight pause for me to say something. I said nothing. So she continued, "My grandfather is a Benson from the Benson and Hedges cigarette company." She said this with a smile. *Maybe she's senile?* I thought to myself.

"Well, that's pretty cool," I said as we slowly walked toward the front door of her building. "Those are some classic cigarettes . . . but I don't smoke," I added, just trying to fill the awkward moment.

"God has amazing plans for you, son," she said. I smiled and helped her into the lobby.

"I'm just glad you're safe now. Don't go outside when it's like this, all right?"

"Thank you, child. You're an angel!" she said one last time. I headed back out into the cold. *That was weird*, I thought.

The weakness in my bones rattled throughout my body

again. I stepped back out into the tire grooves of snow on the road and took a deep breath. *I'll be all right, God has big plans for me . . . I wonder what they are.*

I rationalized that I just needed to eat something. Feed a fever, starve a cold as they say . . . or is it the other way around? I headed toward a sandwich shop and ordered an Italian meatball sub, just like any good Italian boy would. Then I made my way up to Niheer's apartment.

"Dude, I feel like shit," I told Niheer as I threw my sandwich onto his granite countertop and ripped open the paper wrapping. Tomato sauce and green peppers dripped onto the countertop while I inhaled the sandwich. "I'll wipe it down when I'm done."

"You're like a garbage disposal," he told me, and I couldn't disagree. I've always had a ferocious appetite. If I was out for a meal with my friends and they couldn't finish their fries I'd be the one to make quick work of them. It must have been my Italian upbringing. Personally, I blame my nonna for feeding me copious amounts of cake, pasta and my absolute favourite, toasted homemade bread with olive oil and salt. She wouldn't let me or my older brother and sister play until all the food was gone.

I wiped the drips and drabs of sauce off my face with a paper towel and let out a nice belch. "I think I'm feeling a lot better now. Let's go for a swim."

We were the only ones in the pool that night, just the three of us. Niheer (Ni), my Indian friend, who would give his right arm to you if you ever needed it, and Chris, a soft-spoken introvert with a gleaming smile, who loved the ladies as much as he loved his biceps. Chris was the kind of guy who read books like *The Game* and *He's Just Not That Into You*, just to get a step up on a girl he was trying to bring home after a night at the club.

"She was a brunette but I didn't even notice until the next morning," he bragged before dunking his head under the water. "I thought she was a redhead!" he continued after coming up for air.

"What is it with you and redheads, man?" Ni joked.

We jumped into the pool and instantly went into childhood mode, challenging each other to stupid competitions. We started playing this game where we stood on one end of the pool, held our breaths, dove under the water, and pushed off the wall as hard as we could to try and swim all the way to the other end. I was able to accomplish this feat twice.

"Beat that, bro!" I called out. The pool must have been forty feet in length, so I felt pretty good about myself when I came up for air at the other end.

"Yeah, yeah, you're so great," Ni said sarcastically. "Let's go for a sauna!"

"You got a sauna?!" I asked.

"Yeah, it's not, like, gay or anything."

"I never said it was, bro."

By covering the thermostat with a damp cloth, we could outsmart the built-in temperature control and get that baby cooking. "This is good," I said. "Sweat this flu out." The smell of cedar permeated the air. The temperature ticked higher. I felt the weakness in my bones again, and this time I knew it wasn't going to go away, no matter how much sweating or sandwich eating I did. "Guys, I think I gotta get out of here," I told them.

"Cool man, we're gonna soak it in a bit more," Ni replied. I wanted to chalk it up to the fact that we let the sauna get too hot or that I was still hungry, but my friends both seemed fine, and deep down I knew that it wasn't the sauna, it wasn't hunger, it was something else. It was time to go home.

I don't care if Stefan is having sex, I thought. *I need my bed.*

There was something about that moment that I will never forget. It was the one moment that, when I look back on, I knew was the last bit of feeling somewhat healthy that I would get to appreciate for a very long time. And there was something inside me on that day that knew that too. I think they call it instinct. My mind raced, my stomach turned, my gut screamed at me to pay attention. Something was wrong. I wondered if this was the grand plan that God had for one of his angels.

Sick Is Not an Option

The next morning, I woke up back at my apartment still feeling weaker than I ever had before. My head ached, my muscles hurt. The mere thought of taking a shower was daunting. I stumbled through my morning routine and then managed to stumble to the local pharmacy down the street. Every step felt like I had boulders strapped to my legs. A mother pushing a baby in a stroller through the snow whizzed by, leaving me in her dust.

My mind raced. *Now is not the time to get sick. Your acting career is starting to take off and you have too many projects on the go.*

I just finished shooting a pilot for a television special with my sketch comedy troupe, "Fade to Brown." It was a South Asian–based comedy troupe, and I played the token white guy.

"But I'm Italian," I told them.

"That counts. You all look the same to us," my troupe mate and friend, Shawn, assured me. *I can't let them down. Now is not the time to get sick.*

I was getting lots of work from the promotional company I was working for and I was about to go to Kingston for a gig as Captain Morgan. Let me explain a little more here. How do

I say this? I was *Captain Morgan*. Yes, Captain Morgan, the rum guy. Every weekend I dressed up as a swashbuckling buccaneer, glued a moustache and goatee onto my face, wore a long, ratty, curly-haired wig and travelled to bars all over Canada. I would let drunk university students know how wonderful Captain Morgan's Original Spiced Rum and cola was, while frat boys made eye love to a couple of my scantily dressed assistants, aptly called "The Morganettes." I would hand out free T-shirts and swag to those who could beat me in a game of rock paper scissors. It paid the rent and kept me on my toes. I got to act four times a week, which was not bad for an actor starting out. On top of all this, I just finished shooting a couple of episodes for a television comedy series called *Cock'd Gunns*, which would go on to win two awards for best Canadian comedy. Go figure. Life was heading in the right direction. I was young and hungry to practice and perfect my craft. I was finally getting approached by casting directors and producers in the industry who wanted to work with me. I was waiting to hear back from a prominent talent agency in the city that I really wanted to work with. I was working on real TV shows and real commercials; I was in the process of writing a one-person show, which had been accepted into the Toronto Fringe Festival for that coming summer, a rather prominent theatre festival in the Toronto artist scene. *Now is not the time to get sick.*

I pulled my heavy legs up and down the aisles of a nearby pharmacy, looking for the right drugs to do the trick. I asked the pharmacist, "What can you recommend for cough and cold or sinus type stuff?"

The pharmacist, a man with a thick black moustache and bushy eyebrows, looked at me and said, "There's a lot of that going around these days. You should try the Nyquil Cough and Cold tabs."

"Nyquil better than Buckley's?" I asked.

"Sure," he responded, seemingly impartial.

I picked up a box of twelve pills and was out the door.

It all just kept getting worse, though. The coughing was becoming more and more consistent. It was this dry, hacking cough that kept coming back as if on a routine schedule. Like clockwork, every fifteen or twenty seconds, I would cough. At night, I was forced to sleep on my back. It's the standard hospital bed position. I had no idea I was foreshadowing my own future at the time. Then even lying on my back became a challenge. For starters, what felt like the weight of a small child sitting on my chest constricted my breathing and forced me to sit up to let out a tirade of dry, hacking coughs. My solution to this problem was to prop pillows between my back and the wall so I could sleep in a seated position. This mildly alleviated the pressure on my chest and allowed for some semblance of sleep.

When I woke up what must have been only a couple of hours later, my sheets were soaked right through as if I had pissed my bed. I was drenched in sweat. *This flu is brutal!* I thought to myself. *Um, this is more than just the flu,* a little voice piped up, which I quickly silenced. I tried to console myself with the fact that I had sweat in the night before, so it wasn't that out of the ordinary. Those night sweats were the result of really muggy summer nights, however, and this was the dead of winter, but I kept telling myself I'd be fine.

This pattern continued for several days and nights. I flipped my sheets and washed them, or just hoped they dried out before the next time I slept. At 25 years old, I didn't care much for laundry. Plus it was $1.50 a load! Disgusting. You know how much I could get for a buck fifty?

I was determined to not let this flu, or whatever the hell it was, control my life. I carried on with things as I normally would, but with a nagging cough coupled with an aching body. I worked long hours as a promotion rep and actor. I wrote and rehearsed sketches with my comedy troupe. I played indoor soccer once a week and I went to the gym five times a week without giving it too much thought. *It will pass just like every other time that I've been sick. I'm young and healthy and my body will take care of itself.*

I started to feel a sharp pain on the left side of my chest about two weeks after the first ill feelings set in. The pain throbbed inside my chest, increasing in intensity and then easing up. I figured it was just a cramp that I could walk off. It didn't let up. It didn't go away. And I couldn't walk it off. I went to the grocery store in a last-ditch effort to avoid going to the doctor and purchased a variety of different fruits, with the mindset that eating them would help ease the pain. *Fruit! Fruit is full of healthy vitamins, right?* I was dying for relief. *Yeah, fruit will save me! FRUIT!* I was young, dumb and desperate.

I went to rehearsals with my sketch troupe, coughing and concealing . . . I went to work, coughing and concealing, I went to the gym, coughing and concealing, until I finally went to the doctor, coughing and complaining.

It was a small walk-in clinic right beside my apartment, perfectly capable of diagnosing the common cold, or the flu, or at worst, pneumonia. I was starting to think it could be pneumonia.

I got called in to the examination room. Every exam room I've ever been in is the same. A square cube with white or off-white cinder-block walls, a small window that overlooks a parking lot, posters and pictures of the human anatomy hanging randomly on the pale blue cupboards, a plastic office chair and a padded table with a piece of white parchment paper running along its middle. I wondered how many bare sweaty asses had sat on that table in the past and however many it was, did that parchment paper really act as an adequate ass-sweat protector? *I highly doubt it.* The doctor asked me to sit on said sweaty-ass table. I did as instructed.

"What seems to be the problem?" he asked in a thick Indian accent. He looked to be in his fifties, not the most sociable of types, and exuded a very cold energy. He worked at a walk-in clinic, in a pretty shady part of town, so I could only imagine that this was not what he had envisioned for himself when he graduated from medical school. A lot of "Is this herpes?" or "What's this rash on my butt all about?" type of questions, day in, day out. Living the dream, I'm sure.

"I'm coughing a lot and my sinuses are blocked up and I'm having trouble sleeping at night. I think there's something wrong with my left lung. It's something in my chest."

"You have a sinus infection," he said without hesitation.

That was easy. *Of course I have a sinus infection!* My castmate Amish, from my sketch comedy troupe, had a sinus infection when we went to see a movie last week and we shared a bag of popcorn. *This is a no-brainer! Sinus infection, indeed!*

The doctor quickly wrote me a prescription for antibiotics and then started to usher me out of the room.

"Oh, could you check my lungs?" I asked. He rolled his eyes, as though I was certainly wasting his time. He put his stethoscope up to my chest and told me to breathe in and out a couple of times.

"Your lungs are fine," he said.

I let out a big sigh of relief but my aching lungs let it be known that I was still unwell. *A sinus infection! Lungs are fine! All is good!*

But life is strange . . .

Twelve hours prior to that moment, I had this crazy weird "meaning of life" epiphany while lying in my bed. The night before, while I was trying to sleep, the pain in my chest was so great that I looked up to the ceiling and I spoke out loud to myself—well really, I was getting a little desperate so I was speaking to God. I'm not a religious man but, like I said, I was getting a little desperate. Plus, my friend Jane Benson told me I was an angel! You could have called him Buddha, Geisha, Allah, the Sun, Jupiter or fucking Zeus for all I care, I just wanted answers.

"What can this be? This is bad isn't it?" *Then I said it* . . . "Is it cancer? Don't tell me this is cancer, God. You wouldn't give me cancer, would you? I'm an angel!"

As I made my way home from the walk-in clinic, I was relieved to know God wasn't giving me cancer, not even close. He was just giving me a sinus infection! *Thanks, God! I knew you wouldn't shit on one of your angels.*

But after four days of taking the antibiotics, I decided it was time to stop. I was supposed to take them for a full week, but instead of getting better the pain in my chest just kept getting worse. The coughing was becoming more and more intense and the night sweats wouldn't stop. But my sinuses suddenly felt clear, so that was good. *Thanks for the antibiotics, Doc! . . . Fucker.*

A Second Opinion

I knew I had to go back to the doctor, but it was a Thursday and I had a sketch comedy show to perform at the University of Toronto that night. I desperately didn't want to let my troupe down, so I decided that I would do the show and then go see the doctor again the next day before they closed for the weekend.

Backstage, I took a swig of gin and orange juice, like my man Snoop Dogg, in-between sets in hopes to numb the pain. It didn't work.

The show was a disaster. A small audience. Not our usual turnout. Probably a good thing, because throughout the entire show I was doing my best to hold back a number of coughing fits while trying to work them into sketches when I could.

We bowed to a smattering of applause as people grabbed their jackets and quickly emptied the theatre. I passed on "celebrating" with my troupe after the show. "You guys go on without me. I really need to go to bed and hit the doctor's office tomorrow."

"Pussy!" Shawn yelled out, sarcastically.

"I know, I know. I'll catch ya next time!" I called back.

I arrived at my apartment to find Stefan and his girlfriend in the living room, he at his computer, searching the latest statistical updates for his fantasy basketball team, and she on the couch fast asleep. "Man, I'm really not feeling well," I said to Stefan. "My chest is super sore and I can't stop coughing."

"Smoke this, it will make it feel better," he said as he passed me a poorly rolled joint.

"Amateur," I told him as I grabbed the joint. *Smoking weed might make my chest feel better*, I rationalized. I took a really small hit . . . and like a typhoon of razor blades running through my throat, the coughs started coming, more vicious than ever before. I couldn't tell which coughs were from the sinus infection and which were from smoking the joint. "You're gonna get so high," Stefan said, laughing.

"Thanks for the joint, buddy. I'm off to bed," I managed to say between a myriad of coughs.

I did my best to sleep. Stefan's girlfriend was staying the night and our walls were paper-thin. It wasn't me hearing them I was worried about, you sick-minded perverts, but them hearing my coughing, which was so loud and aggressive it would keep anyone up. I tried to lie down, but the more horizontal I got the more pressure I felt on my chest. I could hardly breathe. I forced myself into a seated position to let out another tirade of coughs. I propped pillows between the wall and my back and tried to sleep sitting up for another night. I swallowed my coughs in between twenty-minute intervals of what I guess could be called sleep. It was 5 a.m. My body and mind were completely exhausted and my eyes drooped to a close, finally shutting down to rest.

The sun broke through the window. Moments later, I realized that it was a new day, and on this new day, I was going back to the doctor to get to the bottom of this so-called "sinus infection." My sheets, just like the morning before and the morning before that, were cold and wet, soaked through with sweat.

I rolled out of bed and headed straight back to the small walk-in doctor's clinic, determined to get results. It was a beautiful day, unseasonably warm, but a record-breaking snowstorm was apparently en route. *The calm before the storm, I guess.* On my way, my cell phone began to vibrate. I checked the caller ID and instantly recognized the name. It was a call from the big talent agency I had been waiting on. I answered the phone excitedly while maintaining my cool, stifling the coughs. "Hello?"

"May I speak to Daniel Stolfi, please?" the voice on the line said.

"Speaking."

"We got your submission package and we'd like for you to come in for a meeting, if you're still looking for representation, of course."

"Of course. Yes. I'd love that!"

They wanted to set up a meeting with me in six weeks' time! A sudden surge of adrenalin shot through my body and for a fleeting moment I felt invincible. The pain in my chest and the coughing seemed to subside, so much so that I contemplated skipping the doctor's appointment entirely to celebrate. The adrenalin surge quickly passed, however, as the pain in my chest came rushing back. I wasn't invincible. I continued on to the clinic as planned but felt stronger, armed with a sense of hope for a bright future ahead.

As I checked in at the desk, it was brought to my attention that there was a different doctor working that day. I entered the first available room and waited as I mindlessly stared at the familiar posters that covered the cupboards. I liked to count the vowels in each sentence and then compare that with how many consonants there were. Sometimes, I like to see how many times the same letter is used. *There appear to be a lot of E's on these posters*, I thought to myself.

The doctor entered the room and took a seat across from me. He was much younger than the previous doctor, and he wasn't as rushed, which put me at ease. *I'm in good hands*, I thought. He had a soft Middle Eastern accent. I couldn't quite place it but it was Middle Eastern . . . ish? *Is that politically correct? Middleasternish? Am I allowed to assume he was from the Middle East? You know what? Yes. This is my story, so I say yes.* Anyway, he spoke with a soft Middle Eastern accent.

"What seems to be the problem today?"

"Well, I have this pain in my side and I can't stop coughing. At night, I wake up in pools of sweat and I can't sleep. The last doctor who was here before said it was a sinus infection but I think the problem is in my chest . . . in my lungs."

"Please remove your shirt," he instructed without much hesitation. I did so, quickly. He took his stethoscope and placed it on my back.

The stethoscope was cold but offered a strange feeling of comfort as he moved it around to different areas of my back. "Breathe in and out for me, please," he instructed. Breathing deeply proved to be very difficult. I could only inhale about half a breath of air and then my lungs felt too full to take in any more, and I exhaled quickly. The exhalation of breath was followed by a series of uncontrollable dry, hacking coughs.

Just two and a half weeks had passed since that day after Valentine's Day. It all seemed to have happened so fast. I was just playing soccer earlier that week, able to run and compete without being too winded. I was holding my breath under water through a forty-foot pool with relative ease while making stupid human whirlpools with my friends. I was in the gym lifting and pushing weights routinely in an attempt to add muscle to my tall, lean frame. Now, I was coughing, taking short painful breaths and feeling weak all over. What was happening?

The doctor then asked me to say things like "ninety-nine" and the letter *A* over and over again while he pressed the stethoscope to the side of my left ribcage.

"Ninety-nine," I said.

"Again."

"Ninety-nine."

"Again."

This in-depth conversation went on for another minute or so. He placed his index and middle finger on my back and tapped them with his other hand. It was a strange sensation but oddly soothing. I heard the rhythmic patter of hollow thuds with each tap vibrating through my chest. It was a much more detailed examination than the last doctor, for sure. Really, he could have done anything more than the other doctor and I would have considered him to be miles ahead.

He stopped the procedure, paused for a brief moment and looked at me with determined eyes and with a poker face that all doctors are taught in medical school. His poker face, however, wasn't good. He grabbed a piece of prescription paper and started to scribble an order for what I assumed to be another antibiotic.

"I want you to go get a chest X-ray." He started searching for words. "Do you know where the X-ray . . . place . . . thing is?" I shook my head from side to side. *Also, did he just say "X-ray place thing?"* He went on. "Here's a map, but first I want you to get this prescription filled. Actually, forget the prescription. Go get the X-rays first and then we'll see about the prescription. Right away. Go get the X-rays and hurry. It closes soon. I'll let them know you're coming."

He seemed so nervous, which made me nervous. What did he know that I didn't? The X-ray and ultrasound building was right down the street. *Why the rush?* I began to wonder. *Is it that important?* "Thank you. I'll go . . . I'll go right now," I assured him. I grabbed the next bus and was there in ten minutes.

The clinic was located below a rundown pastry shop on a popular strip in Toronto known as Greektown. From the outside, the building was unassuming: a narrow, white brick building sandwiched between a couple of local businesses. You would never know it was an X-ray and ultrasound clinic by the looks of it. There was no sign on the door or any indication of what type of building it was. Other than a number painted above the door, to indicate the address, it pretty much could have been a door to an adults-only video store. I opened the rusty-framed glass-panelled door and walked down a narrow stairwell. The stairwell led me into a dingy underground office illuminated by humming fluorescent lights.

A woman in a tiny glassed-off kiosk greeted me through a square hole I could only assume was called the speaking hole. "Health card, please," she said in that monotonous tone, as if she'd said it for the hundredth time that day. I handed her my red-and-white Ontario health card, now held together with Scotch tape, the numbers barely legible. She then said my name out loud, calling to the back, "Daniel Stolfi!" I heard some mumbles in the back, from presumably, doctors. One doctor came rushing out of his office and looked at me.

"Hello," he said with a nervousness to his voice.

I found this strange. I don't know why, but he seemed to say hello as though he knew me. *Had we met in a past life? Doubtful.* I could usually get a good read on people's behaviours and mannerisms. I'm pretty good at picking up on social cues and find it funny when other people can't. For example: You know when you're trying to end a conversation with someone but they just keep talking and talking as if you want to hear about how crappy their day was for the rest of your life? You try to give little send-off words and sentences like, "What can you do?" Or "Yeah, well . . ." but they just keep talking. You literally have to resort to "come save me" signals to your friends to get you out of there. Well, I have always been good at picking up on those cues and knowing when it's time to stay or time to go. He said, "Hello" in a way that sounded like he knew something about me, or he knew of me. I knew the walk-in doctor said he'd call to let him know I was coming but it felt as though he told him something else, something more. *Watch out for this Stolfi character . . . he's got something big.*

I sat down with the other patients on a long bench in a narrow hallway. I grabbed a *Vanity Fair* magazine and started reading. Yes, *Vanity Fair*! The pickings were slim, my friends.

There was a pregnant lady to my left. She must have been nine months along or had octuplets, because she was huge! There was an older gentleman to my right with his leg in a cast, groaning as he hung his head in his palms. He was breathing deeply while pressing his thumb and forefinger against his head, trying to calm himself. From the looks of it, I was going to be waiting here a while. I couldn't compete with a pregnant woman and a broken leg.

Three minutes of flipping through the magazine, I heard my name. "Daniel Sto-phie?" called the voice, butchering the pronunciation of my last name. Why do people mess up my last name? It's pronounced how it's spelled. I've gotten Stoffie, Stofli, Stolli . . . What happened to the *F*? Do you not see it? What about the *L*? Where did that go? Why does Stolfi come out Stof-lee? Or Stoffie? I have never understood this and don't think I ever will. This will forever be one of the world's greatest mysteries. Okay, maybe not.

I couldn't believe I was getting called first! The pregnant lady looked like she was ready to give birth right there in the waiting room, the guy in the cast was looking glossy-eyed from all the painkillers he was probably on and I was getting seen first?

The simplest way to explain the Canadian healthcare system is this: everyone gets access to healthcare but there is no official lineup. If you are sicker than the person who was there first . . . you are now first. By using this foolproof algorithm, I was able to deduce that I was sicker than a pregnant lady and a guy with a broken leg. That couldn't be good. But at least I was getting seen first! *Minor victories.*

I jumped up and proceeded to the back room where the X-ray machine was located. The room was cold and dark with faint fluorescent light shining through the window on the door. The operator was behind a glass wall in an adjacent room while he spoke to me.

"Can you remove your shirt, please?"

"Yeah, sure," I said, and did as instructed.

"Could you please lie on the table in the fetal position, on your right side with your feet toward me?"

"What about my pants?"

"Just the shirt is fine." I really wanted to take off my pants for some reason but I did as he asked and lay curled up for the moment. Why did I want to take off my pants? I really don't know. I just remember wanting to do that and thought you should know.

He entered the room and placed a large heavy mat over my lower half. It was a protective apron made of lead that kept the X-rays from getting to my balls, nuking my swimmers, rendering them utterly useless. He left the room and the machine started up. This large scanning device, straight from a sci-fi movie, passed over my chest making a humming sound as it whizzed by. As quickly as it had begun, the humming stopped.

"Same thing but on the other side, please," he instructed through the muffled speaker. He took another scan. "And now flat on your back, please."

After the scans were over the machine operator came out from behind his glass cage, stood over me and asked, "What made you come in today?" He had a seemingly nervous timbre in his voice. I told him the same story I had told the doctor at the clinic.

"I was having chest pain, chronic coughs, night sweats and stuffy sinuses. I went to the walk-in clinic and he sent me here." The operator just nodded his head.

"Put your shirt back on and proceed down the hallway to Room 203. We are going to do an ultrasound on your chest."

"Sure. Thanks."

All things considered, I felt like I was getting first-class treatment here. No waiting, no lines, no papers to fill out. Just door-to-door all-star treatment. *There must be something seriously wrong with me,* I thought.

I left one dark room and entered another. A second specialist greeted me. "Please remove your shirt and lie on the table," he instructed.

"Didn't we just do this?" I asked under my breath.

I lay down on the table, bare chest pushed up toward the

ceiling. I let out a cough. "This is going to feel cold," he said as he squirted some gel on to my chest. He began to move a plastic ball–like apparatus all over my ribs. Sound sexual? Believe me, it was!! I mean, it wasn't. It's not.

He proceeded to mumble doctor jargon to his assistant while pointing at the screen repeatedly. He squinted. *That can't be good,* I thought. *Why is he squinting?*

If a doctor squints at an image, it means, "What the hell is that?" or, "I need glasses," and if a doctor doesn't know what it is or needs glasses, then you know you need a new doctor.

"What made you come in today?" he asked. I told him the same thing I told the X-ray guy and the walk-in doctor.

"I had a chronic cough, sore chest, night sweats and stuffed sinuses so I went to the walk-in clinic and they sent me to get an X-ray and the X-ray guy sent me to you."

He just nodded and smiled, put the device away, handed me a towel and said in this casual tone, "Wipe yourself off." What was this, a porno? The doctor removed his rubber gloves and tossed them in the trash. *This really might be a porno.* He handed me my X-rays in a large brown folder.

"I want you to take these to Toronto East General. I'll have someone call the hospital so they know you're coming. Go right now."

"To Emergency?" I asked, like an idiot.

"Yes, to Emergency," he said calmly. Sympathetically.

The porno was over. This was for real.

Hurry Up and Wait

I left the clinic and hailed a cab. The signature orange-and-green cabs in Toronto are aplenty and they are also the quickest way to get around the city. This was pre-Uber, after all. I instructed the cabbie to take me to Toronto East General, the same hospital where I was treated just three months prior for the self-inflicted star-shaped scar on my chin and the severe separation of my collarbone. My ultimate low.

My mind raced. *How bad could this be? Is it pneumonia? That wouldn't be good at all! I think it's pneumonia. Hands down, it's pneumonia. I was just working with a friend who had pneumonia! It must be pneumonia. I can't believe she gave me pneumonia! I'll get her back for this . . .*

With my X-rays in hand, tightly concealed in the brown paper envelope, I quietly sat in the back of the iconic pumpkin on wheels. I couldn't help but think that where I was going was not the type of place I wanted to become more familiar with. *What did the doctor see on those X-rays that made him want me to go to the hospital so quickly?* I wondered.

My curiosity got the best of me and I slipped the X-ray images out of the envelope and tried to analyze them like they do on television. I held one image up to the rear passenger window of the cab to let the sunlight shine through the black-and-white photograph, accentuating what I was looking at. I had no idea what I was looking for, though, and part of me thought that I was doing something illegal, like the cab driver would say something to the authorities if he caught me looking at my own X-rays. I risked years in prison! I took a quick peek at the images of my lungs. One lung looked completely black . . . the other, white. *That can't be good, can it? What does that mean?* I slipped the X-rays back into the envelope, now more confused than ever as I proceeded to the hospital.

I arrived at the hospital's Emergency unit, used the old "You're expecting me" line, and handed the receptionist my envelope. This did absolutely nothing.

"Put a mask over your nose and mouth and have a seat in the waiting room," the receptionist instructed. *I guess you weren't expecting me? What happened to the royal treatment?*

I slipped the blue sterile mask over my nose and mouth and tucked the elastic bands behind my chunky little ears. I found an empty chair along the back wall of the waiting room, tucked between an old man and woman. They both had masks on too, so I figured I should join the team. I waited for four hours, not moving, not reading, not sleeping, just thinking. With all that time to kill it probably would have been a good time to call my parents to let them know where I was. I rationalized that I couldn't call them, as they were probably still driving to Montreal to see my sister for the weekend and I didn't want them to worry about me while they were away. I figured it would be better for me to get all the information I could and then call them. *Don't stress about something until it's really worth stressing about,* as they say . . . I think I made that one up.

It was 9 p.m. when I heard my name. "Daniel Stophie." *Of course they would fuck it up.* I got up and followed a nurse sporting pink scrubs. "Just sit here for the moment. Someone will be with you shortly," she told me. I was in a smaller, but just as packed, waiting room. Two more hours passed. I sat with my thoughts.

There was an odd similarity between being on set as an actor and waiting in that hospital waiting room. When you are on set for television, film or commercials, you often hear the phrase "Hurry up and wait." Basically, what tends to happen is the creative team will rush you through makeup, hair and wardrobe because the director wants to shoot your scene "right away." Then, when it comes time to actually shoot the scene, you wait. Sometimes they don't even shoot the scene at all. Maybe they ask you to change outfits again and "sit tight," so they can adjust the lights or change the batteries in the camera or argue about the best angle for the shot. Finally, when it's time to shoot the "big scene," they ask you to wait just a little longer because the director has to take a "ten-one," code for take a piss. And then, suddenly, the director comes running out of the washroom and calls "Action!" As an actor, you better be ready because time is money! Someone should tell the director that.

I felt like I'd been on set all day. I was rushed through the walk-in clinic, rushed down to the ultrasound and X-ray clinic and then when I was rushed to the Emergency—my big moment—I was asked to wait. *Would someone just call "Action?!"*

It was a really slow night. Busy as hell, but slow-moving. There was a massive snowstorm on the way, the grainy TV stuck on a repetitive news loop informed me. The waiting patients were beginning to express their frustration.

"I've been waiting eight hours!" one woman yelled.

"We've been waiting ten!" another man complained.

"This is ridiculous, absolutely ridiculous," an elderly woman kept repeating as she looked at me for confirmation. I nodded my head and rolled my eyes for her.

In my mind and in my heart I knew that there was something seriously wrong with me and at that moment I was fine with waiting for as long as it took to find out what it was. I glanced at a bratty teenager with a sprained ankle and an old man with a sore back. *I got these people beat*, I thought, as I lowered my head and kept my mouth shut.

People started getting desperate. The woman who had been waiting for eight hours snuck behind the nurses' station in an attempt to get her father's name bumped up the list so he could be seen first.

"My father is in a great deal of pain. Where is he on the list?" she asked.

"Your father will be fine. It won't be much longer," the nurse assured her.

I knew I was in more trouble than all of these people put together . . . and I was the only one not complaining. I just wanted to prolong the inevitable for as long as I could. They were about to tell me I had pneumonia. I was sure of it. That would sideline me for at least another two weeks! *Pneumonia?* I thought you got that from jumping in a frozen lake or running around in the rain on a cold day. I wasn't really sure how it worked and I still don't. I wasn't one to get sick much. Hurt myself physically by doing stupid things? Yes. Get sick? No. All I could do was wait. Good things come to those who wait, as they say. So the longer I waited the better, right?

"Oh my God, this is taking forever!" the bratty teenager blurted out as her mother nodded her head in agreement. The little shit sat in her wheelchair and propped her nasty naked foot up on her mother's lap.

"What if it's broken?" she continued. "They took X-rays, like, an hour ago and my leg could be broken."

For me, this was the final straw. I couldn't take all the complaining anymore. I took one look at her barely swollen ankle attached to her ugly stupid foot and said, "It's not broken. I've broken my leg before, and your leg isn't broken. If it was broken, they would have let you know by now and you would be getting a cast. They don't let broken bones wait. You just sprained it. They'll give you a pair of crutches, a wrap, a bag of ice, tell you to keep it elevated and stay off it for a bit. It's not broken, now stop complaining."

She and her mother looked at me, stunned. They didn't speak another word. Silence. *Minor victories.*

I returned to my zombie-like state and waited.

I felt a tap on my shoulder, snapping me out of my mini coma. "Are these your X- rays?" a mouse-like voice asked.

A tiny woman, Dr. Jung, who was definitely less than five

feet tall, repeated herself. "Are these your X-rays?"

I stood up and my six foot, 185 pound frame towered over her. I nodded my head yes as I looked down at her holding the brown paper envelope in her hand. She took the X-rays out of the envelope and slapped them on to a light board, which hung just above the girl with the puke face and nasty foot. *Did I mention she had a puke face?* Dr. Jung took a quick look at them and then spoke calmly and directly.

"Have you had a look at these yet?"

"Yes, just in the cab ride over but I had no idea what I was looking at," I replied.

She led me into another room with the X-rays of my chest in hand. She had a smile on her face. Not one of those "I have good news for you" smiles, but one of those "Aw he's so cute because he has no idea how serious this is" smiles. She placed the X-rays on another light board in the room.

"See your lungs? See how one is black and one is white?"

"Yes," I replied. *Is this a trick question? Clearly I can see that. Anyone can see that.*

"Well, they are both supposed to be white. This is your heart in the middle and see how there is a large dark spot right over top of it?"

I nodded my head yes.

"That's fluid. You have a large amount of fluid in your left lung and some around your heart. When we see something like this, it usually means it's something huge."

Huge? What the fuck kind of word is that for a doctor to use? I wondered. *Is that literal, or cool basketball talk? Like, "Yo that Lebron*

James dunk last night was huge!" Or more like, "Have you seen the CN tower? It's huge!" Which one is it?

"We will have to do further tests to see what that fluid around your heart is, okay?" I nodded my head once again, yes. "Just wait in this room and someone will take you for a CT scan."

I was led to a room and instructed to strip down to my underwear and throw on one of those pale blue hospital gowns that are as sexy in real life as they are on TV. I'm calling it right now: hospital gowns will be the next big fashion trend. Maybe not. Ten years ago, I called eye patches as the next hot fashion trend. I wasn't right about that one either. Just sayin'.

The nursing staff hooked me up to an IV. I hadn't had a needle in my vein since I was seventeen and I think it was to donate blood.

A CT scan is a detailed image of the inside of your body. The patient is injected with a dye that illuminates the blood-filled organs and glands. It gives doctors an inside look at the patient's internal system so they can spot any irregularities in certain areas of the body. (This is not from a medical dictionary, this is just in my own words . . . but I think that's pretty accurate without getting too "nerd" on you and having to reference some scientific journal).

At that time, I never really understood the whole, "We need your blood" campaign that the blood donor clinics were always talking about. I just donated my blood a couple of times because I thought it was a good thing to do and I got a cookie and a slice of pizza. Hey, I was seventeen . . . that's a young man's wet dream! But I didn't see any cookies or pizza this time, just a bunch of blank off-white cinder-block walls with really ugly paintings of dogs playing in the snow set in tacky brushed-gold frames.

I got wheeled into the CT imaging room, with my IV pole rolling at my side, to meet a woman with a clipboard who told me she was going to ask me a bunch of questions. She spoke in this sullen, drab, been-there-done-that sort of tone. This obviously wasn't her first rodeo. But it was mine.

"Allergies?"

"No."

"High blood pressure?"

"No."

"Cholesterol?"

"No."

"Diabetes?"

"No."

"Are you pregnant?"

I looked at her... *funny*.

"I know, I know, but we have to ask you, by law."

"I'm sure you do but I think it's safe to assume."

She laughed. "Okay, well, just so you know, we need you to sign this liability waiver. One in one million people have an allergic reaction to the dye we will be injecting you with and, well, die. So just sign here."

"Well, that's not in the least bit frightening." I signed, while taking a huge shit in my pants. Well, technically I wasn't wearing pants . . . but you get the idea.

After the paperwork was signed I was asked to lie on a long white plastic table with my arms stretched out over my head and my feet facing away from a giant tube-like futuristic thing. The table slowly moved back and forth through this circular dome that made a lot of beeps and bops, which sounded like a cheesy '80s arcade game. *Kind of cool.* I've heard horror stories of people feeling claustrophobic in these machines, but I didn't find it to be constricting at all. All things considered, that part was easy.

"On my instruction, I need you to take a deep breath and then exhale when I say so," a man's voice over an intercom said.

Unfortunately for him, I could only hold my breath for three seconds before exhaling and coughing wildly. To think just one month prior, I was holding my breath for the entire length of a swimming pool and now all I could give this guy was three lousy seconds.

After ten seconds he said, "You can exhale now."

It was too late; I had exhaled a long time ago. Three seconds was all this guy was getting.

"We are injecting the dye now," the nurse said.

She attached a long plastic tube to my end of the IV, which sat in the vein at the fold between my bicep and forearm.

Could this be the end? I felt a warm sensation travel throughout my body, starting at the fold of my arm and making its way through the whole of my torso, up to my chest and into my face, then down to my legs and out through my toes. There was a metallic taste in my mouth and I got the sudden urge to take a "ten-one." I could feel the dye working its way through every inch of my circulatory system. I felt like Wolverine from the X-Men cartoons, as he gets his adamantium exoskeleton put in.

The scan ended. The warm sensation passed. And I didn't pee myself. I didn't have claws that could retract from the backs of my hands either. But I was alive.

"Okay, we're all done. You can go now," the voice said through the intercom.

I thanked the guys through the glass wall and made a joke on the way out.

"How did I look?"

"We got some great pictures," they replied.

"I've always been pretty photogenic."

They didn't laugh. I thought it was funny.

Now it was time to play the waiting game . . . again. I was escorted, in my pretty little dress, to another windowless bland doctor's office to sit with my thoughts and await the results. I decided that *now* might be a good time to call my parents and inform them of what "might" be going on. It was roughly 10 p.m. so they had likely arrived in Montreal a couple of hours prior and were just finishing a late meal.

I still had no idea what the diagnosis was or what to tell them. I figured I would let them know it could be something serious, but assure them that they were not to worry. That sounded about right. That shouldn't freak them out too much. A small sign with the image of a cellphone crossed out with a big red X hung on the wall across from me. *Fuck you, sign.* I dialled.

My sister answered the phone. "Hello?"

"Hey, Nadia, can I talk to Mom?"

"What? No, 'How are you?' Don't you want to know how your pregnant sister is doing?" she joked.

"Sorry, how's the belly?" I played along.

"Huge," she said. "Here's Mom."

My mom picked up the phone and before she could say hi, I just went right into it.

"I'm in the hospital. I have some fluid in my lungs and around my heart. I just went in for a CT scan and we will have more results soon." There was a silence. *That didn't come out how I intended.*

"We'll leave now and be there as soon as we can," she said. No further explanation required. Her son was in the hospital, and some sort of motherly magnetic force must have been at play here. Without hesitation, my parents decided that they would drive back to Toronto to be with me.

"But there is a massive snowstorm. Just wait for the storm to pass. It can wait until the morning or after the weekend even," I tried to rationalize.

There was no debating my mother on this one.

"We'll leave as soon as we get our things together," she said calmly.

They're being crazy! I thought to myself. *I'm not dying.*

"Seriously, come home on Monday like you were planning to. The snowstorm is really bad. Why risk driving through it at night?" I continued to push.

Highway 401 from Montreal to Toronto was a rough five-hour drive on a good day, so to drive it in the middle of the night in probable whiteout conditions was completely insane. I tried to convince them not to leave, but they were having none of it. Like I said, mommy magnets. "We'll be there, hopefully, for 6 or 7 a.m."

"Okay. Thanks. But you're crazy," I reminded her.

I hung up the phone and wondered what my parents must be thinking. I never really thought this was an emergency. The way I rationalized it, was that even if there was something really wrong with me, there was nothing we could do about it for at least a couple of weeks. There would be follow-up appointments, tests, a bunch of crying and all that crap. I'm very logical in that way and it keeps my anxiety at a manageable level. *Don't stress about something until it's really worth stressing about.* I definitely made this saying up. It's not even that good, but I'm taking ownership of it.

I continued to wait with all of these thoughts going through my head, plus worrying about my parents driving their shitty mint-green Hyundai Elantra down Highway 401 in a snowstorm.

Another hour passed until Dr. Jung came walking back into my room. Finally, some answers! She sat down in a chair across from me and got right into it. She adjusted her white lab coat and said, "What you must realize is that these tests are all preliminary and aren't necessarily conclusive. What it looks like is that the fluid around your heart is actually a rather large lump. It's quite massive to be honest with you, and—" she cut herself off abruptly then said, "Excuse me one second, I'll be right back."

She must have a phone call or something. I sat there and waited for ten minutes with no sign of her returning. Twenty minutes now and still waiting. Forty minutes . . . *okay, where in the hell did she go?* An hour passed, the longest hour of my life. *What the fuck?!* I sat there in my backless gown, cold, wondering if she'd ever come back. She left me with the words, "a rather large lump." *What does that mean? A rather large lump? My DICK in super tight pants could be considered a rather large lump—under the right conditions, of course, and if you catch it at just the right angle—but a rather large lump . . . in my chest?!* I sat with this information, anxiety now through the roof and the rationalizing now on pause, as panic and fear crept in. You don't really realize how long an hour is until you sit and stare at a clock in the hospital, half naked, cold, alone and terrified.

I couldn't take it anymore. I walked up to the nurse's station outside my room and saw two older women in blue scrubs chatting at their desk, in what was now a much more sparse-looking waiting area. The sprained-ankle snob and old man with what was probably just constipation were back home snuggled in their beds.

"Excuse me, sorry to bother you, but is Dr. Jung coming back?" I asked politely.

"Of course she's coming back." They both laughed. "Just sit down in your room and she'll be with you shortly."

"Okay. It's just, she said that I have a large lump in my chest and then walked away, so I'd just like some clarity."

Suddenly, they spoke in a different tone.

"Oh, we're sorry, she'll be back shortly sweetheart, don't

worry." *Not so jokey now, are we?* I nodded with a smile and returned to my room. To be left with, "You have a massive lump in your chest," was to be left with questions that I wanted answers to. Reality was really starting to set in now. I started to think to myself, *Is it cancer? It can't be cancer, can it? Lumps equal cancer, right? No. It can't be.* I continued to try and rationalize. My logic-driven brain was firing on all cylinders but no definitive answers were coming.

Looking back now, I can see how ridiculous this must seem to you, the reader. How in the hell did I not know this was cancer? Well, cancer wasn't prevalent in my family or in my life for that matter. I didn't have much experience with it at all. Didn't have to talk about it or acknowledge it because it wasn't close to me. I ran the runs for cancer, cut my hair for cancer and walked the walks for cancer . . . but I really just did that because I wanted to do something good for others and feel good about myself for doing it. Cancer is BAD. Running and raising money for cancer is GOOD. Simple as that. Let's just say, I was naïve as fuck. I didn't know what I know now. And I can honestly say that that was a good thing.

Ten minutes later I finally saw Doctor Jung! She was walking toward me, but she had a winter coat on, and . . . *is that a purse? She has her fucking purse!* She walked right past me without the slightest acknowledgement and left out the back door of the hospital. *She's going home? This can't be. At least use a different exit so I can't literally see you leaving me! She's coming back, right? She must be!* She didn't.

I was hurt. My blood started to boil and I became hot all

over, angry that a medical professional would turn their back on me and leave me in such a state of loneliness and confusion. I was left to contemplate this information on my own, sad and alone. I felt pathetic, terrified, anxious, cheated, frustrated and fucking furious. I was desperate to understand what I was dealing with. *What's a lump? Could be just a benign thing, right? I've heard of benign lumps before . . . that means it's not cancerous, right? Just cut it out. Surgery, right? Yeah. Just cut it out and let me get out of here. Right?*

Like I said. I was naïve and it was probably for the better.

Another hour slowly ticked by when a nurse finally led me into another room. It was more of a bed that was encircled by a yellow hanging curtain, separating me from the other patients, than a room. I lay down on the bed and did more waiting. A cute girl in a white lab coat, with a dark complexion and thick black hair, walked through the curtain and came to rest at the foot of my bed. She looked to be my age and, if I were to take a guess, of Indian descent. Yeah, definitely Indian. Why does it matter? It doesn't. I just like to try and place people with their geographical origins of being. I minored in Human Geography in university, so I take a genuine interest in cultures and geography. I'm a bit of an ethnic origin nerd. Jeez, relax.

"I'm a student doctor and am working under Dr. Woo, who is working under the specialist," she informed me. *You're beautiful*, I thought. She asked me a bunch of similar questions that I had answered a number of times already that day. Then she asked that all too familiar question that I had been getting since this all started.

"What made you come in here today?"

It was as though they wanted me to say, "I had nothing better to do," or "I've never been to this hospital before and have heard great things," or "I thought it'd be fun to go to the doctor's this afternoon to pick up chicks!" *What the fuck?!!*

The truth was: *I was in pain and I couldn't take it anymore, so I went to the doctor . . . and he sent me to get an X-ray and they sent me here, where I waited for seven hours wanting to break a 16-year-old girl's leg, which led me to a cold-hearted, shitty doctor, who left me alone in a room for two more hours to dissect the sentence, "You've got a massive lump in your chest," which then led me to you, asking me, "What made you come in here today?" FUCK! Do you not communicate?! I feel like shit. Fix it!*

I didn't say any of that. I just told her the same thing I told the other doctors. "I had a pain in my chest for a couple of weeks and I couldn't stop coughing, so I went to the walk-in clinic and they sent me for X-rays and an ultrasound and then they sent me here."

Why explode? I kept it inside and hid my emotions behind a fake smile. She was very caring, sweet and patient, so of course, I tried to be too. It wasn't her fault. I'm sure she was just following protocol. They must all be taught that in medical school. *There goes me, rationalizing again.*

"The specialist will be in to see you shortly," she said calmly.

The specialist didn't arrive, but his understudy did. He was a tall man with a soothing voice.

He stood with his young protégé and asked me all the questions again. I answered them like I did the first five times. Then, he just laid it on me.

"Well, Daniel, we've seen this a hundred times. You have a large lump in your chest. We also noticed a golf ball–sized lump in your neck and a small one under your armpit. There is also a small one in your groin area. These are tumours, but more specifically, a type of lymphoma." Just like that.

Beat.

"What's lymphoma?" I asked. I had no idea. Seriously, none.

He hesitated for a moment as he cocked his head, now hitting him for the first time that I was completely oblivious to what he just told me. "It's a form a cancer."

Beat.

Time ceased to exist for a brief moment and my mind started to race while I tried to piece together how this could be possible through a series of weird, twisted logistical reasonings. It went something like this:

I don't know anyone who has had cancer except for my aunt. She had breast cancer when I was very young and I never saw her ill or I was too young to even understand it. I think I was five! She's not even my aunt through blood, though, so it can't be that. The professional hockey players, Saku Koivu and Mario Lemieux, had cancer. They're fine now. They lost some hair and got skinny for a bit but played professional hockey again. Lance Armstrong . . . he's doing great! Seven Tour de France titles, right? I don't care what anyone says, I think he cheated, but who knows . . . he's a hero! (I didn't actually think this at the time but lets imagine I did). *He beat it . . . so will I! Looked pretty easy. Those guys were always smiling in their pictures. They just looked a little skinny and had no hair but they were always smiling. How bad could it be? I got this shit! I can still live my life . . . all is good. Did my second cousin have cancer? I think I heard that once. Regardless . . . My agent meeting! I can still meet with my new agent, right? My parents! Oh, shit, my mom! She may be a little worried. Nah, it's all good. She'll be fine, right? Work, acting, friends, partying, Michael Jackson dance-offs at the club. I can still dance, can't I? Working out? Soccer! I can still play soccer, right? I can still do my Fringe show, too. Yeah. I'll be fine. It's gotta be all good, right? They're always smiling in those pictures. Right?! Is anyone there?!! Anyone?*

He went on, "I'm sorry to have to break this to you. Are you okay?"

I just smiled. "I don't know, am I?" I joked as I let out a cough. What he said next blew my mind.

"The good news is there is a cure for this cancer."

"A cure for cancer?" *Fuck off!*

"Well, it's highly treatable is what I mean." *Of course. Mind re-put together after major explosion.* "And because yours is so aggressive, the tumour should respond better to the treatment. It sounds weird, I know, but that's just the way it works. Hey, if you had to choose from a list of cancers, this is the one to get."

Really? Did this guy just say that? If I had to choose from a list of cancers? I choose the one that is no cancer. No cancer is the best kind to get. Where is that one on your fancy list?

"You'll learn more as you go. We're going to send you home for the night and we will get in touch with you as to where to go from here. Are you all right to get home?" I nodded my head yes and let out a cough. The cute intern doctor gave me a sympathetic smile and a pat on the foot. I touched my neck and felt the golf ball–sized lump under my skin. I couldn't believe it had been there the whole time and I never noticed. Then a pea-sized node under my armpit and one in my groin, just like the doctor said. I shook my head in disbelief.

I got my stuff together and left the hospital. It was now 2 a.m. and the blizzard outside was in full swing. I called an orange-and-green cab and went back to my apartment. I was alone and I was afraid.

The Actor. The
Comedian. The Girl.

I was born in Guelph, Ontario, Canada, in the summer of 1982. Guelph was a smaller town at the time with a population of about 60,000 people. Growing up there, I realized that not much happened in Guelph. I think it's where the wire coat hanger was invented and it was recognized as one of the cleanest cities in Canada once, but that was about it. My parents were Italian immigrants who raised my older sister, brother and me in a very traditional Italian way. We ate lasagna instead of turkey at Thanksgiving and Christmas, we canned our own tomatoes every year, butchered pigs in our basement to make sausage and crushed grapes in my uncle's garage to make wine. This was totally normal. Being the youngest, in not only my immediate family but also in my entire extended family, which consisted of 30 aunts and uncles and over 50 cousins, I was able to observe many different characters and pick up on quirks and tics that make people unique and humorous. I remember my mom telling me that when I was two years old, I would make people laugh by making funny faces and apparently I was doing it intentionally. As I grew older, I fell in love with making others laugh. Bringing ease to people by breaking the tension in the room or just changing someone's bad day by making them laugh made me feel good. I knew early on what I wanted to do for a living. I wanted to entertain people by making them laugh because it was the best feeling in the world.

Eventually I used school as a testing ground for material. I would test out the timing of when to make the off-hand remark or play on word. It was all about the timing and how I delivered the joke, which proved to be the most important thing to getting a good laugh. I'd kick myself if I let too much time pass before making my clever remark. The timing had to be perfect!

I became obsessed. I created and filmed dozens of comedy sketches on my camcorder with my friends every weekend during my middle school and high school years, editing them through a method called "tape to tape." I'd edit from one VCR to another VCR by pressing the Play button and Record button simultaneously on one machine and then the Stop button on the other. Video editing has come a long way since then.

From there, I applied to four universities to study theatre. I chose the University of Guelph, striking a deal with my parents that if I stayed in Guelph to go to school they would let me live on campus and outside our home for the next four years. I also had a girlfriend at the time who lived in Peterborough, and I was obviously "in love." Cue the "No, I wasn't" record scratch. *That Rod Stewart song is playing in my head, "I wish that I knew what I know now..."* Words of wisdom to the students of the future: Don't date your high school girlfriend in university. It's torture for the immature and insecure mind. It took three years of breaking up and getting back together before we realized that we weren't right for each other. I had squandered quite a bit of valuable time and focus to develop my craft, and quickly realized that I had a lot of catching up to do. In my fourth and final year of "higher education," I was finally single and soaking up all of the acting I could handle. I learned, not only about acting but creating my own work too—writing, producing and all the other technical jobs, which take place behind the scenes of a theatre production. I learned how to hang lights on the theatre grid, how to build sets in the theatre's studio shop, and how to design costumes. It all helped push my development as an artist forward, and although I didn't know it at the time, I met so many people that would prove to be huge inspirations and pillars of support in the years to follow.

The biggest pillar of them all? Her name was Jenny. Like Forest Gump and Jenny, Jenny. That's what everyone called her. In my graduating year of university, I was introduced to her. A year my junior, she stood all of five feet five inches tall and had long pin-straight brown hair. Her eyes always seemed to have this subtle squint to them. I immediately thought she was a beautiful mix of Asian and some Anglo-Caucasian hybrid. Turned out she wasn't Asian at all, she just smoked a lot of weed and smiled a lot! My type of girl.

"Yo, she's totally available right now, if you want to just hook up or be friends or whatever," my classmate Mike told me as we sat on the lighting grid above the small university theatre space. We watched Jenny working away, hauling fifty-foot electrical cables across the grid. She seemed so confident and cool with the whole process. Jenny was working on the lights and sound for the main stage show that semester and I was working on the set.

"I don't know, man. I just got out of a long relationship and I don't want to get involved right now," I told him.

"Bro. Like, whatever. Hook up, friends, all good. She told me to give you the green light."

"Green light?" This piqued my interest. "I'll think about it."

Later that night, I was busting out some mean Michael Jackson dance moves at the campus bar. Thursday nights were cheap drinks and old-school hip hop from 7 to 11 p.m. Two-dollar beers and three-dollar mixed drinks were the key to making this bar the place to be. Without that, it was nothing more than a dirty, gross, seedy dive in the middle of campus. I guess that was part of the charm as well. It was officially called The Brass Taps but was originally called The Keg, and due to legal reasons, the actual restaurant, The Keg Steakhouse + Bar and Grill, forced them to change the name. It was campus tradition to continue a silent protest and still refer to it as The Keg, so everyone did. Just a little Guelph history lesson for you.

Outkast's, "Hey Ya!" started blaring through the speakers, the jam of the year no doubt. I made a little circle on the dance floor, ushering people to step aside and spread out to give me some space. My feet were about to let the music take over. Spinning, kicking, breaking it down into a robot and then shaking it like a Polaroid picture, just like the song told me to. Across the way, I saw her, Jenny, dancing in big brown Ugg boots, blue jeans and a light blue top. She did this train-chugging motion thing with her arms as she kicked her legs in the air. Not sure you could call it dancing, but it was super adorable. I pointed at her across the dance floor and reeled her in like a fisherman casting his rod for a big catch, but in this case it was a petite smiley brunette catch. She danced her way toward me and I danced my way toward her. We danced, getting closer and closer. Our drunken slurs blended into meaningless jargon like, "Love this song!" and "Yeah!" . . . Riveting stuff. And then, it happened. We kissed. A sweaty make-out session broke out on the black sticky dance floor. She had these big full lips like a young Angelina Jolie. Her bottom lip was so big I just pretty much kissed that one with both of mine and hoped for the best. She was more like Bubba from Forest Gump than Jenny for the moment, except way less everything Bubba and way more everything Jenny. I don't know why I said that . . . but it's staying in.

"You like me?" I asked her after coming up for air.

"You like me?" she asked in response.

"Uh, oh yeaahhh!!!" I shouted. We continued to dance and kiss for the rest of the night.

The next morning, I saw her in class sitting alone in the back row of the tiny black box theatre. I wasn't sure if she remembered what had transpired the night before, but I sure did. We kissed, that I knew. *Should I sit beside her today? What's the protocol after a night of making out, drunk on the dance floor? Are we a thing now? Should I get her number?* All these questions went racing through my head. I just went with, "Hey."

"Hey," she replied. I sat down beside her, and the class

began. The professor assigned us our tasks for the day and sent us on our way. I had to make a move before we separated to work in completely different areas of the theatre for the rest of the class. It was now or never.

"Could I get your number so I can call you outside of class, maybe?" I blurted out.

"Sure," she said all cool, like she wasn't that interested. She wrote it down on a piece of paper. It was 2004 and pen and paper was still the method of choice for getting a girl's number.

"Jenny De Lucia," I said as I read her name off the small square of torn paper.

"Great pronunciation! Everyone gets it wrong," she said.

"That doesn't sound Chinese at all!" I said.

"That's because it's Italian."

"You're half Chinese, half Italian?!" The perfect combo!

"I'm half British, half Italian," she corrected me.

Ah, so you're part insane, part guilt-tripper but probably a decent driver, I rationalized. (I'm not apologizing for that cheap joke.) I took the piece of paper, folded it in half and nervously placed it in my pocket.

The weekend came and went quickly without me calling and I knew I was going to see her again in class on Tuesday. It was on me to call her before then or else it would have been too late and she'd think I wasn't interested. *This is the logic of a 22-year-old male.* It's like a three-day rule or something like that. I wasn't too keen on getting into a relationship, but she seemed really cool and I'd be an idiot to let her get away. She had that aura about her that made me think she was a girl I could marry.

What the hell am I thinking!? Marriage!? Get your head out of your ass, Stolfi! You're 22 years old and you just got out of a long, crazy relationship. Why are you pretending this is the girl? Just have fun. Jeeeeez.

I paced in the narrow kitchenette of my apartment contemplating whether or not I should call her. I lived in a two-bedroom apartment with my friend and university "relationship coach," Mark Mathews. He was a hockey player who charmed his way through a number of girls throughout the years. I'd watch him bring home girl after girl from the bar in envious wonder. They would just throw themselves at him and his blond-haired, blue-eyed chiselled physique. It was really quite impressive to watch from the sidelines as his official wingman. I could never figure out how he did it, until one day he told me, "I just lie to them."

"Come on!" I responded in disbelief. "What do you mean?"

"I tell them what they want to hear. If they want me to say I love them, I do, and then I . . . you know, fuck 'em." Sage wisdom from a proper gentleman.

"Hey man, should I call her?" I asked, as he sat on our blue two-piece sectional, playing R.B.I Baseball on old-school Nintendo. Yes, the original NES.

"Nah, man. You don't want to get involved in that shit," he told me.

"Let's play two-player then," I said. We struck up a new game of R.B.I and after an hour of playing nine innings of hard-hitting eight-bit graphic baseball, I decide to pass on his advice and give her a call. I couldn't stop thinking about her. It was Monday at 10 p.m., now or never. I dialled every number but the last one . . . I paused . . . then hung up. I took a breath and dialled *all* the numbers this time around. The phone rang. "Hello?" It was Jenny.

"Hello, Jenny? It's Dan. From our theatre class," I said, feeling the need to clarify. *I'm sure she has a lot of friends named Dan.*

"Of course. How are you?"

"Good. You?"

"Good." Again, riveting stuff.

"So, do you want to maybe go see a movie together or something?" I asked.

"Uh, sure. That would be great!"

"What about *Hitch*?" I suggested.

"I love Will Smith!" she said excitedly.

"Me too!" Remember, it was 2004. You gotta give it up for Will Smith. I mean, come on!

It was on!

We dated here and there, went to a movie once or twice (*Hitch* wasn't Will Smith's finest work), and I spent a night or two at her place. Okay, a few nights . . . many nights. The closer we got, the more terrified I became. I decided to make it very clear to her that what we had was not "a relationship" and that no one could think that we were "a couple." I didn't want to get into another relationship, and I promised myself that no matter how great the girl, the time just wasn't right. I was being such a dick, I know! It's painful. I'm having a hard time writing this it's so painful. Stop judging me . . . I blame the underdevelopment of my frontal lobe.

As my final year rolled to an end, I decided that it would

be in both of our best interests to not see each other anymore. I couldn't handle another "deep, long-term, meaningful" relationship. Plus, I was about to begin my professional career as a famous actor. I couldn't afford to split focus on a girl and my sure-to-be-extremely-successful career. *I was being stupid and selfish, I know. Shut up. I know!*

One night, after we smoked a joint in her room, I looked her in her beautiful brown eyes and told her that I couldn't date her anymore. There was no lead-up, no subtle hints along the way, I just broke it off with her. She was NOT HAPPY.

I broke her heart that day and knew that I was potentially making a terrible mistake. I stayed firm on my decision, though, and figured we could leave it up to fate. If we were meant to be together then I was sure it would happen when the time was right. For now, I needed to be on my own. I was so cool. *So not cool.*

When I graduated from the University of Guelph Theatre program, I instantly wanted to get a talent agent and move to Toronto to pursue my career in comedy. I gathered all of my savings, roughly $600, spent it on headshots, and got my very sparse list of acting credits together to submit myself to twenty agents around the city. Two out of the twenty agents wanted to see me for an interview. I couldn't believe it. Two agents wanted to see me? *They must think I'm great*, I thought. I was pretty sure I was well on my way to dominating the acting world right out of the gates.

Reality check, I had no idea what I was doing . . .

I signed with the Violet Group Talent Agency. My agent

was Violet Pierce, a chain-smoking, relatively young ex-model, who was very new to the business. Her house, which doubled as her office, was located in a pretty sketchy area, just off the downtown core in Toronto. It was filthy. It reeked of cigarette smoke and was covered in cat hair. Her walls were plastered with about a hundred different pictures of all the actors and actresses she represented on her roster. The first time I walked into her office, she was on the phone yelling at a client about an audition they had missed. All the while a cigarette dangled precariously off her bottom lip, while her two cats rubbed up against my legs.

"I told you two-thirty p.m. How clear do I have to be? Are you stupid?! Don't let it happen again!!"

I sat down in the chair across from her, she hung up the phone, took one look at me and said in her smoky voice, "There are a lot of parts for Indian guys right now. Because of nine-eleven. You'd be great for that."

"I'm not Indian, I'm Italian," I corrected her. *And the 9/11 guys weren't from India . . .*

"You could pass," she said. "Also, do you play gay? Would you kiss a man? 'Cause that's big right now, so I'm not going to say you have to, but it's much better if you would."

That's interesting. "Yeah, I'll totally play gay," I blurted out, fearing that if I said anything other than that, she wouldn't represent me. I was young and naïve and I just wanted to go out on auditions and work, so of course I said yes . . . to everything. The one thing that the University of Guelph didn't prepare me for was the harsh reality of the business of acting for film and television. She brought up race and sexuality in the first two sentences out of her mouth. I was getting a crash course. That being said, I signed with the Violet Group but was rarely sent out to anything substantial and I never kissed a man or played any Indian characters for any of the auditions she did manage to send me out on. It was a learning experience to say the least.

During that time, I was still living in Guelph, so I would have to drive into the city for the odd audition that she would get me. The drive from Guelph to Toronto would become very familiar to me over time. What should be a 45 minute to one-hour drive could sometimes take over two hours due to the heavy traffic. I remember one audition in particular where, in the waiting room, there were about ten 14-year-old boys and their mothers sitting outside the audition room doors. Then there was me, a 23-year-old fresh-out-of-university student, feeling very much out of place. It was a commercial audition for the new Nintendo DS. I didn't even know what that was! I was still rocking old-school Nintendo! Needless to say, I felt I was too old for the part. I walked into the audition room and the casting director took one look at me and laughed. I shook my head and gave him a look like, *Right? What the hell am I doing here? I'm 23! All these kids outside have dirty peach fuzz moustaches and are being chaperoned by their mothers!* I didn't get the part.

At that time I was also driving into the city on Wednesday nights to take improvisation classes at the Second City Training Centre and working my weekend promotional gigs as Captain Morgan, which had me driving into the city as well.

The long drives for the five-minute auditions, three-hour

improv classes and late nights of promotional weekend work were getting to me. I knew it was time to fully lean into the work, leave the security blanket of my childhood home and peruse my passion fully. In the spring of 2006, I decided to move to Toronto with my friend and fellow University of Guelph graduate, Kevin, who desperately wanted to move to the city to pursue his acting career as well. It was a spur-of-the-moment decision of sorts to move. I was at his apartment in Guelph one afternoon and he blurted out, "Do you want to move to Toronto with me?"

"Sure. When?" I asked.

"April 1st."

"It's March 15th," I said.

"Well then, we better get looking!" he exclaimed.

I was immediately on board. We looked up some places on the magic of the Internet and picked the first place we saw. I grabbed my few belongings, which consisted of a single bed, a bike and my shitty run-down desktop Dell computer, dumped them in my parents' van and left for Toronto!

We moved into a small 300-square-foot (yes, 300-square-foot), two-bedroom apartment in the heart of Kensington Market. If you have never heard of Kensington Market, it's a pretty hip, fruit-fish-and-meat-market, hippie-dog-walking, vintage-shopping, weed-smoke-filled part of town. All of the amenities were at arm's length and the food was fresh, local and cheap. Perfect for a wide-eyed, 23-year-old actor, ready to take on the big city.

Rent was $500 a month each. The apartment was tiny. Tiny

doesn't even begin to do it justice. Our two bedrooms were located beside each other, measuring eight by ten feet. Our washroom was literally in our kitchen, which also doubled as our common living space. Our sink, fridge and stove were all one appliance. How is this possible? Imagine, if you will, two stovetop burners sitting beside a small steel sink, and underneath that sink, a beer fridge. It was an engineering marvel! We had a 12-inch grey Toshiba television that sat directly on our kitchen table. Space was at a premium but that was the apparent norm for Kensington Market. Our air conditioner got to sub-zero temperatures and homelessness ran wild in the streets. The sounds of drunken ramblings were heard from our windows on a daily basis and would often wake us at sunrise or rock us to sleep at night. It was a major culture shock for me.

My first morning there, I remember opening up my blinds to let the sun shine into my bedroom. I looked across the street and there, in an alleyway, was an elderly homeless woman, squatting with her pants around her ankles. *Is she? Oh God! She is. She's taking a shit!* Welcome to T.O., baby!

But, with all the chaos that surrounded me on a daily basis, the energy was unlike anything I had ever experienced before in my life. It was a fabulous mix of art, culture, food and music. I was in love.

My life really seemed to be heading down the right path and things just seemed to keep getting better. I was happy, single, independent and living the dream.

In 2007, I had been accepted into the Second City Conservatory Program for improvisation and I was working on a solo show for the Toronto Fringe Festival. I had also joined a South Asian sketch comedy troupe that was selling out shows all over the city, and on top of that, our troupe received grant funding to shoot a thirty-minute comedy special for television that upcoming year. I was really flying on a high and ready to celebrate, so I rang in 2008 with a bang. We threw a massive party, in what was now my new apartment in the east end of town (yes, the mould-infested apartment). On January 1st, 2008, my Bulgarian roommate and I got into a car and drove to New York City for a three-night tour of continued drunken debauchery.

It was my first time in New York and when we got back from that trip I was so inspired by the energy and hustle of the people there that I knew I needed to work even harder than ever before. I came back to Toronto reinvigorated to take my acting career to the next level. I knew I couldn't do it with my current agent, so as soon as I got back, I let her go and it felt so liberating. I was going to start a new chapter in my life and really go for it. But then, as quickly as things seemed to be heading in the right direction, *it* happened.

Denial

The cab ride from the hospital to my apartment was a long slow trek. The snowstorm was really bad, and as a result the cab driver felt the need to keep apologizing for the ride taking so long. "There's nothing I can do, I have to drive slow, for safety," he kept saying.

"It's really all good, my man. Just get me home safe." We arrived at my apartment around 2 a.m., I tipped the driver more than I could afford, but money and time seemed irrelevant at that moment.

Stefan was still awake, checking on his fantasy basketball stats again. He was the best in our league and this type of nightly commitment was what it took for him to be a champion. As I passed him to go to my room, I casually broke the news. "I think I might have cancer, man." Just like that.

"Oh shit. Want to smoke a joint?" he asked, unfazed.

I don't think he understood the severity of what I was telling him. I don't think I really understood it either. I laughed for a moment, coughed into a clenched fist and this time, I passed on the offer.

There was still no proof, though, right? my head reasoned. The doctor mentioned a biopsy would be needed to confirm the results of the CT scan. So, until I had that information, I wasn't going to believe anyone. *Cancer? Me? No way. I'm Daniel Amedeo Camillo Stolfi, for fuck sakes! Not this body, baby! Not a chance.* My name may be Daniel . . . but for the moment you could call me Denial.

My parents called my brother and asked him to drive to Toronto from Guelph to be with me for the evening. They wanted someone with me while I waited for them to not die on their treacherous adventure down 500 kilometres of snow-covered highway. My brother arrived at my apartment at 6 a.m., after spending four hours in whiteout highway driving conditions. There was an awkward silence as he and I sat and watched the early morning news. We made small talk. "Snow is still really coming down, eh?" he said.

"Yeah, it's brutal," I confirmed. "Did you hear from Mom and Dad?"

"No. Last I heard, they were still on the highway."

"Cool."

It was 7 a.m. when my cellphone started to buzz. It was the signature number that came up on my phone's display when someone was calling from the lobby doors. I'm not sure how my dad does it, but no matter what the road conditions, no matter how far away he is, he can accurately give you the time of his arrival within minutes, and he's never late. I get my punctuality from him. (And he doesn't use GPS or Waze).

They made it. They were safe. We were all safe.

I had packed a small bag of clothes and basic toiletries

in anticipation of their arrival and my trip home. My parents entered the apartment and there was this eerie silence, a silence that cut through the room with an uncomfortable calm. No one said it, but we all knew my life could be in for a real change. There was no need for words. I threw my bag over my shoulder and left my apartment, not knowing when I would return. I anticipated that I would need to stay at my parents' house until I got the official word from the doctors that I did indeed have cancer. My lease was up in five months so I figured I would pay the rent until the end of it and jump that hurdle later. Again, money and time were irrelevant now. We left the apartment in silence. I didn't get a chance to say goodbye to Stefan. He was sleeping. *I'll text him later,* I thought.

The next week of my life was spent trying to break potentially life-altering news to friends, family and co-workers without freaking anyone out. I felt that I had to prepare them for the potential of me being out of commission for the next little while. How long? I had no idea. It could be forever . . . *Cancer does that, no? It does and it has. But it won't, right?*

Many people were supportive and hoped the best for me. Some friends didn't know how to react and joked around about it. "Can we incorporate cancer into our sketches?" one of my troupe members joked.

"If you want, but I won't likely be in them," I replied.

"My cousin had cancer and all he did was eat chocolate!" another one chimed in.

"Hey, if you're tired of being hairy, this is the best way to remove it!" they went on. What in the hell were these guys saying? I felt like I matured ten years in two days. I was terrified on the inside but kept smiling and laughing along on the outside. I tried to make it as positive an experience as possible, not necessarily for me but for everyone around me. I couldn't spend too much energy engaging with their comments, as I would have likely made the same sort of cracks to ease the tension if one of my friends was dealing with the same kind of shit. We all knew it was a serious moment, but us comedians have a curious way of dealing with heavier issues. Maybe we were all in denial.

~

The house smelled like garlic, olive oil, onions and tomatoes. I love that smell. It's a familiar smell that permeates throughout my parents' house and always reminded me of home whenever I was in Toronto heating up a batch of my mom's sauce. I was home now, reflecting and waiting. Sports highlights played on the television as I coughed quietly into my sleeve and waited. I was waiting for the all-important phone call to confirm that the lump in my chest was indeed cancer. Just one week ago, I was waiting for the all-important phone call from a premier talent agency in Toronto, and now, I was waiting for the all-important phone call from the premier oncology specialist in Toronto.

I paced around my parents' kitchen, circling the granite-top island as I ran my finger along its smooth edge. The phone rang and the call display read "Unknown Number." I later found out that any time the call display read "Unknown Number" it meant the hospital was calling. "Hello?" I answered in nervous anticipation.

"This is Sarah speaking from the office of Dr. Sebastian Di Augostino. Is this Daniel Stolfi?"

"Yes, it is. Speaking. Yes," I managed to spit out, trying to conceal my nerves.

"We have a meeting scheduled for you for tomorrow at Toronto East General for two p.m., third floor, G-wing, Room 206. Just want to confirm."

"Can I bring my parents with me?" I asked.

"Of course," she said as if it was a silly question. It wasn't silly for me. I needed them to be with me, desperately.

"See you tomorrow, then." I hung up the phone and exhaled. Then coughed uncontrollably.

Dr. Di Augostino's office was unlike anything I would have expected. I was sure I was going to walk into another sterile-looking room with the parchment paper sheets, stirrups, cotton swabs and fluorescent lights. But this doctor's office was more similar to that of a CEO of an ad agency. It was a large office with a massive bay window overlooking the parking lot. The walls were completely covered in solid oak panels. Photos of his family and crayon drawings, signed by his daughter, sat framed on his Victorian-style cherry-wood desk. He, a dapper looking man in his forties, sat in a big brown leather chair. Gone was the white lab coat, replaced by a clean, pressed blue button-up shirt. His demeanour was calm, as he greeted my family with a smile. "Hello, I'm Dr. Sebastian Di Augostino."

Italian. Definitely Italian, I thought to myself. Now the oak panels made sense. My parents also confirmed this quickly.

"Di Augostino? You're Italian? So are we," my mother said

with a smile.

"Yes, well my parents are Italian and I was born here. It doesn't get much more Italian than Di Augostino, though," he joked, to ease the tension that painfully hung in the air.

I felt a reassurance and comfort with this man. He had a sense of humour, and that made me feel good.

After a bit of banter we got right into the details and he quickly calmed my anxiety by saying the most reassuring thing a doctor could say to you when you are about to enter the fight of your life. "We are going to do whatever it takes to save your life." That's all I needed to hear.

My mother inquired about the world-famous and number one cancer care hospital in North America, located in Toronto. "Would we be able to have Daniel treated at Princess Margaret?" she asked. "We hear it's the best." We were such amateurs at this, it was painful.

He replied confidently, "I would like to recommend Sunnybrook Hospital for Daniel's care. I know a great team of young doctors who specialize in lymphomas and Daniel would be much better served there." Sunnybrook was considered the fifth best hospital for cancer care in North America at the time. I was not really sure how they rank these things, but if this was what he thought was best, then I wasn't about to argue. I trusted this doctor. When someone tells you they will do whatever it takes to save your life, you don't challenge that.

"You the man, Doc. You have my full trust," I told him.

Feeling a bit more comfortable, I asked the questions that had been floating around in my head over the last 48 hours.

"How long do you think this *thing* has been growing?"

"Due to its size, fifteen centimetres by ten centimetres by ten centimetres, it could be anywhere from six months to a year," he informed me.

And to think the whole time, I had no clue. A tumour, the size of a grapefruit, had been apparently sitting over top of my heart and growing inside my chest for six months and I never had a clue. "How long do you think the treatment will be?" my mom asked.

He replied, "With this type of cancer, and the stage that it's in, stage three, it will likely be anywhere from four to six months. We still don't know the exact type of lymphoma. There are over thirty kinds. We'll know for sure once we have the results of your biopsy."

I didn't hear what stage, or what type of cancer it was or the word "biopsy" at that moment . . . all I heard was: *Four to six months.* Then my mind started to wander and rationalize. *I can handle that. I may even get to do my Fringe show in the summer! Our rental lease will be up and then I can move back to Toronto and have a place of my own. I can sign with the new agency too! Four to six months!? That's a cakewalk.* We thanked him and left his office, now armed with a sense of relief and optimism. It was going to be okay.

I still wanted to hold on to the fact that there wasn't full conclusive proof. Until a biopsy was done, I would cling to the fact that it wasn't cancer and they had this whole thing wrong.

But I guess Daniel was still in Denial.

My Balls

The next day, I was on the phone again with Dr. Di Augostino, "There is an off chance that the lymphoma can spread to your testicles, so in order to cover our bases, I'd like to send you in for an ultrasound." I hung up the phone, plopped myself down onto the living room sofa and took a deep breath. It was all so overwhelming. I really didn't want to lose my baby production line of Daniel Stolfi's Manhood, Inc. I had heard of other men who had had testicular cancer and they sometimes got their testicles removed as a result. I was 25 years old and didn't feel I'd made the most use out of my clang-clangs yet and really wanted to hold on to them for as long I could. *Didn't they say it was lymphoma? What do my balls have to do with a tumour in my chest?*

It was all so new to me.

The appointment was scheduled for the coming Tuesday afternoon in Toronto at Sunnybrook Hospital. "I want to go on my own," I told my parents. They didn't argue. My dad had to work that day and my mom was, well, my mom and it was kind of a private procedure.

"I've seen you naked before, you know. I am your mother,"

she tried to joke.

"Yeah, I think the last time you saw me naked was when I was three and I need to keep it that way."

I wrote an email to my friends in Toronto to let them know I would be in town for the day (I didn't go into why), and that it would be nice to meet up. No one was available except for one of my friends from my sketch comedy troupe. Her name was Jessie. She was the other token white person in the group and by "white" I mean super white. Like, if she were to stand out in the sun for more than three minutes she'd go up in a ball of flames, leaving nothing but smoke behind like a cheesy magician doing a disappearing act. She was my best girlfriend and our friendship often revolved around taking jabs at each other and other people's annoying nuances. Mostly, we'd joke about our own respective cultures. Italian vs. Jewish. Who does it best?

"What are you coming in for?" she asked over the phone.

"I don't really want to tell you. Kind of embarrassing," I told her.

"Oh, come on. What—you gotta get your hairy Italian ass examined or something?" she teased.

"No. My hairy Italian balls," I shot back.

"Oh, I am totally coming with you!" she responded excitedly.

"You're such a weirdo. But that's cool. You can come. Would be nice to have the company."

We met at the hospital entrance, and she greeted me with, "Did you have to shave your gross hairy balls to do this thing?"

"Yeah, but I waxed 'em. They're like Chinese medicine balls." We laughed and made our way inside. (I didn't actually have to shave them or wax them, FYI.)

I was back lying on a cold parchment paper–covered table in a super dark ultrasound room, wearing my fancy blue gown, this time completely naked underneath. Jessie patiently sat in the waiting room like the great friend she is. A big hairy technician walked into the room with a nurse. *Wow!* She was smoking hot. Blond hair, tied back in a bun, no makeup required, just a bombshell. So many porno scenarios seem to apply to the healthcare system. Sexy nurses, sexy doctors, gels, darkrooms with padded tables and my balls on the verge of being exposed for "examination." It had all the makings of a classic. I could feel my boys suction themselves up tight to my body. *Now is not the time,* I said to myself, trying to think of warm sweaty thoughts to release my babies to free-swinging glory. It was no use; my balls were about as impressive as an old lady's change purse after church.

"Can you tuck your shaft underneath the towel and expose your testicles?" The big hairy technician instructed. *Did he just say shaft? Why, thank you good sir, but you must have me mistaken for someone else . . .*

"You're going to feel a cold gel on your testicles and then we will begin. Just try to relax," he told me. I looked at the nurse, her eyes glued to the screen, thank god. The specialist applied the gel and began to move the plastic ball–like wand over my good friends. *Just keep looking at the screen, hot lady. They look way bigger on the screen. It adds ten pounds.* "Do you see anything?" I asked them . . . *aside from my massive balls on the screen, of course.*

"Even if we did, we can't divulge that information. We just take the pictures and send them off to the specialist," he informed me. *Well, that's no fun.* He finished the procedure then said the all too familiar porn line, "Wipe yourself off with the towel, and come out when you're ready." *Porno music would inevitably fizzle out right here.* There was no music. I wiped myself off, zipped up my pants and met up with Jessie, who was still patiently waiting in the waiting room.

"So, do they have to tear your balls out?" Jessie asked as I slinked by her.

"Don't know yet. They just took pictures. Now let's go get coffee, please."

"Couldn't find them, eh?" she continued.

"Shut up, ya ass."

We went for coffee, shared some laughs and talked about anything other than cancer. Exactly what I needed.

The Biopsy

My biopsy appointment was set very quickly, and within a couple of days from my meeting with Dr. D, I was back in the hospital getting prepped for the "minor" procedure.

I lay on a CT scan table in my blue ball gown with a clear plastic tube extending from my right forearm. A nurse asked me if I was ready for the chemical dye to be run through my veins. I nodded my head, yes. I felt that familiar warm feeling of the liquid dye coursing throughout my body, again. It was all going as it did the last time: tin flavour in my mouth, warmth from head to toe, the sensation to take a piss, deep breaths in and out for three seconds and the video game sound effects in full swing. They wanted a 3D image of my chest so they could get a good look at the lump before they

> A biopsy is when a doctor takes samples, or in my case, chunks, from the tumour or lesion for further testing. The biopsy would allow them to determine the exact type of lymphoma that I had . . . there are over thirty different types, after all. Based on these results, my eventual oncology team could decide on the best course of action for treatment.

performed the procedure. The mass was literally sitting on top of my heart, so it was best they were sure which mass in my chest they should be poking at. I would have hated for them to mix the two up.

After the beeps and bops came to an end, a porter transferred me onto a rolling bed and off to a room where the actual biopsy procedure would take place. It was another room just like the rest of them.

I lay on my back, chest exposed, as I stared up at the doctor while holding a nurse's hand for support. She had a firm grip. Only the doctor's eyes were visible. The rest of his face was covered by a pale blue paper hat and cotton mask. He had piercing blue eyes and a rather nice tan. *Must have just gotten back from Turks and Caicos or some fancy place like that.* He rubbed cold iodine onto my chest with a cotton swab. Like spreading tomato sauce onto a pizza, he swabbed the brown liquid in concentric circles, moving outward, covering the whole of my left pec. "I'm going to give you a local anesthetic," he told me in a firm and direct tone. I was wide awake for the moment and would remain that way throughout the procedure. No sedative required. I felt the pinch of the needle and the sting of the freezing solution make its way into my chest. He removed the needle from my left pectoral and pushed firmly on the area with his index and middle fingers. His touch quickly became numb and distant, with only the sound of latex-covered hands crinkling as they moved over my bare skin. "You ready?" he asked.

"As ready as I'll ever be," I replied.

He took a large needle, the size of a meat thermometer, and held it firmly upright in his hand. With a front-row seat for the whole procedure, I watched as he brought the needle down and pierced my now completely numbed chest, between my fourth and fifth rib.

"You're going to feel a little pressure," he warned. That was an understatement. The tumour was resting on my heart, so from my vantage point it looked and felt as though he was literally stabbing me right in the middle of my most vital of organs—besides my penis of course, wink and the gun. He put his weight behind the needle and pushed it hard into my chest. The needle popped through the muscle tissue and pierced into the tumour like a knife ripping through raw meat. I felt a sudden sting of sharp pain in my heart and became breathless for the moment. *Was this what being stabbed in the heart feels like?*

"Are you okay?" he asked.

"Yeah, sure," I said, breathless, now squeezing the assistant's hand even harder.

"Most of the time we only need three or four samples to get accurate results but I'm going to take five just for good measure. Now, you're going to feel a little pressure."

I'm pretty sure all doctors call everything "pressure." No matter what they are doing to you, whether setting a bone in your leg or stabbing you with a giant needle through the heart, they just chalk it up to "pressure." I'm pretty sure it's more commonly referred to as "pain" but we wouldn't want to scare anyone, now would we? *Just call it pain, you fuck!*

"Wait!" I shouted. He stopped for a moment. Stunned.

"What is it?" he asked.

"Before you start, how are my balls?" I began to ramble. "I never got the results from my ultrasound." The doctor shot his assistant a quizzical look.

"Sorry, what are you referring to?" she inquired.

"I had my balls tested for cancer and no one told me if I had testicular cancer or not."

There was a silence. Confusion. "I'll quickly check your folder," she assured me. She let go of my hand as the doctor leaned back in his chair and crossed his arms. He let out a sigh. *Sorry to waste your time, Doc.* I thought to myself as the large needle protruded from my chest. We waited as the needle moved rhythmically up and down with every breath I took. After a moment . . .

"No cancer in the testicles," she said kindly.

"Cut away, Doc!" I told him. He leaned back in and got back to work. He started pressing a trigger-like button on top of the needle, resulting in a loud clicking sound, with each *click* indicating the removal of a piece of the tumour. Each *click* was followed by a sharp sting to the inside of my chest. It felt like he was taking chunks right from my heart. I was in a lot of pain but squeezed harder on the nurse's hand to push through it. After he removed the fifth and final sample for the biopsy I let out a deep breath and let go of the nurse's hand, which I was pretty sure I had rendered completely crushed.

Before he removed the needle he asked, "Do you want to have your lung drained of all that fluid while we're at it? You'll feel much better once it's done and since the needle is already in there, we may as well take advantage and suck the fluid out."

I looked at the needle buried deep into my chest, then up at the monitor, and back toward the doctor.

"Go for it, Doc."

"It won't hurt. I promise."

This time, he was actually right, it didn't hurt. I just felt "pressure." I couldn't help but take a look at what he was doing. I looked down at my chest and saw blood and pus being sucked out of my lung through a large clear syringe. Once full, he emptied it in multiple loads to a large clear container with markings along the side to measure the volume, like you would use for baking a cake. Instead of a sweet strawberry-shortcake batter, he was mixing up a nasty new recipe of blood and some other awful gelatinous liquid. I reached out to hold the nurse's hand again but this time my grip was much weaker. I felt a rush of blood race away from my face as the lights became brighter and the room began to spin. "I'm about to pass out, Doc," I mumbled. He immediately stopped and looked me right in the eyes, his sharp blue specs locking in.

"Don't you faint on me now, kid. If you faint, we will have a whole slew of other problems that we don't need to deal with right now."

I was terrified to close my eyes, willing them to stay open, stretching my eyelashes toward my eyebrows.

"Get him a cold towel, stat, and place it on his forehead," he ordered the nurse. She did so quickly. The coolness of the cloth calmed my nerves as the blood started coming back to my face. I pushed the thought of the pink ooze being sucked out of my body deep into the recesses of my brain.

One point two litres of fluid, pus and blood were drained from my left lung. The needle was removed from my chest, the cold towel now warm from my overheated forehead. I took a deep breath with my new lungs. Clearer now, I *breathed.* "Thanks, Doc," I told him. "Did I break your hand?" I asked the nurse.

"No sweetheart, but you came close."

I smirked. She patted me on the foot.

It's Official

My brother sat across from me at our dining room table. He was recently engaged and worked full-time as a physiotherapist in Guelph. He's handsome as all hell, with a darker complexion than mine. His black hair was meticulously formed into a perfect coif. When describing his hair, he would tell you it's "jet black." Can't just be black, it's jet black or nothing. He took a sip of his water and motioned toward the pad thai "Can you pass me that?" I picked up the bowl and handed it to him across the table. My sister, the oldest, now six months pregnant, chewed her vegetarian spring roll slowly while admiring the homemade red wine she couldn't drink. My dad, however, happily sipped away. My mom, beside me, fiddled with her chopsticks as a quiet calm settled over the table.

It was a Friday night in March, now just a few days after the biopsy. My parents had recently returned from a trip to Asia, which had widened their worldly palates, so of course we were eating Thai food from a little restaurant in Guelph, population now 115,000. Authentic Thai cuisine at its best, I'm sure.

The phone rang, cutting through the silence, jolting us all momentarily. Four sets of dark brown eyes settled on mine. We all knew it could be "The Call."

"Don't they know we're eating?" I said sarcastically, in an attempt to lighten the mood. I got up from the table and proceeded to the ringing telephone on the kitchen counter. I took a deep breath and answered the phone. "Hello."

"Hi, is this Daniel?" the voice on the line asked.

"Yes, speaking," I replied.

"This is Dr. Richards. I know you're probably out with your friends or something right now, so I'm sorry to call you so late on a Friday night."

"Actually, I'm at home with my family waiting for your call," I told him.

"Well, I'll cut right to it then. It is what we thought it was. You have cancer." Just like that. No peas and carrots, just the meat and potatoes.

"I figured as much." There was a brief awkward silence.

"It's a form of non-Hodgkin's lymphoma. Acute T-lymphoblastic. Stage three by the looks of it." More awkward silence, as I didn't really know what to make of that. "Ok. Well, we will call you shortly to set up a time for you to come in. Sorry again for calling so late," he added.

"HA! Do you think I give a shit? You are telling me I have cancer . . . you could call me at 4 a.m., and I wouldn't give a shit! Cancer!"

I didn't say that. What I did say: "Oh no, that's fine. I'm just glad you called."

I hung up the phone and broke the news to my family. There was a certain unsettling calm that hung over the table. I had no idea what my family must have been thinking. They did a great job of keeping their collective poker faces on, remaining still. No tears were shed, just a silent knowing calm. It was the first moment when we could unequivocally say that I had cancer and that my cancer had a name, a long and complicated one: "Stage Three Acute Non-Hodgkin's T-Lymphoblastic Lymphoma." This was for real. No more questions about what it might be or what we hoped it could be. Anything other than cancer would have been ideal, but the reality was, it was cancer. It had come for me. I had never been so scared.

ACT II

Easter Weekend at the Fertility Clinic

Holy Thursday. It was one of those rare Easters that occurred in March. It was also the day my oncologist had me come to the hospital to start my chemotherapy treatments. Happy Easter!!

I arrived at Sunnybrook Hospital, with Mom and Dad. We began to make our way to the C-Wing of the massive complex. A man in a white lab coat greeted us at a service kiosk on the main floor. "Would you like to use a wheelchair, Mr. Stolfi?" he asked. *Is this guy for real? I'm 25 years old and my legs are working just dandy, thank you very much!* But part of me wanted to be wheeled around.

"No, that's fine. I can walk."

We were ushered along a never-ending sterile hallway toward a set of elevators that took us up to floor three of the hospital. Floor Three, Ward C, or "C-3," as it was referred too, was the cancer ward. Fitting to name the cancer ward with the letter *C* and seeing as my cancer had progressed to stage three, it was all so fantastically convenient and easy to remember!

My room was located at the end of another long hallway.

I passed a nurses' station and a number of rooms with sickly looking people lying in beds. I heard some moans and groans and one girl just fuming about how she didn't want to be there anymore. She sounded young and terrified. The hallway reeked of hand sanitizer, poorly cooked hospital food and traces of . . . what's the word? Urine? Definitely urine.

We entered my room. It was a shared room but I had the window with a view . . . of the parking lot. My roommate wasn't there, and I was glad to have the room to myself for a bit.

The crinkling sound of plastic echoed off the yellow cinder-block walls as I sat on the cheap, thin hospital bed mattress. The sheets, white, with a thread count of possibly two, were so thin they were practically see-through. "No pillow?" I asked the porter.

"We're working on it," he replied. *We're working on it? Seriously? No pillow? Where am I?* "Your oncologist will be with you shortly," the porter assured me. I sat patiently in silence with my parents casing the room for what it had to offer in terms of perks.

"Great view of our car from up here," Dad remarked. "You have your own washroom too! And room service!" He always tried to crack a joke to cut the tension. It kept my mind at ease. I laughed along.

We sat in silence for a while when a young man, wearing designer frame glasses and a white lab coat, entered the room. This was my first encounter with my oncologist. My first thought: *He is so freaking young!* He had an aura of wisdom about him, though. He looked wise beyond his years. He had this youthful glow about him too. He smiled widely and adjusted his glasses as he awkwardly waved hello with his other hand. I could see Mom's face melt with concern. She clearly thought he was too young to be treating me and later confirmed this with me. I, on the other hand, was all for it. He had a warm, caring presence about him and a genuine smile. The true test would be how he reacted to a little dark humour by yours truly. After all, laughter is the best medicine.

"I'm Dr. Michael Chang," he said.

"What's up, Doc? Penthouse suite. Not too shabby," I joked. He tilted his head slightly and chuckled. Sort of gave me a look like, "You know why you're in here, right?" I smiled back. *I know.* He passed the test.

It would be me and Dr. Chang from now on. We were a team. This was the man who was going to save my life.

As he spoke to me about the treatment, I couldn't help but notice he was talking about a lot of drugs, and a lot of "phases of treatment." The timeline seemed to be much longer than the four to six months which I was given by Dr. Di Augostino just a little while back. "Phase one and phase two are the hardest but they are the shortest and will be complete after two months. Phase three is about six months long and then if all is going well, we move on to phase four until the full two years are up."

Alarm bells went off in my head. Mom perked up and blurted out, "TWO YEARS?!" then calmed herself quickly. "Two years? We were told four to six months." Dr. Chang looked at us a little funny and then shook his head sympathetically.

"After looking at the sample from the biopsy, we decided

that the two-year protocol we want to put you on is the most effective for this type of cancer. It has a ninety-five percent success rate. The treatment protocol has been around for thirty years and, albeit it is one of the most difficult chemotherapy treatments out there, you are young and your body can handle it. In the grand scheme of things, two years now for forty to fifty years of life is worth it." We couldn't argue with that logic, but what went through my head in that moment was the following: *I won't be able to perform my show at the Toronto Fringe Festival. I won't be doing any comedy anytime soon. I might never act again! I might never dance again!! I love dancing. I love it. Ninety-five percent is 5% shy of 100% and I'm all about 100%! Soccer, basketball, stand-up comedy, acting, working out, eating the foods I love, partying with friends, sitting in the sun, sex, going on vacation, sex! (I wasn't currently having any sex, but the potential for sex, ya know?) To be without these things, these passions of mine, for four to six months, I can barely handle, but two fucking years?!! In the prime of my life?!!*

"Think of it as a two-year vacation," he said, snapping me out of my thoughts. *Think of it as a two-year vacation? Question: who in the hell would ever sign up for a two-year cancer vacation? Two years of hair loss, weight loss, nausea, vomiting and erectile dysfunction, all in the comfort of your parents' house in Guelph, Ontario, Canada! Quite possibly the worst sales pitch for a vacation ever!*

I took it all in, and held my breath.

"Can we start after the Easter long weekend?" I asked him. *It's Easter. The death of Christ and all that good stuff . . . Last Supper and such.* I just wanted to spend some time with my family. Not for religious reasons but for just being with the people who loved me unconditionally, but I could play the religious card if I had to! I was also desperate to delay all of it. *I mean, two years? What's a couple of more days?* Dr. Chang seemed very supportive of the situation but also hesitant. "We really should get you started right away, but you can start on Monday, okay?"

"Deal. That's when Jesus rises and lives again and all that stuff, right?" No reaction. *Maybe too far?*

He gave me some steroids that would sustain me for the weekend to keep the tumours at bay. "I guess I am going to get my 'Last Supper' after all," I joked. *Still probably a little too dark for the moment, but he'll come around, I think.*

He quickly changed the subject. "Oh, before you leave, I should tell you that the heavy amounts of chemotherapy can make you sterile." *Just keep dropping the bombs on me, eh, Doc?*

"Okay. Good to know." I was still so caught up in the two-year protocol thing—he could have said anything and I would have been all for it. He could have said, "By the way, your mom will have to give you sponge baths from now on," and I would have been like, "Cool. All part of the deal, I guess." He could have said, "You will have to wear a diaper for a good part of the treatment, just in case, you know . . . you shit your pants," and I would have been like, "Of course! I LOVE diapers." Thank goodness he didn't say any of that stuff, but he did go on to add one more gem and said, "Oh and we do have to test you for AIDS, too." Aaaand, scene.

Excuse me? Did he just say AIDS? Before my head blew right off my body, he explained, "The type of cancer you have is related to the immune system and sometimes we find that this form of cancer is found in AIDS patients. As a precaution, we will have to test your blood to see if you have the virus. Just to rule it out officially."

So at that moment, I was seriously clenching my butt cheeks to prevent myself from shitting my pants, while trying to rationalize. *Based on my sexual history of hardly any, and my lack of experience swapping blood with people for all these years, I am pretty sure I am good on the AIDS front, but I still think those diapers might come in handy!*

"So what do I do about the sterility thing?" I asked calmly, while my insides turned.

"I can set up an appointment for you," he replied. "We'll get you in tomorrow."

So, on the day of Jesus's death, I'd be off to the fertility clinic to freeze my baby makers in case I wanted to make life rise again in the future through a virgin birth kind of thing. Was that irony? Coincidence? I never could tell the two apart.

~

Back home now, my parents, my sister and I ate pasta for dinner. No one was speaking. We sat in silence. "Do you want me to come with you to the fertility clinic?" Mom asked.

"No, I do not want you to be anywhere near me when I jerk off into a cup!" I replied. My sister laughed. *Moms are weird. My mom is weird.*

"You know, I've seen you naked before," she said (again) like a bratty teenager who thinks they know everything.

"We've been through this . . . that was when I was, like,

three and this is not the same thing!"

We all had to laugh.

I arrived at the fertility clinic the following day. It was a sunny Friday afternoon. The air was crisp. Perfect for ejaculating into a plastic cup! The façade of the clinic was a townhome-looking building in a complex of attached houses. It looked more like a residential complex than a specialty health clinic. I entered through the front doors and headed directly into a waiting room with leather chairs lining the walls. Coffee tables with various magazines scattered about the surface sat in front of the chairs. It was packed with young couples looking very apprehensive and nervous as indicated by the restless leg syndrome that everyone seemed to have. Eyes locked on me from all directions, each couple looking at me wondering, "What's this guy's story?" Everyone who was there was either:

1. Trying to get pregnant.
2. Having a vasectomy to avoid getting anyone pregnant again. Or
3. Just found out they had cancer and needed to put their sperm away in case the chemotherapy zapped all of them to death over a two-year span.

I fell into the "C" category. *C* is for cancer. I went to school.

I approached the receptionist, a blond bombshell, with seriously large boobs. Like huge. Cleavage on full display. *I'm just stating the facts.* "I have an appointment to make a deposit," I said, trying to hide the awkwardness of it all.

She was about my age, wore glasses and spoke in a high

whiny voice, "You'll have to see the specialist first to discuss the procedure to make your deposit." *I'm pretty sure I know how to jack it into a cup . . . but if I have to talk to some dude who "specializes" in masturbating to show me the ropes, then so be it.* Had I been doing it wrong all these years? I wondered.

"You can just wait in his office," she continued.

His office screamed fertility. It was covered in posters and charts; one that said IT ONLY TAKES ONE, and the other, FAMILY FIRST. Images of the male and female reproductive organs were everywhere. I felt like I was in my Grade Ten sex-education class all over again. I sat down in one of the two chairs on the other side of his brown oak desk. Dr. Exian came into the office with a big smile on his face, full of energy and excitement. He clearly had a hard-on for fertility. Boom! Fertility puns!

After some general conversation and friendly banter, he went straight into his sales pitch. "When do you start treatment?" he asked.

"Monday," I replied.

His face lit up, and like a dirty car salesmen he began upselling me. "Well then, why don't you make your first deposit today, another on Saturday, we're closed Sunday, and then we can squeeze you in on the Easter Monday morning? We might as well get three samples in if we can. The more the merrier, am I right?"

"Sounds good to me." *I think he just conned me. Your poster says it only takes one. Well played, sir.*

Back in the waiting room with all the young couples again,

the receptionist called me over to her desk. "There is someone downstairs using the room right now, so just have a seat and I'll let you know when he's all done." She handed me a clear plastic bag with an orange-capped, clear plastic cup on the inside. A couple of minutes later, I saw an awkward-looking hairy, sweaty man come up from the basement stairs. The receptionist looked at him, and then at me, and said loudly, "The room is ready for you, Mr. Stolfi!" *I have to follow this guy? Did they even have time to sanitize the room?*

The receptionist led me down the stairs and into a room on the left side of the hallway. Not so much a room, but a box. An eight foot by eight foot box with two windows. One window looked out into the parking lot and the other actually looked out into the hallway of the basement. Nothing but a set of thin, grey venetian blinds separated me, masturbating to my heart's content into a plastic cup, and a group of dudes with ice packs on their balls as they recovered from vasectomies.

I looked around the room and saw nothing but a leather chair, a television, some magazines and a roll of toilet paper on the floor. The nurse looked at me and said cheerfully, "There are magazines, DVDs and VHS videos to aid in your deposit." *VHS? That's disgusting! Is this the '80s? Who watches VHS anymore?*

"So just go in the cup, put your name, date and time on it, seal it up tight and then ring the doorbell on the wall outside when you're all done." She handed me the cup and left the room but not before saying, "Good luck!"

So there I was, standing in the middle of this room, with a plastic cup in my hand and my pants around my ankles. I wasn't going to sit in the leather chair the hairy, sweaty-ass awkward dude was just sitting in, so I went for the DVD, but I couldn't seem to get it to work. It was stalling and skipping. No image, nothing. *I guess I'm not as technologically savvy as I thought.* So, I popped in the old reliable VHS, and sure enough, it was old . . . but reliable. There was this Russian prison guard locking up these female inmates into a clearly studio-fabricated jail cell. They asked him if they could make a telephone call and he replied, "I got your telephone right here." (He was referring to his dick.) And, so it began. The '80s music kicked in and the pubic hair started flying everywhere. I did what I had to do because I was twenty-five years old, feeling fly and had the sex drive of a dog in heat 24/7. But I was a little disappointed with the amount. You know, of baby making juice. So, naturally, I tried to do a double up, a double take. My thoughts were, *when I ring that doorbell and the cute nurse sees my weak performance, she's going to laugh at me.* But it was no use. For the first time since I could even produce the sweet goods, I just wasn't performing. I didn't know if it was the steroids I was on or the fact that I was digesting the "I have cancer" thing, but it would be a one-shot deal this time around.

I left the room and rang the bell on the wall. This cute Asian nurse—*Why does she have to be so cute?*—answered the door, wearing a blue gown and white latex gloves. I handed her the plastic cup and smiled. She closed the door and I was left standing there feeling sort of used and dirty. I looked down the hallway and saw the group of men dressed in hospital gowns with ice packs on their balls. We gave each other a supportive nod. *I wonder if Dr. Exian upsold them on a two-for-one sale?*

I went back upstairs to wait for my results. They had to make sure my boys were "good" before they could freeze them. The room was still full of young couples and the receptionist told me to take a seat amongst them. The phone rang and the receptionist answered. She then yelled out across the room, "Daniel Stolfi!" All eyes locked on me. "Your counts are in and everything looks fine! So we'll just go ahead and freeze them for you!"

Thanks for telling everyone! What if my counts were bad?! Would you yell that out too? "Daniel Stolfi! Your counts are in and it looks like you're a little low, sweetheart . . . yeah, there are a couple of guys with two tails and one of them just keeps running into the side of the Petri dish . . . he must think it's the egg!" Come on! I just thanked her and told her I'd see her tomorrow.

On Saturday, it was the same deal. Same box, same TV, same VHS . . . but a little further along in the jail cell this time. The Russian prison guard was now fast asleep as the girls were ready to make their escape—but not before the warden had something to say about it. *Ziiiip!*

~

Monday, March 24th, 6 a.m. I had one last deposit to make before going to the hospital to start treatment. The dry cold air bit my fingers as I climbed into the ugly toothpaste mint-green Hyundai Elantra with Mom, Dad and my pregnant sister. My brother drove up separately. It would be a full family affair. I was so grateful for that. I held on to the ziplock bag containing the sterile plastic cup with the orange lid. Dr. Exian gave me an extra cup to take home so I could bring it to the clinic and make my deposit. They didn't open until 8 a.m.—well, at least the receptionist who prints the labels and distributes the cups wasn't working, but the lab was open and the porn was still running. Porn doesn't take time off. There was an awkward silence as we drove toward the fertility clinic for my last deposit. "That's an awfully big cup, isn't it?" my sister joked. We laughed. She loves awkward humour.

We got to the clinic and I hopped out of the car. "Go to Tim Horton's and grab a coffee and I'll call you guys when I'm all done," I told them uncomfortably as they stifled their laughter.

They didn't even get halfway to the coffee and doughnut paradise when I called them to let them know I had done the deed. I was never much for marathons. More of a sprinter.

"That was quick," Mom joked.

"Thanks. This isn't awkward at all," I replied. We all laughed.

Three hundred dollars a year to keep my boys frozen in time and space. My folks paid for it. I mean, it was their grandchildren, right?

Day 1 ... Sort Of

A little lighter in the sack now, I arrived at the hospital with my parents and sister and proceeded to the infamous C-3 wing of the building. I entered my room and sat at the edge of my bed. My friends and family didn't let me arrive to the hospital empty-handed. Gifts, consisting of books, DVDs and even a Nintendo DS—yes, the same system I had auditioned for with the dirt-stash kids and their mommies just a couple years ago—was there to entertain me. *So that's what it looks like. I was mime-playing it all wrong*, I thought. The aim of these gifts was to occupy my mind for the eight-to-ten-day stay in my luxurious sterile hospital room with a view, while my body was pumped with chemical drugs. My bootlegged DVD movie haul consisted of *Rambo IV*, *Dumb and Dumber* and the complete *Best of Oprah* series.

My brother took the morning off work and met us at the hospital. He and my sister gave me a bag of goodies, too. My sister placed the shiny blue paper gift bag down on the window ledge of my 300-square-foot, two-bedroom hospital apartment. It all felt quite similar to my apartment in Kensington Market but with a bunch of cancer patients for neighbours instead of homeless public poopers. "We got you lip balm, magazines and a journal so you can write things down, you know, if you want," my sister said.

"No pressure," my brother chimed in, in his baritone mumble that only my sister and I had come to understand.

It was a brown leather-bound book, with 400 blank pages, ready to be filled with my thoughts and feelings.

"Write in it whenever you can. Just track your progress, or just write about the experience. You know, whatever," my sister continued.

"Yeah, no pressure," my brother said again.

"Yeah, I got that part," I assured him. I laughed. Their collective nerves and anxiety were poorly masked by trying to encourage a passive, keep-it-cool attitude. I love them for it.

"I'm not really one to keep a journal, but it's never too late to try something new," I told them. "Thanks."

Three doctors entered the room a little apprehensively. I don't think they'd ever seen so many Italians in one room at the same time before. Dr. Chang spoke with a sheepish smile on his face. "Just wanted to let you know that we aren't quite ready to go through with the chemotherapy treatments just yet. We don't have all the results from the biopsy and it would be best to proceed once we have all the information we need."

I guess you'd hate to start treating me for cancer and then find out that you misdiagnosed me. Wait, come to think about it, what would have happened if we started treatment on Friday like you had initially said? "We want to check to see if the cancer has advanced to stage four and spread to your bones," he continued. *So still cancer, but maybe worse cancer . . . got it.* "We will have to take a bone marrow sample now and then we should have all the results in the morning. We can then proceed from there."

"Is the bone marrow test going to hurt?" I asked.

"You'll feel some . . . pressure," he said. He exited the room and everyone else followed. My family waited in the visitor waiting room while I waited for the doctor to start the "pressure"-filled bone marrow extraction.

A short Asian man named Dr. Wong waddled into my room pushing a metal table on wheels with what looked to be a number of sterile-looking pokers and pinchers. He spoke in a broken English. "I'm a bone marrow specialist . . . best in business," he said with a smile. "Turn on your side and I freeze your hip," he instructed. Then, "Pull down pants." *Not even going to take me out for dinner first?*

With my pants down and my butt exposed, he started pushing his thumb deep into the boney portion of my hip just above my bum. *He must be feeling around for the perfect spot to extract the juice.* "Bee sting," he called out before plunging a large needle into my skin to inject a general anesthetic around my hip. He was so aggressive and routine about the whole thing while smiling the entire time. "I've done this hundred times! Nothing to worry about," he assured me.

"Okay, but this is my first time, so go easy," I told him. He didn't. He grabbed a meat thermometer–sized needle from his rolling table. *Are they running a hospital or a butcher shop here?* He pushed it with some force into my skin until it reached the bone. That part didn't hurt so much because the skin was frozen. I just felt . . . pressure. What came next, however, was a world of hurt that no human being should ever have to endure. He put all his weight on top of the needle and gave a heavy heave downward, forcing the needle into my hip. I heard a *pop* and felt a *crack*. The pain shot through my body like a lightning bolt of electricity, down my leg and through my toes. "We in," he said. *You think!* I bit my tongue and swallowed the pain. He began to extract the marrow and I immediately felt a stinging sensation, like a dozen bees planting their stingers in one spot. It was a sensation of pain that I had never felt before. I wanted to scream. "Hum—*hmm*," Dr. Wong instructed.

"Hum!?" I asked loudly.

"Hum! No scream. Helps with pain," he reassured me. So I hummed, loudly, but the pain didn't stop. I couldn't believe this type of implausible stinging could even exist. It seemed never-ending until finally, he yanked the needle out of my hip and the pain subsided after one final shock. "Okay, we all done," he said matter-of-factly. "You pull up pants now." He packed up his equipment and left the room as I rolled onto my back and let out a deep calming breath. *I'm alive. I'm alive.*

Moments later, a nurse entered the room with some rubber bands, needles and empty plastic vials. "I'm going to take some blood," she told me. With no time to think we were back in the ring.

"Okay, sure." She found a nice plump vein in my arm between my bicep and forearm and inserted the needle. The blood flowed easily into the plastic tubes, four in total, varying in colour and size. She snapped the rubber band off my bicep and in no more than 30 seconds, she was gone, off to her next patient.

Before my head hit the pillow, another nurse walked in wearing pink scrubs with her hair in a bun. She was young and pretty. I figured she'd want to chat with me for a while because we were about the same age and she probably didn't come across too many younger patients. She dropped off some pills in a white paper takeout ketchup cup. "Where are the fries?" I joked. She didn't laugh. There were exactly 19 pills of varying shapes, sizes and colours. "Take these with some water," she said.

"All of them?" I asked.

"Yes, please."

"Why am I taking so many?"

"It's a combination of drugs that were prescribed to you by your oncologist. There are steroids, Tylenol, Gravol and other drugs to counter the side effects of the chemotherapy." She watched me, while holding my wrist, feeling for my pulse. *She's pure business. Wonderful. No small talk today!* I took the pills, a couple at a time, each one making me gag slightly from the chalky flavour and texture. "You should just shoot 'em all back at once," she suggested.

"Seriously?"

"Down the hatch, in my opinion."

After I swallowed my final pill she gave me a pat on the foot and turned to leave. "Are you my nurse for my stay?" I blurted out, in a desperate attempt to keep someone my age around a little longer.

"This is my final shift for the day, another nurse will be in for the rest of the day." And just like that, the youth quota was cut in half.

The routine for the remainder of my stay was starting to take shape. Blood work at 5 a.m., 11 a.m., 5 p.m. and 11 p.m. with 19 pills every morning. At the time, I don't think I had ever taken 19 pills in total throughout my entire 25 years of existence, let alone 19 pills in one day. It was incredibly daunting and the actual chemotherapy hadn't even started yet!

"Is it okay to come back inside?" Mom whispered from the hallway.

"Yes, please," I replied.

She was joined by my good friend and former roommate from university, Jeff. He was a crazy Northern Ontario boy from Timmins with a tough exterior but kind heart. My dad, brother and sister poked their heads in too to say goodbye and head back home. My dad's school work week beckoned him early in the morning. My pregnant sister was off to the airport to head back to Montreal to be home with her husband, and my brother had to get back to work at his physiotherapy clinic. Life goes on. "We'll see you soon," they assured me.

"Thanks for coming," I told them.

Mom, Jeff and I chatted into the evening. We grabbed a bite in the hospital cafeteria and I scarfed down a rotisserie quarter chicken dinner from Swiss Chalet. Mom paid for it. One of the perks to having cancer is people just feel the need to start paying for your food. I mean, she's my mom, though, so of course she paid for it.

Visiting hours were now over and it was time for Jeff and Mom to go home. I went back to my room, put my headphones on and listened to the 25th anniversary edition of Michael Jackson's *Thriller* album. I opened my new journal, heard the crisp spine of the book crack, clicked my pen and began to write.

March 24, 2008

Day 1 of 730

Night 1 in the hospital. Should be fun. The day was pretty good. I had my bone marrow tested and that hurt like a bitch!! But I'm alive. Tomorrow's going to be a rough day but I think I will have some more visitors to make it easier. I'm going to attempt a shower and shave tomorrow. Gonna try to make this cancer thing look good. I gotta get in the shower before they hook up the IV. My roommate seems a little weird, and there is this guy in another room that sounds like fucking Chewbacca from Star Wars. This hospital life is gonna be fun. Seven days, I'm out. Gonna watch Rambo then hit the hay. I'm gonna beat the shit out of this thing. JUST WAIT AND SEE!!

- 19 pills
- 1 bone marrow test
- 5 vials of blood

Fighting Cancer = Priceless.

Day 2

Tuesday, March 25th, 2008. A major US recession and housing market crash was all the rage at the time. That meant absolutely nothing to me because I had cancer and I was about to start two years of chemotherapy. What recession? Three doctors entered my room, one of whom was my oncologist, Dr. Chang. "Are you ready to begin?" he asked.

"As ready as I'll ever be," I said, surprisingly quite confident.

My cousin Davide and Mom had arrived first thing in the morning and sat by my bedside the entire time. "I'm going to make this shit look good," I joked. They laughed it off, nervously. I was 185 pounds and feeling great, relatively speaking. My curly hair was as thick and as dark as ever, I smelled good and I was looking dapper in my red Adidas soccer shorts with the signature three white stripes. My bare chest was puffed out, screaming, "Bring it on!" At least that's what was going on in my head.

The IV nurse entered my room with her tool kit of needles, elastic bands, surgical tape and cotton balls. She inserted a needle into a plump blue vein on the back of my hand. The needle pinched and stung as it broke the skin but took hold with relative ease. She placed a piece of clear dimpled tape over the needle and all I could think was, *that tape is going to hurt like hell when they rip it off.* Italian hairiness and tape don't do well together.

Before they began the first round of treatment, my doctors introduced me to the oncology pharmacist. He entered my room with a big goofy smile on his face. *Probably nervous*, I thought. He began to list off all the side effects of all the drugs I'd be taking. He really seemed to be enjoying it too. "The Doxorubicin is red in colour. It's injected intravenously and causes hair loss, vomiting and nausea…" He adjusted his glasses before continuing. "But we can counter that with Gravol. Your urine will likely appear red, due to the colour of the drug."

What the fuck? "Red?" I asked. He just kept going, nodding and smiling as I interjected with the odd "Really?" Or, "For real?"

"It will likely also cause headaches but we can counter that with Tylenol. The Methotrexate is yellow in colour and is injected intravenously as well. It causes infertility, which you have already taken care of, I've been told. Oh, and constipation."

"Awesome!" I said sarcastically. He didn't even flinch.

"Severe constipation . . ." he clarified.

"Even better!" I exclaimed. He just kept talking.

"So we will be giving you a mix of stool softeners and laxatives to help you through that." He continued to list off more and more side effects followed by a list of drugs to help counter the side effects and then the side effects of *those* drugs that should be tolerable enough without *more* drugs. "It's my first day here at this hospital and you're my first patient, so I'm a little nervous but admittedly a bit excited too!" he informed me. *Now the awkward smile on his face made sense. This guy was such a dork.* I sort of wanted to punch him in his dorky face. *It's all new to me too, bro, but I'm not as excited, so please curb your enthusiasm.* I just wanted him to act as though he understood that it was all so overwhelming. A little empathy, ya know? He was so clinical.

After he handed me a stack of paper, with all the drugs listed on them and all the side effects that could potentially happen as a result of taking them, he left the room and wished me luck. It was time for the treatment to begin.

A large clear bag filled with a bright, almost fluorescent, yellow liquid was hooked up to a metal hanger at the top of my IV pole. The IV pole stood on a set of squeaky wheels at the side of my bed. I couldn't even begin to think of how many patients before me had had this trusty pole as their sidekick throughout their treatment on C-3. My mom, cousin, oncology team and I watched the yellow liquid drip slowly out of the bag, down a long clear tube and into the back of my hand. It felt warm. I was terrified.

Phase 1: Initiation

My oncologist informed me that the best course of action was to put me on a heavy cocktail of drugs called the Acute Lymphoblastic Lymphoma (ALL) Dana Farber protocol. The protocol consisted of a four-phase intensive chemotherapy regime that began with heavy doses of drugs, which gradually declined over a two-year period or until full and complete remission. The first phase, aptly titled the "initiation phase," lasted fifteen days and would prove to be extremely difficult, not only mentally but physically as well.

March 26, 2008

Day 3 of 730

I couldn't write last night 'cause I was pretty sick. My family and friends hung out with me and kept my spirits up, which made me feel good. But when my friends left I got nauseous and started puking . . . I also had a pretty bad headache. I puke when I take the pills. The taste or thought of them turns my stomach. So I missed a couple of pills last night. Fuck it. I have taken quite a bit.

Today, I am gonna get some red drug shit . . . I think they missed a couple of other pills but I took so many of them yesterday I think it was enough for one day. Keep on trucking, baby!

> *- 17 pills (supposed to be 19) . . . oops*
> *- 5 vials of blood*
> *- 2 spinal taps*
> *- 2 IV pushes*
> *- 2 bags of Gravol*

Fighting cancer = Hard.

"This is the one called Doxorubicin," the nurse told me, as she sat at my bedside. "Nicknamed, 'The Red Killer.'"

"Well, that's reassuring," I joked sarcastically.

"It's given this name because it is very potent, red in colour, highly poisonous and extremely effective in killing all the white blood cells in your body." She said this as though she'd said it a hundred times. I was pretty sure she had. I consulted my stack of papers the goofy pharmacist gave me, as she continued to speak.

"Is this the one that turns my pee red?" I asked.

"Sure is," she replied with what I think was a smile. The nurse was covered in a blue protective uniform from head to toe as she handled a large syringe filled with the ruby red poison liquid.

"Why are you wearing so much protection?" I asked.

"If I were to spill this on my skin it would burn," she replied matter-of-factly.

"And that's going in my veins??!!" She didn't respond and began to push the plunger on the needle. The red liquid slowly passed through the clear plastic tube connected to the back of my hand.

"This drug will be the main cause of hair loss," she told me. "Within seven to ten days your hair will fall out completely."

"We'll see about that," I challenged. She just nodded her head and smiled with her eyes, "Sure." I could only see her eyes.

My Hair

When I was told that I would lose my hair, it was one of those moments where I felt like I wasn't allowed to be upset about it. "It's just hair," the doctors would say. "It will grow back."

"It's a lot easier for guys to lose their hair during treatment because guys can walk around bald all the time and no one will think anything of it," a friend told me. This may be true for some, but for me, it was different. My hair was always a defining feature of mine. Throughout my entire life I had thick, tight, dark brown curly hair. During my childhood, my parents would cut it short, so I never really knew just how curly my hair was until I was nine years old. I remember coming out of the shower one day and running my hands through my hair. I walked down the set of large wooden steps at my parents' house and looked at myself in the mirror at the bottom of the stairs. I remember seeing for the first time these dark wet ringlets of brown curls glimmering on my head.

"Mom, I have curly hair!" I yelled out.

"Of course you do! Just like me," she called back.

"You don't have curly hair," I said.

"I straighten it," she replied.

"Why would you do that?! This is awesome!"

From that day forward I kept the locks. I'd grow them out, pick them into a 'fro and walk—no, *strut*—with confidence to wherever my feet would take me. My hair was my trademark and the first attribute people would use to describe me. "Dan Stolfi. You know, the guy with the curly hair."

As a comedian, my big curly hair came in handy. I could pin it into a ponytail. I could wet it and slick it back to play the Italian mobster, or I could pick it out into a big 'fro and play a smooth-talking ladies' man from the '70s.

When the chemotherapy started, I believed that my hair was so thick and so curly that the roots would be impossible to break. I had heard of people who didn't lose their hair because of chemo and I thought, *why couldn't I be one of those people?* Only time would tell. There were other side effects to deal with at the moment.

As the pharmacist and nurse said it would, "The Red Killer" began to rear its ugly head. I went to the washroom to take a pee after the initial push of the cherry red Kool-Aid, and what landed in the toilet bowl was this odd red and yellow–coloured substance, a combination of apple and cranberry juice. Initially I thought it was blood, and almost had a panic attack, but then quickly remembered the smug pharmacist and his giant list of side effects.

My hair seemed to be holding on, but it was feeling drier and more brittle than it once did. *It will hold on. It has to.* I was willing it so.

My Appetite

I have a ferocious appetite, but you'd never know it once they started me on the drugs. The hospital volunteers brought me food three times a day but I assure you, just the thought of it, the look of it and the smell of it was enough to make you vomit . . . and that's without being on any chemical drugs.

Each morning a porter would come into my room and give me a piece of paper with food items written on it to be checked off for breakfast, lunch and dinner for the next day. A regimented schedule was in place for when the plastic trays of plastic food would be left on my retractable plastic side table. The menu looked appetizing enough, but what they actually put down in front of me was anything but. Mushy, processed microwaved food at its finest. I asked my doctor, "What should I be eating during my treatment?"

"Eat whatever you want. You want to take in as many calories as you can," he assured me.

"Fruits, vegetables? Should I be at least eating healthy? Organic and all that shit?"

"Anything with lots of butter and high in fat. Whatever you want."

"Seriously?" I asked.

"I'm not a nutritionist. The chemotherapy will cause you to lose a lot of weight, so just let the drugs do their thing and you eat as much of anything that you want," he insisted, now seemingly frustrated with my general interest and what I thought was common sense for eating healthy.

This sounded so backwards to me, but at the end of the day, it didn't really matter because I couldn't stomach anything anyway. Whatever I took in was coming up shortly after, so . . . *fuck it. I'm not going to eat whatever I want, I'm going to eat whatever I can!* What made this even worse was I also had my disgruntled roommate next to me chirping away with the odd comment here and there every time he heard the snap and crunch of one of my mini carrots being masticated by my mouth. "You know you're burning more calories chewing those stupid things than they provide."

Thanks for the tip, ya dick.

Mom's take on the food was something to behold as well. One look at the hospital food and she was insulted that the tomato paste-covered noodles they were serving me were being passed off as spaghetti with a marinara sauce. I think I saw a vein begin to throb in her neck at one point. Her Italian soul was slowly being crushed like the fresh tomatoes she crushed every year to make authentic homemade tomato sauce.

The next day, Mom brought me some homemade cannelloni, a traditional Italian pasta dish that consisted of a flat pasta noodle rolled and stuffed with ricotta cheese and covered in tomato sauce. I loved cannelloni and therefore scarfed it down quickly. *Real food for once*, I thought. But my stomach began to turn. This warm sensation started to swirl around in my belly. I felt like I just woke from a massive night of drinking. The nausea was relentless. "I think I'm going to throw up," I called out to Mom. She hurried over to my bedside with a green plastic kidney-shaped bowl and held it under my mouth. A burning sensation crept up my esophagus and as quickly as I threw the cannelloni down, I threw it right back up into the small plastic container, almost over-flowing with chunks of pasta and bits of tomato sauce. "Sorry, Mom," I said, while a string of saliva, mixed with Parmesan cheese, dangled from my lower lip into the puke-filled basin.

The nurses gave me Gravol and other medications that were "great for countering nausea." None of it seemed to want to work for me. I just kept throwing up everything I threw down. I was now taking in 200 calories a day if I was lucky. I was normally taking in 2000 to 3000 on any given day and my 185-pound frame was quickly wasting away, transforming into the body of what felt more like that of an 80-year-old man.

My roommate, separated from me by only a thin yellow curtain, was well into his '70s and I was starting to think we were looking quite similar. His name was Marley and he had lung cancer. He was generally a quiet man but had no remorse about being loud when it came to passing gas. This guy smelled like ass! At first, I felt sorry for Marley because he was ill, old, and dying of cancer. But after being locked in the gas tank with this guy for a few days, I was thinking, *maybe now would be a good time for Marley to give up*. Let life take its natural course. Free the bed up for a young twenty-something. *Just a dark thought.* At the end of the day though, we were in this thing together. So, fart away, Marley. Fart away!

SIDE NOTE: To this day, I don't eat cannelloni or anything made with ricotta cheese.

~

The chemotherapy regime was a carefully calculated routine that operated like clockwork. Every day, I would get pumped with a different mix of drugs at the exact same time of day. Subtle variations in the process gave each injection, or blood test, its own charm that made it a little more tolerable, but it was really all the same. Sometimes, the chemo would be hooked up to my IV for up to four hours, sometimes it was just 20 minutes, but every drug had a different effect that put more and more strain on my body. I couldn't keep up with what drug was doing what. There was no time for a break to try to figure it all out. It was constant. My white blood cells were being destroyed, my immune system was being shattered and the cancer cells were officially under attack. The war was just getting started and I felt like I was already losing the battle. My soldiers were looking at me like, "Sergeant, what do we do now?" and I was like: "I don't know. Just act cool! Ah, fuck it. Run like hell!"

The Dos and Don'ts
of Cancer

I was lucky. I am lucky. Lucky to have had a wonderful support system of family and friends visit me on a regular basis at the hospital. Mom stayed with me every day from about 10 a.m. to 10 p.m. and without her I'd be dead. *I will say this repeatedly throughout this book. Without my mom, I'd be dead.* Not because she gave birth to me and without that, I'd never have been born. More like she was always by my side, day in, day out, and acted as my primary caregiver on most days. She was there to bring me water, make me homemade soup and played the role of nightclub bouncer between visitors to let me rest when I needed it. It was a lot of work for her, but I rationalized, at least she had just retired. I mean, she must have been bored anyway and needed something to do. My cancer diagnosis couldn't have come at a better time, right? I'm sure she loved spending her first years of retirement watching her baby potentially die. Did I mention I'd be dead without her? Moving right along . . .

Books, books, books! Everyone kept bringing me more and more books. I was super grateful but I don't think they understood how difficult doing anything was, let alone picking up a book, keeping my brain functioning for long enough to read a sentence and then continuing this process to read past that sentence.

CANCER SUPPORT TIP: Hold off on the book giving until your loved one is out of the hospital. It's like giving a person without legs a soccer ball to just kick around whenever they feel like it. Let me put it this way: reading seems like the easiest thing to do when you're trying to pass the time, on a sandy beach, in sunny South Florida, sipping on strawberry daiquiris and soaking up the rays. But, when you feel like you are literally dying, getting poked with needles every four hours, vomiting on the regular and passing in and out of consciousness . . . reading is like running a marathon, in Mongolia, in the summer, naked, without legs. *Maybe I should leave this part out of my book. I mean, I love that you're reading it, but if it's going to make you vomit, best you wait a bit before carrying on!*

~

"Stay positive," one of my improv classmates told me as she patted me on the leg. *Positivity can suck a dick when you are throwing up in a hospital room toilet*, I wanted to tell her. I just opted for the nod and smile instead. I knew she meant well.

It seemed like everyone who visited had my best interest at heart and really wanted to stay positive for me, but I really just wanted people to say, "Fuck man, this is so fucking shitty." Or "Son of a bitch! Cancer can suck it. I hate that you are going through this and I want to punch someone in the face!" These were just some of the sentences that would have been nice to hear. I don't know why, but maybe it would have validated my true feelings inside. It sucked and I wanted to be supported in how badly it sucked.

CANCER SUPPORT TIP: So, what do you say to someone who has cancer? It's actually a lot easier than you may think. Over the years, friends, family and even strangers have reached out to me for advice on what they can say or do when it comes to offering support to a loved one going through cancer. I see the helplessness in their face or hear it in their voice, but the simple truth is, you don't have to say or do anything grand. Just *be* there for them. Tell them you love them. Tell them that you are thinking about them. Tell them that if they need anything, you will be there for them. Check in on them. That is all you can do. You don't need to do or say anything else.

So, that being said, what absolutely don't you say to someone who has cancer? *And, just a note: The following are all things people actually said to me or wrote me, while I was going through treatment.*

Don't say: "My cousin had the exact same cancer as you at the exact same age as you . . . and he died." *Yes, someone said that!*

Don't say: "So because you have cancer, does that mean I could get cancer? Like, is it contagious?" *No joke, it happened.*

Don't say: "So how did you get it? Was it something you ate? Or something you did? Because I think it could be deodorant." *What the fuck?*

Don't say: "So, if you beat this, are you going to be, like, different? Or are you going to be yourself again? Like drinking and partying and stuff." *Oh dear. We are in trouble. Just nod and smile. Just nod and smile.*

Now, this last Don't was a big one for me. This was the Don't that pushed me the hardest. One of my improvisation classmates asked me if I was going to do anything with my experience. She wasn't the best improviser. Actually, quite brutal if I'm being perfectly honest, but she had this air of confidence about her. Like she knew everything. I briefly mentioned that I was thinking that maybe I would write a show about it . . . a live show for the stage. *I'm an actor and comedian, and I was working on a show already, and it's ingrained in me to tell stories, so it only made sense to have a creative goal to strive for.* She said, "Like a solo show thing?"

I nodded my head yes. "Just thinking about it."

She went on, "Well, I wouldn't if I were you. My friend had cancer and did a show about it, so it's already been done." She then added, "And it's really good." I just nodded my head and smiled, locking her high-pitched, self-righteous voice in my head for fuel later. Just nod and smile.

It's sometimes the negative things people say that have the most positive impact.

After visiting hours were over, my friends and family were

gone, and I was left alone with nothing but the beeping sounds of heart monitors and the squeaking wheels of passing carts. My eyes fell in and out of focus as the fluorescent-lit hallways began to blur and I was rocked to a restless sleep.

March 27, 2008

Day 4 of 730

Yesterday I had another push of the red stuff and I didn't feel so good but people stopped by and lifted my spirits. Today was a rough one. I had a massive dose of chemo and threw up a bit. I have never taken so many pills in my life! My appetite is non-existent but I am trying to get some food in me. This headache is rough but nothing a little Tylenol can't handle. Fuck, my head hurts and I think I gotta take a shit but my roommate may have just destroyed the washroom for the next hour. MARLEY!!!

> *- 16 pills*
> *- 1 bag of chemo*
> *- 4 vials of blood*
> *- 1 bone density scan*

Killing cancer = Very hard.

Breaking Out of the Big House

It had been six days of intensive chemotherapy, locked in my hospital room prison cell. My beeping buddy, attached to my veins, was my best friend and literal lifeline. Over the course of six days, I had been given more drugs than I had ever taken in my entire life. My energy had been completely stripped from me. My body felt like a damp towel after it had been wrung out of every last bit of water. I was getting restless to get out of there. The doctors told me I would be in the hospital for seven to fourteen days while they killed all of my white blood cells. They needed to make sure my immune system was completely shattered before the chemotherapy could crush the cancer cells. It's a messed-up process and still feels backwards to me, but whatever it takes, right? I was determined to get out of that room in eight days.

The level of Methotrexate, a drug running through my bloodstream, had to be at a sufficiently low-enough level before I could leave the hospital. It had to register below .001 parts per milligram of blood, or something scientific like that. I was kicking around .003 by day seven and had been at that level for the past 24 hours. I didn't know what any of that meant. All I knew was I wanted out of there and if that meant I had to get to .001 parts per milligram of blah blah blah, then I was going to will my way to .001 parts per milligram of pee pee poo poo bum bum!

The doctor, who was working the weekend shift, knew I was eager to get out of the hospital. He entered my room, looked at my chart and said, "Your counts are still registering at .003, but it's your lucky day. I'm going to let you go anyway." *Woohoo!!* He was probably bending the rules and taking a bit of a chance letting me leave early, but a couple one thousandths of a point couldn't hurt anyone . . . could it?

"Hey, you're the professional," I told him with a smile. *Seven days and I'm out, baby!*

"One last thing before we let you go," he said.

"What's that?" I inquired.

"You have to have a bowel movement." After a brief pause.

"Okay, sure. No problem," I assured him as he left the room. *Shit! I gotta shit before I can leave this shit hole?* I thought to myself. A few hours passed and still no shit in sight. A nurse entered my room. "I have a laxative for you to help you go," she said.

"Oh, that's great!" I replied as I stuck out my hand to get the pill.

"Not that kind of laxative. Turn over on your side," she instructed as she put on a pair of rubber gloves.

"Wait! What?"

"I need to put this"—she showed me a blue "pill" about

the size of a mini lighter—"up your anus."

"Oh, come on! Really?" I said, as I turned over in a huff.

"Sorry, sweetie. It's the only way. I'll be gentle." She lubed up her plastic-wrapped finger and jammed the pill up my butt. *Okay, maybe she didn't jam it up there . . . but even if it was a "gentle insertion," it felt like a jam!* My ass puckered up like a kid taking a bite of lemon. She left the room. I felt violated. I waited.

After about an hour of waiting, I still didn't feel the need to go to the washroom. My logic was that I hadn't really eaten anything anyway and anything I did eat I'd throw up. So how much poop could I really have in there? I went to the washroom and sat on the toilet. Then, I made the biggest mistake I could have made throughout my entire treatment. One I would come to regret for years to come. I pushed . . . and I pushed . . . and I pushed . . . as hard as I could. I felt the blood rushing to my brain, a vein throbbing on my forehead. Nothing. Finally, I felt a twinge in my backside followed by a "pop." It wasn't painful. But I for sure felt something. I eventually gave up. *I'll just tell them I went. What's one little white lie going to hurt?* That "pop" would prove to cause a world of hurt down the road that still causes me regrets to this day. But, with that pop, and that little lie, I was out!

I couldn't believe it; I was on my way home. I felt like someone had just put my body through a pasta maker, starting with my toes and slowly turning the handle as the rest of my body was squeezed through the rollers, pressing every last ounce of energy out of me.

Mom grabbed the crazy and ridiculous amount of

thoughtful and generous gifts from my room as I shimmied my way off the bed with my dad's help. I reeked of what smelled like sliced onions and blue cheese. Not having taken a shower for a week, I was not surprised that my hairy Italian body could produce such a wretched stench. I was unhooked from my bedside beeping buddy and shuffled down the hallway with the support of my dad's shoulder. My red Adidas shorts were now hanging off my hips as I struggled to walk. My parents helped me into the back seat of their tiny, tacky, mint-green standard-transmission Hyundai Elantra and we drove back home to Guelph. I gently lay curled up in the fetal position, as we raced down the highway, my dad trying to beat the rush hour traffic. I felt every bump and pothole rattle through my bones as we weaved in and out of the cars and transport trucks. I knew I would have to get used to this, though, as this would be how I travelled to and from the hospital for treatment every week for the next two years of my life. *FUCK!!*

One Second at a Time

My parents weren't necessarily ready for me to be home again. All the kids had moved out and lived on their own for almost three years, so the house was all set for two semi-retired adults, waiting to be grandparents for the first time.

My old childhood room now had two single beds in it and was acting as a guest room. My sister's room wasn't being used but it had an old mattress in it that wasn't all that comfortable. Feeling like Guido Locks and the Three Bears, I slept in my brother's old room. It was just right . . . sort of.

The mattress was new, but the bed frame was old and just slightly too big. Dad doesn't like throwing things out, so if he could use an old bedframe for a new bed, he was all about reduce, reuse, recycle. He's frugal. I couldn't blame him, though. He grew up poor, with ten siblings in Italy. Frugality was a way of survival. I slept in my brother's bed for my first night at home. My brain, however, didn't want to shut off and I began to toss and turn causing the bed to shift slightly. Little by little, the bed eventually worked its way out of the frame, causing the bottom right corner of the mattress to fall with a thud to the ground. I lay on an angle fighting gravity as I slowly felt myself slip out of the bed onto the hardwood floor. "Dad! Help!" I called out. My parents' room was at the other end of a relatively long hallway, so they couldn't hear me. My voice was hoarse, and I didn't have the strength to project loud enough to wake them. My once booming theatre voice was reduced to a weak, rasping cry for help. I was too drained to get out of bed and fix it myself, so I lay on an angle and just waited it out until morning. I didn't sleep that night. The next morning, I nestled the bed back in the oversized frame and hoped that it was just a one-time thing.

The next night, the mattress fell out of the frame again. This time Dad heard me calling for help and came rushing into my room. He laughed a bit at the sight of me lying on the broken bed and swiftly lifted the bottom corner of the mattress, with me still on it, and nestled it back into the frame. "I will have to fix this for good in the morning," he assured me.

A wonky bed was just one of the many things I had to contend with, and it was really the least of my worries. It's all relative.

Sleeping had become more problematic since my return from the hospital. No matter what I did, I just couldn't shut off my brain. I was so restless! The most random images and words kept reverberating in my head and there was no way to stop it. I couldn't stop humming the same songs over and over in my head throughout the night. The song, "Umbrella," by Rihanna just played on repeat in my brain and it was maddening! It wasn't even the whole song either! Just the part of the song that goes, "Umbrella, ella, ella, eh, eh, eh..." I don't even like the song! It didn't matter. It just kept playing and playing and playing. It was driving me insane! *Thanks, Rihanna for having such a terribly catchy song and haunting my dreams.*

I tossed and turned trying to find a comfortable position on the bed. I tried everything. I lay on my side, my back, I held a pillow, I used no pillow, I lay on my stomach, propped myself up against the wall and then promptly slid down. It all felt so

> **SIDE NOTE: To this day, "Umbrella" by Rihanna stirs up haunting memories. If I hear it on the radio, I immediately switch the station.**

uncomfortable to me. Aside from Rihanna in my head, I heard this other voice, which played on repeat too. It was this dark little voice that just kept whispering in my ear. Until now, I had never heard this voice before. It said, "I'm going to get you." *What is this voice?* I thought to myself. *What* is *this voice!?* I was alone and scared. I just wanted it to stop. "I've got you," it kept saying. "I've got you."

I shook the voice out of my head and pulled myself out of bed and began to pace in my room. Coupled with the creepy voice from hell and the song from hell in my head, my stomach was in excruciating pain. It felt like someone had put their hand inside my stomach and was squeezing my intestines. At 2 a.m., in search of relief for my stomach, I made my way downstairs to the kitchen. It turned out that the only thing that settled my stomach was a glass of 2% milk. It was a short-lived remedy, as the relief only lasted about ten minutes at a time, but it cooled and coated the inside of my stomach and released the grip that was squeezing my insides. I abandoned ship on this remedy after the sixth trip to the kitchen fridge as it was impossible to continuously consume milk over the course of a night no matter how much relief it provided. I needed to sleep!

I was so hopped up on steroids my body couldn't sit still. I tried to exhaust myself by walking in endless circles around the kitchen. It was three in the morning now and my parents were fast asleep. I walked like an old man with my elbows back and hips out, shuffling my feet from the living room to the kitchen. I was incredibly skinny, and I couldn't eat a thing. The pain was so intense. I had pain in my mouth, my arms, my legs and my back. There was now a permanent humming and drone sound filling my head that wouldn't go away. It sounded like I was in a huge cave that was echoing my pain back to me over and over again. I wasn't sure if I was the only one who could hear it. It was so loud my parents would surely have woken up. They, however, stayed sound asleep.

Eventually, I found myself back in my room lying on my bed and struggling to find a comfortable position again. I turned onto my stomach with no pillow for my head to rest. This appeared to be the best position for me. I finally settled and found a moment of stillness. The stillness gave my mind and body a break, but it opened up an eerie calm that allowed the quiet darkness to creep back in. It was here, where I had my first conversation with death. That voice was starting to make sense now.

I opened my eyes and saw a dark faceless person sitting at my bedside. He was staring at me, almost toying with me, teasing me, and laughing maniacally. *Is this a dream?* I asked myself. The voice drove me out of my bed and out of the bedroom. My plan was to go downstairs, pace around the kitchen and drink another shot of milk until the voice went away. I stood at the top of the large oak steps leading down to the main floor below. The voice whispered into my ear, "Maybe you can trip and fall and this will all be over. Just one missed step and this could all be over . . ." I fought these dark feelings and forced out the visions of falling down a flight of stairs from my head. The voice was eventually replaced by my own. I began my slow and careful descent down the stairs, one step at a time. I started a mantra that I would carry with me for as long as this marathon would last: *One second at a time, one minute at a time, one hour at a time, one day at a time. I am going to get through this. I am going to beat this.* I repeated this over and over again as I reached the bottom of the stairs, safe. These were the longest nights of my life.

I walked endlessly around my parents' kitchen until I got the urge to go to the washroom. *Could this be my big bowl movement moment?* I found myself sitting on the toilet now, at around 4 a.m. I pushed. I strained. Then, "plop." Success! A bowel movement!! I looked down into the bowl and suddenly my mind began to race: *Mom and Dad are asleep. I don't want to wake them. I will sleep it off and deal with it in the morning. I have already put them through so much. Why should I wake them up? It can wait until tomorrow, right?*

What is happening to me?

The toilet paper was beet red, covered in blood, and the

sight of it terrified me. I began to panic. I thought I might be hallucinating, so I grabbed another piece of toilet paper and this time there was even more blood than before. The water was now completely streaked red with fresh drops of blood floating on the surface as it slowly mixed with the clear water. My mind raced again: *Colon cancer. I have one kind of cancer, why not two?* I was scared. I didn't know what to do. I took a deep breath. *This can't wait.* A wave of confusion and fear washed through my body and I began to cry. I had to wake my parents up.

"I think I need to go to the hospital," I called to them through their bedroom door. After little explanation and without hesitation, they took me to the Guelph General Hospital emergency wing.

The emergency wing had quite a few people in it for 4 a.m. on a weeknight, so I figured I would be waiting for a while. But, hot tip, the word "cancer," is a powerful thing. As soon as I dropped the C-bomb at the check-in desk, it was like this magical portal opened up and I was immediately given a room in the back to wait for a doctor. *All it takes for a little service around here is a bit of cancer?* It dawned on me at that moment that I was now part of a pretty exclusive club. Call me a VIP, a Very Immune-suppressed Person.

A doctor entered through the curtain, which surrounded my bed. Mom, who was by my side, stepped out to give us some privacy, I mean, he was about to look up my butt and all.

"What seems to be the problem, son?" he asked.

"I was diagnosed with cancer a few weeks ago and since taking treatment, I've been having some issues going to the bathroom. I went to the bathroom tonight and my butt is bleeding pretty bad," I told him.

"Let's have you turn over and I'll take a look." He snapped on some rubber gloves as I turned over on to my side. I pulled my shorts down, my butt now in his face.

"It's not colon cancer, is it?" I asked nervously.

He chuckled a bit as he spoke. "It's probably just a hemorrhoid that ruptured."

"Hemorrhoids? Aren't those for pregnant ladies and old people?" I joked.

"They can be for anyone and everyone," he replied. "And by the looks of it, they are for you. I've actually never seen one this big before." I felt like I should win a prize for that or something. *Biggest hemorrhoid of the year!* No prize was awarded, just an ointment to rub up there three times a day. "Stay regular and apply the ointment routinely," he instructed. Then he hit me with the worst news ever. "It probably won't fully heal until you are finished treatment. Your immune system is pretty much non-existent. The cream should help alleviate some of the discomfort, though." He could read the pain in my eyes. "How long is your treatment?" he asked.

"Two years," I said, defeated.

"What?!" he said, in shock. "I don't think I've ever heard of a treatment being that long. That's officially the longest I've ever heard of."

"So, you're telling me, not only do I have the biggest hemorrhoid you've ever seen but I will also get to have said freakishly huge hemorrhoid for the longest time on record?" I joked. He laughed.

"Just apply the cream and it should help. If it gets worse, come back." He patted me on the foot and left through the curtain.

Mom and I broke the news to Dad who was still waiting patiently in the waiting room. "I used to get hemorrhoids all the time!" he exclaimed. I think he was proud that we were bonding over similar ailments. As a kid, I can remember going through his bathroom closet and seeing his tube of Preparation H and thinking, "Ewwwww, gross. Old-people butt cream." Now? Now, I get it. I'm Old People Butt Cream. We went home. It was time to rest.

CANCER SURVIVOR TIP: When the nurse shoves a laxative up your butt and tells you to take a shit before you leave the hospital, you wait for the laxative to work. Bottom line: try to manage constipation at all costs! Eat beets, grind up some flax seed or do anything that can help keep you regular! In retrospect, getting out of the cancer ward two hours early was not worth the two years of war between me and my butt! So, stay regular my friends!

That morning. Back home. Seven a.m. It was all so difficult. I was exhausted and hungry. I knew I needed to eat, as I hadn't been doing much of it for the last ten days. My stomach was still in excruciating pain, I felt dizzy, and the thought of food made me nauseated. I made it a goal to have a bowl of fresh fruit and cereal every morning. Just the act of chewing my food and swallowing it was excruciating. As I sat at the kitchen table, staring down at my overflowing bowl of Happy O's with a spoon in my hand, I said, "Mom, this is the hardest thing to do in the world right now." Mom thought that if she put more food in the bowl I would naturally eat more. This is Italian logic at its finest. It turned out, more food in front of me had the opposite effect and made me more nauseated than ever.

"I know, honey, but you have to eat," she replied. I put the spoon to my mouth and took a bite of the circular oats floating in milk and chewed very slowly. Each bite came with its own individual struggle. I forced my throat to swallow the food down as tears streamed down my face. I was a mess.

~

The sleepless nights and unbearable mornings continued like this until my first in-clinic meeting with my oncologist four days later. I arrived at the Odette Cancer Clinic at Sunnybrook Hospital at 8:30 a.m. This is where I would come for weekly chemotherapy injections and blood work for the next 100 weeks of my life. The lobby was huge. A large atrium with a glass ceiling was at the centre of the clinic. It was spacious and clean. Rows and rows of chairs filled with grey-haired and bald patients were waiting for their names to be called for their respective appointments. I scanned the clinic. I was the youngest one there by far. I took a seat and waited. A woman, about 60 years of age with wispy strands of grey hair, sat across from me. After a moment, she leaned in across the aisle and said, "Are you here supporting your mother?" It took me a second to realize that she probably didn't assume I was the one here for treatment, because, by all accounts I still looked somewhat healthy. My hair was holding on, for the moment, and I was presumably too young to have cancer.

"I'm actually here for me," I told her awkwardly. She leaned back, in a bit of shock.

"I'm sorry to hear that, sweetheart. Is this your first day?"

"Yup. You?"

"Oh, no. Ten years a survivor. Breast cancer," she said proudly.

"Lymphoma for me."

She then said something that has stuck with me to this day.

"I've been coming here for ten years. And this place hasn't changed a bit. They got new chairs, but everything else is the same. Same system, same sick-looking people, same treatments. Sometimes I wonder if we're making progress at all. I wonder what it will look like in ten years from now." I let this sit with me for a moment. I wanted to hope that they'd find a cure by then. Maybe, during my treatment, some doctor would find the cure and I'd get to go back to normal. And just as I was about to say something, I heard a loud voice calling my name. As I got up I finally said, "I'll let you know in ten years." I gave her a little smirk. She smiled and gave me the thumbs up.

I sat patiently with Mom in one of the medical rooms and waited for Dr. Chang. After a few minutes he walked in the room rubbing his hands together, having just lathered them up with hand sanitizer.

"Good to see you again. Are you having any challenges?" he asked nonchalantly.

"Aside from everything and the record-breaking hemorrhoid in my butt . . . I can't sleep," I told him.

"I can prescribe you some sleeping pills," he said quickly.

"Sleeping pills?! I can take sleeping pills? That would be amazing."

"Of course." He laughed, as he began to write down the prescription. "We'll also look into the hemorrhoids, but if you have a cream, keep applying that for now and we will check in on it at a later date." He handed me the prescription for the sleeping pills and as soon as we got home, I got Dad to fill it for me.

The moment I got my hands on these pills my life became just a little bit easier. It by no means alleviated me of all the other hellish things I was going through, but the minor victory of a few hours of sleep and shutting out the voice of death was a nice one. Without a doubt, the pills helped me sleep, but I would still wake up once a night to go to the washroom. But I didn't care. I was so grateful for the opportunity to sleep

SIDE NOTE: I still have trouble sleeping to this day. I haven't gotten a full night's sleep since I began treatment in 2008. If you are reading this, whatever day it is, trust me I didn't sleep well last night. I went to a sleep clinic to figure it out in 2018. They couldn't prescribe anything except for a more regimented night-time routine. It hasn't worked. I find meditating is helping, so I'm sticking with that for now.

for a few consecutive hours. I will never take sleeping for granted ever again.

~

Day 10 into treatment: I woke up in the morning and swung my legs to the side of my bed, the frame now fixed and the whole bed itself relocated to my original childhood room. It was closer to the bathroom and my parents' room, so it only made sense. I scratched the top of my head to relieve an itch and noticed something was different. Ten strands of curly dark brown hair clung to the tips of my fingers, the roots still seemingly attached. I picked at another set of curls and pulled out a cluster of hair. I held it, squeezed between my thumb and pointer finger. I looked down at my pillow and saw even more curly strands scattered about the white fabric case. Just like they said it would, in ten days, like clockwork, my hair was falling out. It was completely painless, but extremely surreal. Every time I ran my hands through my hair, hundreds of strands of dark curls got gobbled up by my palms. The legend of, *if you masturbate too much your palms will turn hairy,* was starting to ring true, although I hadn't masturbated since the Fertility Clinic. *Wink and the gun.* So that myth has been officially busted!

I put on my track pants and gingerly made my way downstairs, my curls barely holding on now, patchy atop my head. I looked in the mirror at the bottom of the steps. The same mirror I looked into when I was nine years old, discovering my curly hair for the first time. This time I yelled, "Mom, my curls are falling out!"

"They said they would, my darling," Mom called back. *Damn.*

I called my brother, the resident barber of the family. He had no formal experience but made up for it with an unexplained joy for cutting hair. He apparently used to cut his roommates' hair in university, so I bestowed him the honour.

Back in the bathroom he took his electric clippers, which I believe he used to trim his pubes, but we won't go there, and started to clip away. In a matter of seconds, my thick majestic 'fro was no more. "At least you have a nice-shaped head," he said. He's a glass-half-full type of guy.

"I look like I'm eighty years old!" I told him.

"Oh, you do not," he said. "It's all a part of the process."

"I have a mole on my head!" *Who knew?*

~

The first 15 days of the protocol were finally over! The longest days of my life. They were the most consistently painful and scary, when I put it all into perspective. But there would be a close second later on. I will never forget those days and I know that no matter how much pain I ever have to endure again in my life, if I could get through those 15 days, I can get through anything. And to think we were just getting started. This is a marathon. Not a sprint. One second at a time. One minute at a time. One hour at a time. One day at a time.

Phase 2: The Central Nervous System

I was now poised to enter phase two of my chemotherapy treatment and, as the name suggested, this phase of the chemotherapy protocol focused on my central nervous system, or as it is more commonly known, the spinal cord and brain. On top of many chemotherapy drugs that would be injected into my body intravenously and taken orally in pill form, I would also be introduced to the wonderful world of cranial radiation and a number of lovely lower lumbar punctures, also referred to as spinal taps. Just like the hit '80s flick, *This is Spinal Tap*, only way more painful and without the music and laughs.

Before all the spine poking could begin, I'd have to get some lovely radiation treatments . . . to my brain. I was to come into the chemotherapy suite, Monday to Friday, for the next two weeks. The Sunnybrook Hospital Odette Cancer Clinic was where all the "routine" chemotherapy and radiation treatments took place. This would be my new office, or in my case, theatre space for the next two years.

The clinic was just as it was a few days prior when I met with my oncologist for the sleeping pills. I entered through the sliding doors, took a couple hits of hand sanitizer and soaked in my surroundings. Dad, the scheduled driver for the day, took a couple pumps of the foamy cleanser as well before we made our way to the reception desks. I saw so many . . . heads. I just saw heads. Bald heads, heads covered in pink scarves, old heads, lots of old heads, and the odd head with scraggly pieces of hair scattered about. *Anyone my age this time?* I wondered. I took a quick glance around. *Nope.* We made our way downstairs to the radiation centre. A digitized board hung over the closed double doors leading to the radiation rooms. The board had names scrolling across it in red flashing lights, like a theatre marquee, only way less exciting. Like clockwork, at five-minute intervals, the names would change and a new patient would get up and slowly shuffle their way through the doors. A lab technician in a white lab coat, holding a clipboard, greeted each patient. He was like a bouncer at a club that no one actually wanted to get in to. The doors closed and we waited for the next name and time to flash up on the digitized board. I saw my name, STOLFI – 8:05 A.M., in shiny red lights. "Look Dad, I'm up next," I said excitedly. "My name in lights . . . Broadway!" I joked. Dad chuckled.

We entered the doors, and the radiation doctor—a tall, hairless gentlemen—adjusted his spectacles and explained to me, "You will need to receive radiation on the brain because this portion of the chemotherapy regime can cause brain tumours down the line. The radiation shows significant results in preventing tumours of up to ninety-nine percent but if not used, only seventy percent. There is also a ten percent chance that the radiation itself can *cause* tumours." *Jesus . . . anything else, Doc?* "There is also a good chance the radiation will cause cataracts later in life." *Yup!* "…and it could potentially burn your skin. Some people get nauseated too . . . but that's very rare. The option is always left to the patient to proceed." *WOW.* He paused, waiting for my response. Needless to say, it was a lot to take in, but here's what I rationalized.

"Ninety-nine percent? That's closer to one hundred percent than seventy percent, right? A ten percent chance of tumours is lower than the thirty percent chance of tumours . . . Is this a trick question?" I joked. He didn't laugh. I made the choice to go for it. Seemed like the logical decision, and we were there anyway!

Radiation

The process of radiation was really quite simple. But again, it's all relative. If my entire cancer treatment consisted of only doing radiation therapy, then that in and of itself would be scary enough . . . and fucked up as all hell. But since I had just taken down a few litres of chemo and was still peeing red, while dealing with the world's largest hemorrhoid in my butt, radiation seemed like a cakewalk.

I was one of the first patients that morning, but before we could get started, the specialist needed to fit my head for a plastic mesh mask. The mask would be used to keep my head secure to the radiation table and act as a roadmap for where to focus the radiation. I was instructed by one of the specialists to lie face up on a cold steel table. The room was dark, frigid and sterile. "Just stay on the table and we will get your mask ready for you," the specialist instructed. On the wall, I saw at least fifty moulds of different plastic mesh masks. It looked like a museum of famous stone busts.

"Are those other people's masks?" I asked.

"Yes, they are. Once we finish yours, we'll put it up there as well." *Well, isn't that exciting.*

"Like the wall of fame only way worse," I joked. They laughed.

I lay on my back and the cold metallic table sent shivers up and down my spine. "The mask is just warming up in the liquid solution. When it's ready we will be pressing it onto your face quite firmly. We have to make sure it's a very tight fit. So please don't move," he instructed. This was serious business.

One specialist took the flat plastic mesh out of the liquid and quickly carried it over to the table, holding it out in front of him like he was carrying a naked, diaperless baby on the verge of peeing. The two of them quickly began to press the naked baby onto my face, almost as though they were smothering me with a pillow. They were pressing and pushing and really seemed to be struggling, mumbling things like, "It's not warm enough" and "We should have left it in longer." They stopped and let out a sigh of frustration. "Turns out the liquid solution isn't quite warm enough, so the mask isn't fitting properly," one of them said. "We have to throw it out and give it another go." *Yippee! Two masks for the price of one. Can they both go on the wall of shit!?*

The second time around was much more successful and they didn't have to push nearly as hard. My big Italian nose was sore from the first mask but this one just seemed to fall nicely into place, almost melting over my facial features perfectly. The warmth of the mask countered the biting cold permeating from the steel table. I felt the sensation to pee.

The mask was quite handy and a huge advancement in the radiation game. Apparently they used to actually place permanent tattoo marks on a patient's face until they discovered that they could mark up a mask instead. In retrospect, my nose was a little sore and I escaped a sad attempt to be smothered to death by a naked baby, but the tattoo-less mask was probably the way to go.

I lay there, motionless, as they placed my mask over my head and clamped it tight to the table locking me in place. One of the specialists, a young Indian man, looked at the T-shirt I was wearing. It had my sketch comedy troupe's logo, FADE TO BROWN, on it. "Fade to Brown? They're great!" he said.

"I'm in the troupe," I mumbled to him, my jaw locked shut because of the mask.

He got excited and said, "Really? That's awesome! You guys are great!"

"Have you seen any of our shows?" I asked.

"Yeah, a bunch. Me and my friends go all the time."

I was feeling like a minor celebrity for the moment. That feeling quickly went away as it suddenly dawned on me that he didn't recognize me at all. The reality that I looked so different than I did just a few weeks back suddenly kicked in. The excitement on his face wore off as he realized the new reality that my life had taken on as well. For a brief moment, though, we forgot why we were there. We forgot I had cancer. We connected about something other than my illness and that made me feel a bit more normal.

He made some markings on my mask with a blue Sharpie and then hid behind a wall, but not before he gave me the standard sympathetic pat on the foot. He turned off the lights. The room was now almost pitch black, lit only by the blinking blue lights on the various pieces of hospital equipment. My eyes shifted around, seeing very little else through the tiny holes in the mesh mask. The two specialists hid behind their wall to protect themselves from the evil deadly radiation. I couldn't blame them . . . *who would want to be radiated??* Suddenly, I heard a buzzing sound and I shut my eyes; the radiation process was about to begin. Even with my eyes closed, I could feel and see a blue light cover my face as the back of my eyelids lit up like a blank IBM computer screen from the '90s. A warm sensation covered my head, slowly moving from my jaw, past my nose, through my eyes and right up and over my head. It all took a total of twenty-five seconds. In less time than it took for them to leave the room and hide, it was over. The specialist came back in the room and released my head from the clamps that kept my mask bolted to the table. He took my mask as I got up on my feet. "See you tomorrow," my super fan said.

"Yup, thanks," I replied.

I stumbled out of the room with a pounding headache, barely able to walk. Outside the double doors, I found Dad and put my arm around his shoulder for support, leaning all of my weight on to him. I wasn't quite sure if it was the radiation or the chemotherapy that caused it but a wave of nausea swept through me and I left my Dad's side and stumbled to the washroom. I burst through the door, fell to my knees and proceeded to vomit uncontrollably into the toilet bowl.

I exited the washroom and wiped my mouth with a brown paper towel. It felt like sand paper against my skin. I looked at Dad and I hung my head, disappointed in myself. I felt like I was failing. Dad was convinced it wasn't the radiation that caused the vomiting. "It's all in your head," he said. "Subconsciously, you are associating the radiation with throwing up." My dad is a really smart man, but he ain't no doctor . . . although he seemed to think he was.

STORY BREAK: "Dad the Doctor." My dad's self-doctoring practices date back to my childhood. When I was in Grade Three, I had an incident at school that ended with me in the emergency ward of Guelph General Hospital. It was my dad who provided the eventual diagnosis and my release from the emergency waiting room. Story goes like this: I was eight years old, sitting at my desk in one of those big yellow portables that acted as my classroom. I was leaning back on my chair, the two front legs off the ground with my human legs dangling in front. I was bouncing a 2 HB pencil off my desk. The tiny eraser acted as the mechanism to propel the pencil upwards. It would bounce straight up, two or three inches off the table and back down as I rocked back and forth on the hind legs of my plastic chair. I was toying with gravity. Suddenly, my balance was compromised, and without warning, I crashed forward toward my desk and the pencil. My right nostril, as small as it was at the time, managed to find the end of the recently sharpened pencil tip, and jammed deep into my nose, stabbing me, causing me to rear my head back and cry out in pain. My nose started bleeding uncontrollably. My teacher sprang into action and applied pressure with tissues as she tilted my

head back. Spots of blood were scattered around the floor and the taste of iron seeped down the back of my throat. The school called my dad. He rushed to the school, picked me up in our grey station wagon and accompanied me to the emergency room where we registered my name and waited patiently. The bloody rag I was holding to my nose seemed to be slowing the trickle. Upon inspection of the pencil/weapon, we noticed there was a chip in the lead portion of the recently sharpened tip. We feared that this chip could be lodged up my nose somewhere. Lead poisoning? Death? Only time would tell. We waited for an hour, two hours, three . . . until my dad finally said, "How are you feeling?"

"I'm okay," I replied.

"Let's go to the washroom and take a look," he suggested.

In the washroom, he tilted my head back and tried to move my nostrils directly under the fluorescent lights that hung from the ceiling. He squinted his eyes and moved his head from side to side trying to get his shadow out of the way. Finally, he settled for a clear look. "Nope, nothing there. Let's go." And just like that, he gave me a clean bill of health. No lead poisoning, and no more waiting at the hospital. He was no doctor but you'd be damned if you were to tell him that.

After my radiation and barf session, I was sent upstairs for my spinal tap. I could barely walk myself to the doctor's room where the procedure was to take place. I sat in a chair and waited with my doctor—I mean, dad. What I wanted, more than anything, was to lie down to alleviate the headache that was now pounding my brain into mush. The pain was unbearable. "We have a bed you can lie in down the hallway if you'd like," one nurse said.

"That would be great," I replied. *Minor victories.*

After an hour I was brought into a room that looked like all the others. I was instructed to lie down on the parchment paper–covered table, as Dad waited patiently outside. I turned on my side and pulled down my black tear-away pants and red soccer shorts to expose my lower third and fourth vertebrae. "I haven't done too many of these but I'm getting better," Dr. Chang said, as he rubbed a cold brown liquid solution over my lower back with a wet gauze pad.

"Well that's reassuring, Doc," I said sarcastically. We made small talk as he organized his equipment for the spinal tap procedure.

The pinch of the needle caused me to twitch as the local anesthetic was injected into my lower back, numbing the area thoroughly. It was painful, but I had felt this pain before. The sharp bee-sting sensation increased in intensity as the anesthetic was pushed through the needle. The pain declined gradually as the freezing took hold. Dr. Chang removed a six-inch needle from a package and showed it to me by reaching out from behind my head. "You ready?" he asked.

"Whenever you are," I replied.

"You're gonna feel a little pressure."

"Sure." Then . . .

"It's in," he said.

"Really? I didn't feel a thing," *If I had a dime for every time a woman said that . . . Hey, oh!* I continued to lie motionless on the table, staring out the window into a vacant parking lot, the sun shining brightly, as the heat of the April sun warmed my face. "We're going to extract the spinal fluid now. We'll then send it off for testing and inject the chemotherapy," he told me.

"Okay."

"Your spinal fluid is dripping very slowly, so we may be here a while, but it's okay. We'll wait." He took three vials of 5 mg of fluid, put them in a plastic bag and set the bag on a side table. After about 15 minutes of lying on my side, curled up in the fetal position, he injected my spine with the yellow liquid drug, Methotrexate. The fluid worked its way

> Spinal taps are used to collect spinal fluid for testing to see if blood cancer cells are present in the spinal column. They are also used in conjunction with the chemotherapy to inject certain drugs directly into the brain through the spinal column. The chemotherapy, injected through my veins, can't access the brain directly, so the solution was to replace my spinal fluid with a drug called Methotrexate and allow it to work its way up to my brain. A side effect to Methotrexate on the brain is what people like to refer to as chemo brain or foggy memory, but more significantly, in the long term it can cause brain tumours. *Excuse me? Did someone say brain tumours?* In order to counter the brain tumours, I received brain radiation, which significantly reduced the chances of obtaining tumours. It was an intricate dance of attack and counter-attack, sort of like playing chess . . . only much more dangerous and way less fun.

through my spine and up to my brain. I didn't feel much, but the thought of it happening made me extremely uncomfortable. I started to shake, now feeling cold, the sun not standing a chance against my fatless frame and the hospital's industrial-style air-conditioning system. The thought of a giant needle sticking out of my spine started to creep its way into my imagination. *Just breathe and hold on, it's almost over. One second at a time, one minute at a time . . .* I told myself. He took the needle out of my spine and a shock of electricity shot down my left leg and into my foot, causing me to kick as I shouted out a mumbled version of the word *fuck.* "Sorry about that, must have hit a nerve," Dr. Chang said calmly as he placed a tiny bandage over the pin-sized hole in my back. "I want you to turn over on to your back and just lie here for twenty to thirty minutes. This will allow for all the fluids to disperse evenly throughout your spinal column." He left the room and let Dad in. Dad sat by my side and we waited.

When I felt ready, we returned to Guelph in the 2005 mint-green shit-box Hyundai Elantra. I lay in the back seat, curled in the fetal position the entire way. Seatbelts are for suckers.

What came in the next 24 hours and lasted for the next four weeks, was a world of hurt that I had never experienced before in my life! The only words available in my repertoire of the English language are *migraine* and *headache.* Let's break these words down here first for a second. The words, *head* and *ache* would imply that one's head is aching or sore, maybe even throbbing. Aching, just sort of sounds like mild pain or discomfort, like a sore shoulder or something. *Migraine* is a word that is used to describe a really strong headache, where you can be sensitive to sounds and even light. I even heard migraines can be paralyzing at times. Well, these were not headaches, and they were not migraines. They were who-the-fuck-knows-what-the-fuck-this-shit-bitch-ass-cockmouth-fuck-shit-is! That's the word! I found it. A new medical definition has been created! You can use it if you ever experience it, but for the sake of brevity, I will just call them headaches from here on out.

The headaches were supposed to only last a few days, but because I was receiving spinal taps every four days, my head was never given a break. The headaches kept building on top of each other, increasing in intensity over time. Nothing was alleviating the pain, except for lying on my back . . . all day. I consumed all the Tylenol that was legally allowed without overdosing while lying on my back. I drank gallons of water while lying on my back. I even ate my meals lying on my back. Nothing else did the trick. All I could do was lie on my back and wait it out. *One second at a time. One minute a time. One hour at a time. One day at a time.* I watched the clock on the TV's cable box, and willed the time to move forward. *Keep moving forward.*

From that moment on, I was doing anything and everything lying down. Eating, drinking and even going to the washroom were all activities done lying down. *How the hell did I do that?* you may be asking. Well, I didn't fully lie down when I went to the washroom but it was more of a keeping my head below my heart type of move I had developed. Just to get to the washroom, I'd roll myself off the sofa and crawl on my hands and knees, keeping my head down, staring at the floor. I laughed a bit at the thought of me crawling to the washroom as I took note of the crumbs scattered on the off-white dimple-tiled floors. "Mom, you need to do a better job sweeping," I joked.

"That's not funny!" Mom laughed, trying to mask her concern. "But clean the floor while you're at it, please," she joked back. I laughed.

When I returned to my sofa, I felt my phone vibrating against my leg through my pocket. The caller ID read "Jenny D." My heart began to pound and my mind began to race. *I guess word has gotten out. But this can't be Jenny, Jenny . . . can it? Why would she be calling? Pretty sure she hates you. But, of course it is! You idiot! Okay. Just pretend you don't know who it is. Pretend you don't have her number in your phone anymore. That's the move.*

"Hello?" I said, acting confused.

"Hi," Jenny's voice came through clear as day. There was a pause. "It's Jenny!"

"Jenny?" I asked, continuing my silly charade.

"Jenny De Lucia!" she said, clarifying.

"Oh, hi Jenny." *Solid work, Stolfi.* There was another long pause.

"Nelson told me what happened. So I hope you don't mind that I'm calling you."

"No. Not at all."

"I just wanted to tell you I'm thinking about you and I hope you're doing okay. I'm really sorry you are going through this. You're a rock star. If there is anything I can do, please let me know. You got this, Stolfi. We all love you."

I didn't know what to say. But her words seemed to melt the pain away for a brief moment.

"Thanks, Jenny. I really appreciate you calling. It means a lot."

"Love you, Stolfi," she said.

"Thanks, Jenny."

"And . . ." she said, leading.

"Oh. Love you too," I said.

"There you go." She laughed. I laughed. After a bit of friendly banter our conversation came to an end. I hung up the phone and smiled. Mom called to me from the kitchen. "Who was that?"

"No one," I said sheepishly.

"Sounded like a girl. Was it a girl?"

"Mom. Please."

"I love you too," she said, teasing. She chuckled. I shook my head and smiled.

Clarity

Phase two of my treatment lasted 30 days, just as they said it would, and it was finally over. Over the course of roughly 50 days, I had lost 35 pounds, received ten brain-radiation treatments and was administered seven spinal taps. As a result, my hair had completely fallen out, my appetite was non-existent and I couldn't get a boner. Yeah, you read that right. No bones.

I was eager to enter phase three of the protocol with the hopes that things would start to get easier. The doctors told me that after the first two months of treatment, it would all get easier. Reality check: THEY WERE LYING!!

I struggled each day with, "Why me?" I was filled with the worry and fear of losing my life. "I'm a good person, Mom! I don't deserve this," I would tell her from the white living room sofa, shrouded in a blanket to keep me warm.

"I know, sweetheart. *Sempre coraggio*," she said. Something my grandfather used to always say when times were tough. It's Italian for "always have courage." I was trying to stay courageous but I was getting tired of it. I was getting angry. I needed a reason to keep fighting. I needed some clarity.

The morning of my sixth week of chemotherapy, I awoke

with a pain in my chest similar to the pain I felt that started this whole journey. It was this sharp, stinging pain that seemed to linger with every breath I took. Conveniently enough, I had a chemotherapy appointment that day so I figured I should mention it to Dr. Chang when I met with him for our weekly consultation. He ordered a chest X- ray and discovered something quite shocking. He noticed that I had quite a bit of fluid collecting in my left lung, so he decided to admit me as an in-patient to monitor me in the dreaded C-3 wing of the hospital. It all happened so quickly, but there I was, six weeks later, back where I started—in a hospital bed, wearing my red Adidas soccer shorts, but this time, much skinnier and with much less hair.

As I sat in my hospital bed I took note that my chest was a little bit sore, but the initial pain had subsided and was nowhere near the type of pain I was feeling when I was first diagnosed. My overall appearance, compared to the other patients they normally dealt with, seemed to perplex even the nurses. "You should be showing much more ill effects from what your X-rays are indicating," one nurse told me.

"Sorry to disappoint you," I mumbled as she exited my room.

My team of doctors ordered three more tests on top of the X-rays, including a lovely CT scan, an enchanting echocardiogram, and an undulating ultrasound. These extra tests were necessary to check my legs for blood clots, a common side effect to the chemotherapy. I was informed that blood clots could possibly lead to a stroke if they were left unattended.

Yippee!

Finally, they ordered to have my lung re-drained of the fluid and get it tested for the possible spreading of cancer cells. *Amazing! Keep piling the shit on the already massive pile of shit I'm currently sitting in. I was just about to go into the third phase,* I thought. *I just want this to get easier!*

"Sorry, it's part of the process," the doctor told me. "Better to be safe than sorry," he continued.

The tests came back and all was looking good. They found no cancer in my stomach from the CT scan, no clots in my legs from the ultrasound and my heart was ticking away quite nicely, according to the echocardiogram. *So what was I doing here?*

You know those moments of clarity that seem to come from nowhere? Those moments that suddenly slap you in the face and put things into perspective? This was that moment.

I just wanted to know why this was happening. I was frustrated and angry. I had come so far and then had to take a step back before I could move forward again. I just wanted it all to be over with and I didn't want to wait anymore. I didn't want to be a patient. I just wanted to be done with it. I felt like the world was against me. I was pissed. I wanted to shout from my room, "I don't deserve this! I'm a good person! This shouldn't have happened to me!" But then, there was this moment of clarity.

His name was Jamie. Jamie was my roommate. He also had lymphoma and at the ripe old age of 27, he was two years my senior. He had been diagnosed around the same time as I had and he had just had his first child, with his lovely wife, who was by his bedside day in, day out. Jamie was in much worse shape than I was. Jamie had a blood clot in his left leg, which left him immobile. Just three days prior to my arrival, Jamie had a stroke and the doctors had pretty much told him that he wasn't going to make it. Jamie was eating through a tube inserted into his nose and was hardly able to speak. Jamie had been there every day for the first two months of his treatment. I, on the other hand, was sitting upright in my bed, drinking ice water, and actually chewing and swallowing the questionable hospital food I was being served. I was walking around the hospital floor and talking to visitors and nurses like the host of a hot party in a swank downtown condo. I looked and felt great in comparison to Jamie. Moment of clarity: *Quit your whining, Dan! You're 150 pounds? Jamie is 110 pounds! Hemorrhoids? Jamie is eating through a tube stuck up his nose! He has a wife and a newborn! He has been in this hospital hellhole for two months straight! He hasn't breathed a breath of fresh air since he's been here! So they're going to stick a needle into your chest and suck some fluid out? Big deal! Then you go home. I will go home. I don't have a wife or child to leave behind. I'm lucky.*

I was feeling a lot less "woe is me" about this whole thing now. I wanted Jamie to make it. We were in this together.

It was my second night in the hospital and the procedure to drain my lung was scheduled for the morning. Before going to bed, I heard a voice come from behind my curtain. "Hey, man." It was Jamie.

"Hey," I said.

"This sucks, right?" he said.

"One hundred percent," I replied.

We laughed.

The next morning, a short man with glasses came into my room. He carried a meat thermometer–type needle with some other equipment in a clear plastic bag. The needle, which I had now become oh-so familiar with, would be used to extract the fluid from my lungs . . . again. He seemed to be in a rush as he quickly placed a few glass bottles of local anesthetic on my lunch table. He looked at me and said, "You look pretty good."

"You're not so bad yourself, Doc," I joked. He laughed. I went on, "It's weird. I feel pretty good but everyone keeps telling me there is fluid in my lungs."

"Should we double-check the X-ray before I go poking around in there?" he asked.

"I'm good either way. Let's get this over with."

Mom, who was always by my side, piped up, "I think you should double-check."

"Good idea. I should know what I'm aiming for before I start poking around in there, shouldn't I?" he joked.

"I think that's a great idea," Mom chimed in again.

I don't really care, I thought to myself as I sat patiently at the edge of my bed. Mom helped me lift my blue gown over my shoulders to expose my back. Twenty minutes went by as I sat with my arms draped over my lunch table, my back waiting to be poked and me wondering what the delay was. Finally, the doctor returned. He looked at me and then looked at the X-ray. He showed me the image, throwing it down on the table tray. "Do you see any fluid in that lung?" he asked, leading.

"I don't think so?" I replied, a little surprised, not really knowing what I was looking at.

"They look pretty good to me," he said. "That's because there is no fluid in that lung. If I were to have gone in there, I would have punctured your lung and we would have had a whole other set of problems to deal with. I'm going to give your oncologist shit. The X-ray he gave me was from your original results when you were first diagnosed . . . in March."

"So what does this mean?" I asked, confused.

"I'm not touching you," he said. "I'm going to get you to fill out some papers and you are going to go home."

A break! A minor victory! I was so happy. *Dr. Chang, you really blew it!* I chalked it up to his youth and forgave him quickly. If Mom hadn't asked the doctor to double-check the X-rays, who knows what could have happened. A collapsed lung? Another few weeks in the hospital, leading to other complications? But Mamma knows best and like I said, without her, I'd be dead. All of this didn't really seem to sink in as much as it did when I had time to reflect back on it because, regardless of my oncologist's almost disastrous mistake, I was going home! I didn't care. I got to go home.

Then, I thought of Jamie. I was going home. Jamie was not. It dawned on me: *Not everyone gets to go home.* Jamie really gave me something special in that moment. Perspective. I knew I had it bad, but he had it worse. It didn't mean it all still didn't hurt, or that I couldn't feel frustrated or sad when I was in pain, but it definitely changed my mindset. It gave me perspective. A perspective I carry with me to this day. It could be worse. *It could be worse. Could it be worse?*

May 15, 2014

Day 51 of 730

It has apparently been 51 days since I started treatment. It has been very difficult but I have quickly learned from my recent stay in the hospital that it could be much more difficult. I'm at home now, trying to get through each day, trying to stay positive. Sempre coraggio. I don't think I can write much more today. This feels impossible. I will beat this!!

I left C-3 inspired by Jamie's perseverance to fight, but at the same time, saddened by the fact that he had the same cancer as me but was travelling down a much more arduous path. I believe they call this guilt? I was able to leave the hospital no better or worse than when I came in and was expected to continue my treatment for the remainder of the protocol. Jamie, however, was potentially going to continue to suffer for who knows how long in the same shitty hospital bed he started in. All fights are not created equal. But then, something strange happened.

~

A few weeks had passed and I was now getting one of my spinal taps from an oncologist, who was filling in for Dr. Chang. She was quite lovely and carried a calming energy. She appeared to be much more skilled and confident about the whole sticking-a-needle-into-my-spine thing than Dr. Chang.

"I love doing these. It's my favourite procedure," she said with a smile as she prepared the needles.

"You do know that sounds insane," I told her, as I lay curled up in the fetal position. She laughed. Then, she casually inserted the needle between my lower vertebrae and I could feel that familiar "pop" that indicated the needle was in.

"There was a gentleman about your age who was doing the same treatment as you recently," she told me as my spinal fluid slowly dripped into a vial.

"Really, who?" I asked. Selfishly, I was a little excited by the prospects of meeting a new chemo buddy.

"His name was Jamie," she said.

"Was!?" My mind began to race: *No! Jamie? Not Jamie, Jamie. That's not fair. I just saw him! He's too young. He has a child. He has a wife! He has his whole life ahead of him. What in the hell happened? Oh shit . . . am I next!? Give me an answer!*

The clear liquid continued to drip slowly out of my spine. "What happened?" I asked calmly.

"He quit," she said with a pinch of disappointment in her voice.

"Wait, what?" Now my emotions were all over the place. *Did I hear her right? Did she say, "He quit"?!*

"Yup. He wanted quality of life. He figures he'll take his chances that the amount of chemo he's had will be enough to keep the cancer at bay," she explained. *What is he, a doctor or something?!*

I started to feel a twinge of anger in my stomach. I was trying to remain calm as my reality warned me that there was still a giant needle sticking out of my spine and any sudden movements could prove disastrous. So, while staying as calm as I could, I asked, "What's going to happen to him?"

"Well, the cancer will surely return and he will either be back here or . . ." She paused. "He'll die." *Well, that's fucked!* I was pretty sure she was breaking the patient-doctor privacy code thingy, but she seemed like she needed to vent and we weren't going anywhere for a while, so vent away! Jamie was one of her patients and to lose a patient because they quit on you must feel like a slap in the face to a doctor. I knew it felt like a massive slap in the face to me! *He was one of my rocks, my pillars of support, my moment of clarity; he was put there to remind me to keep fighting, no matter what. We were a team!* My mind began to rage out! *Moments of clarity!? FUCK clarity.* Now, I was just right pissed off! I'm not sure what came over me but I felt so betrayed. I had this giant needle sticking out of my back, my spinal fluid was being replaced by chemical drugs, I was sick, sad, hot, cold, pale, hairless, skinny, weak, nauseous, I still had 90 weeks of treatment hell left, and this guy just quit! I wanted to yell at him, tell him to think of his kid, his wife. Tell him that he was making a huge mistake! But instead, I said, "That's too bad," as she pushed on the plunger to inject the yellow liquid drug into my spine. I took a breath. It wasn't for me to make those decisions for others. Everyone's journey is different and they have to go through it the only way *they* know how. They can't do it for anyone else. They can't be expected to fight a certain way. Who was I to judge?

When it really came down to it, I had to ask myself, how

important was it to me that I stayed on this planet and lived? How badly did I want it? I was 25 years old, I didn't have a girlfriend, I didn't have kids, I didn't have a job that needed me so badly that without me they'd be lost. I lived in a shitty apartment, pursuing a dream that my friends and family thought I was insane for pursuing. But, I knew I wanted my heart to keep beating, my lungs to keep breathing and my legs to keep moving. I wanted to keep making people laugh, I wanted to keep making people cry, I wanted to keep making people laugh so hard that they cried. I wanted to keep being a person on this fucked-up planet. I wasn't about to give up. There was more for me than this illness and I was not going to just be this illness. *I'm going to own you, cancer.* At that moment, I decided that I wasn't going to only complete my treatment for me but I was going to do it for my parents, my family, my friends and anyone else who was going through it. If I didn't make it, I didn't make it, but at least I'd go out knowing I gave it my all.

The doctor removed the needle from my spine and I turned onto my back. Breathe.

An Unexpected Letter

This was quite possibly the nicest thing ever written.

May 17, 2008

Hey there, friend. I have been thinking about you daily and just sending all the love and support and wishes of good things to come for you . . . I hope you have been feeling them . . . there is no doubt in my mind you will get anything but better than ever before and this will all be a little bump that had to happen to make you work that much harder when it was all over . . . and hey, it's great for the tell-all book about your life, no? Oh Stolfi, you're the happiest face I have ever met and I just know that through all this you're smiling and even when you're not, don't worry because you're allowed to feel and be anything you want right now . . . and there are so many people around who will smile and laugh and just love and support you even when you don't have the strength . . .

I hope to be able to come to Guelph and visit you soon...

You are going to get through this and you are going to continue to be an amazing person and lead a life that whatever you choose, be it acting, writing, whatever, you will be a success because, Stolfi, you got it . . . you know, that thing you either do or you don't and you do . . . you always have . . .

Much love and if there is anything, anything at all, I'm there with a smile and the making of thriller VHS. That's right, and we can marathon MJ, the man of style—sickest style ever!!!

All right, I'm just rambling now which I tend to do . . .

Peace, love and only great things for you.

Jenny

And sometimes it's the positive things people say to you that push you to do the things you'd never imagine yourself doing.

Phase 3: Intensification

May 2008. I was roughly seven weeks into treatment. The first two phases of my treatment were officially over and it was now time to start the intensification phase of my chemotherapy protocol. I was happy to be over the first two major hurdles of treatment and had high hopes it would all start to get easier and that the cancer would go away, but with a phase name like "intensification," I was keeping my expectations in check. *This is already super intense and NOW you're going to intensify things?!!* The intensification phase would take place over thirty weeks, consisting of weekly injected chemotherapy drugs, pills and spinal taps. The "Red Killer" was back for more Stolfi on three-week cycles, as well. *YAY! Intense.*

Thirty weeks sounds like a relatively short period of time to deal with hell, but when you are living it, it feels like an eternity. "Time flies when you're having fun and grinds to a halt when it sucks." If you ever find yourself wondering, *what happened to my life? It all seemed like just yesterday* . . . it means you are having fun, so keep rocking it. Let time fly, baby!

Getting the needle to stay inside my veins for the duration of the treatment sessions was becoming increasingly difficult.

Over the past seven weeks of treatment the veins in my hands had transitioned from thick, plump and purple, to grey, wiry and weak. The nurses explained to me that the chemotherapy caused internal scarring, resulting in thinner, weaker veins over time. To help alleviate this, they introduced me to a device that would help deliver the chemotherapy into my body without having to inject it directly into my veins. It was called a port-a-cath (port for short) and consisted of a small plastic ball-like apparatus with a clear rubber tube extending from it. Sort of looked like a giant sperm, *something I was sure to be lacking for the moment.* This device would be surgically inserted into my chest, just underneath my skin and directly above my heart. More specifically, the ball portion (sperm head) of the device would sit underneath my skin and the tube (sperm tail) would then be fed over and around my collarbone and into my aortic vein, which is connected to the heart. Blah, blah, blah. Jargon, jargon, jargon . . . it's weird.

The doctors explained that the nurses could now insert a needle into the port and the chemotherapy could be pumped directly into my heart. This would relieve my veins of the added stress from any direct contact with the chemotherapy and needles. The port could also be used to draw blood for testing, which was an added bonus. The only time they would draw blood directly from my thin, wiry veins would be if I was ever admitted to the emergency wing of the hospital or back to C-3. Why? Because, as the doctors told me, "the blood is more pure" when it is drawn directly through the veins, or something random like that . . . which made no sense to me at the time and still doesn't to this day. But what the fuck do I know?

"I really don't want to have this thing inside my body," I said to my nurse as he presented the port pamphlet to me. The Odette Cancer Clinic was packed that day and he knew I'd be waiting a while, so what better time than now to upsell me on all the benefits of the port-a-cath?

"It's a really simple procedure and it will make things much easier for the remainder of your treatment?" he continued. Nurse Joseph, my personal nurse, who worked as my oncologist's head nurse, always had a smile on his face and finished all of his sentences with a raised inflection like he was asking a question, even when it was a statement. "Your veins are getting weaker? So you should really think about it?" He was such a dork sometimes but damn good at his job.

"I just feel like this thing is like a pair of handcuffs and if I put it inside my body, I'm giving in to the disease. Like, permanently shackled, you know?" I explained. He looked at me blankly. Mom stood behind him shaking her head at my stubborn logic.

"Okay, well I'm going to give you some time to think about it, but we really do think it should be done sooner rather than later, okay?"

"Okay." I took the pamphlet and handed it directly to my mom.

My pride kicked into overdrive. *If I have a device implanted into my body for the sole purpose of injecting drugs into my heart, the cancer would be winning, right? That's how it works. That's how cancer gets you.* The loss of control, the feeling of helplessness and the idea of giving in to cancer was not an option for me, but there was no time to think about it in too much detail as I heard my name being called. "Daniel Sto-fli!" My name, butchered of course, by one of the chemotherapy nurses. It was time to begin my chemo session. The port would have to wait.

I shuffled my way through the doors and into one of the small rooms with two pink puffy plastic "chemo chairs" in it. The nurse, a tiny Filipino lady with an endearing accent, said my name. "Daniel Stolpee?" She pronounced the F as a P and I thought it was the cutest thing ever. If anyone was going to butcher my name, let it be Filipinos! She prepared my IV and searched for a healthy vein to inject the needle.

She opted to use a vein in my wrist just below my thumb. "Don't worry, I pined the right beins all the time." I felt the cold saltwater solution work its way up my arm, but it felt unusually cold this time, as though it was pooling in my wrist more than coursing up my arm and through my body. I looked down at my wrist and the skin around the injection site was bulging! My wrist was swollen and filling with liquid like a water balloon. "My wrist!" I yelled out to the nurse, her back now turned to prepare more bags of liquid drugs. She turned quickly, bee-lined her way toward me and ripped the wire out of the vein. A shot of saline solution oozed out of my arm. She quickly applied pressure to the area with a cotton gauze pad. "Shoot, I'm sorry. The bein burst. It's no good," she told me, pushing down on my wrist as the liquid continued to ooze out of my skin, dripping down the back of my hand and onto the floor.

"I guess I should start thinking about getting that port put in, eh?" I said.

"They make everything easier. Por you and por me, sweetie," she said. With that, my decision was made. Bring on the port!

May 21, 2008

Day 58 of 730

Big day tomorrow. My chest will never be the same again! Getting the port put in. Little nervous but want to get this done. Must dominate this cancer . . .

May 22, 2008

Day 59 of 730

Got the port in today. I am puking up a storm and have a headache and am in serious pain as a result of the surgery. Like, serious pain! What the fuck! Was it the best move? Hope so . . .

Once the nausea passed and the pain subsided, I felt the port through my skin, pushing on it with my thumb and forefinger. It was like a firm little bouncy ball. I couldn't help but think, *This little device means a significant reduction in needles to the veins. That pinching, stinging and pushing feeling will all be replaced by one little prick accompanied by some gauze and surgical tape. It should all get a little bit more manageable from here. Minor victories . . . and on a really cool note, I think I am now part cyborg . . . so that's pretty sweet.*

~

For the intensification phase, I was set to start a weekly chemotherapy cycle of three-week intervals. I would receive my heaviest cocktail of drugs intravenously the first week, followed by a mix of less intensive drugs the second week and even less intensive drugs the third week. All of these drugs, however, still came with their own special side effects and challenges, sort of like a roller coaster but with zero exhilaration and all the fear. These cocktails were prescribed with a combination of pills to be taken every day in the morning throughout the day and before bed. Drugs, drugs, drugs. Exhilarating!

The Red Killer continued to cause nausea, vomiting, loss of appetite and the loss of hair. I didn't know I would lose hair in places other than my head but, oh yeah, I lost it there too. I was still losing weight and was, at that point, 137 pounds. A loss of forty-eight pounds and counting. *Eat your heart out, Jenny Craig.*

Setting Goals

June 12th, 2008. My sister was almost nine months pregnant! When I was first diagnosed, one of my biggest fears was that I wouldn't be able to meet my new nephew when he was born. I set a goal for myself to at least make it to the birth of this newest family member. It was a motivating force behind waking up every morning, getting out of bed, putting on my socks and putting food in my mouth. I was determined to walk, rest, take the treatment and get through each day no matter how difficult it was. I needed to set benchmarks for myself like they do in marathons. I would run my cancer race in five-mile increments, each marker getting me one step closer to the finish line. The five mile was my sister's belly. *How many miles is a marathon again?* On the days I felt like giving up I would think about my sister and the baby. I was determined to meet this kid!

June 12, 2008

Day 80 of 730

My sister had a baby boy! I'm an uncle! I'm a Zio, baby! A baby! Zio! I am now to be referred to as Zio Daniel.

Dad and I are going to try and make it up to Montreal tomorrow, but I may not be able to make it because I have treatment in the morning. I hope "it" lets me go. It will let me go. This is my "off week." I'm only going to get better . . . I've decided. Anyway, back to the baby. I am super excited and can't wait to see this little guy!

Beat this! Fight this! Win this!

YOU ARE BIGGER THAN THIS.

Mom was already in Montreal to help my sister through the birthing process. Dad took me to Toronto to get my chemotherapy. I could see how excited he was that he was now officially a nonno. My dad never gets overly excited about much, so I took some joy in watching him squirm and shift uncomfortably in the chair of the hospital room as we waited for my name to be called for treatment. The last few drops of chemo slowly dripped through the tubes and into my new port at about 2 p.m. My chemotherapy infusions were finished but the cumulative toll of the treatment had been such that I now had to lie in a bed for my appointments, too drained and weak to sit in the pink fluffy chairs. Dad was pacing. He wanted so badly to be there in Montreal to meet his grandson. I really wanted to be there too . . . so . . . *fuck it*. "Hey Dad, wanna go?" I said with a dry grin.

"Now?" he asked excited but reserved.

"We can be there by seven if we leave now." Just like in the emergency room washroom when he played doctor, it was now my turn to make the call. He shifted his head back and forth a couple times, making sure the coast was clear, helped me out of bed and just like that, we were on our way! No spare clothes, no deodorant, no toothbrush, no worries. Just two guys screaming down the 401 in the green machine on our way to Montreal. The excitement of seeing this kid made the trip seem easy. "Don't tell Nadia we're coming. We'll surprise her," I told Mom over the phone.

"Ok, I won't say anything, but hurry, visiting hours are over at 7!" she whispered, already trying her best to keep it a secret. Mom is the worst at keeping secrets, but it seemed like she was going to pull through on this one. I reclined my chair all the way back and rested. Dad's lead foot did the rest.

We arrived in Montreal and were at the hospital at 6:30 p.m. The traffic just seemed to vanish on the trip up. Mom stood outside the door of my sister's hospital room waving us on. "Would you hurry up already?" she urged, whisper-shouting.

"I'm shuffling as fast as I can!" I whisper-shouted back.

We poked our heads in the doorway, quiet and calm, holding our excitement in as my sister, still drowsy from the painkillers, smiled in dopey disbelief. "You're here!?" she said, as tears began to stream down her face. My sister never cries. NEVER.

"You think a little cancer is going to keep me from seeing my nephew?" I joked.

"Want to hold him?" she asked.

"Of course!" I was too weak to hold him while standing up. I took a seat and she handed him off to Dad who rocked him for a brief moment before handing him off to me.

"He is so tiny," I whispered. His abdomen pumped up and down in perfect rhythm as he took his first little breaths. When I held him in my arms for that first time, it all became so clear. *A new reason to keep fighting,* I thought. *I have to watch this kid grow up!*

June 15, 2008

Day 83 of 730

Went to Montreal to see my nephew, Adrian! Very happy I was able to go and that I was strong enough to do it! I think I may have overexerted myself, though, and should take it easy this week. Gotta go to Toronto tomorrow and get some chemo again. Not looking forward to it. I am tired. I must go to sleep now.

Back in the Big House

It all happened so fast. I was roughly three months into treatment back in my bedroom, ready to take on a new day. I woke with soreness in my chest. *Not again*, I thought to myself. The pain was stronger, sharper this time. It was different. I could feel something was wrong. I made my way downstairs, sat in front of my bowl of fruit and Happy O's and said, "Mom, my chest is sore again." Tears of sheer terror streamed down my cheeks.

"Let's mention it to Dr. Chang today, okay?" she said calmly. And just like that, the next thing I knew, I was back at C-3 lying in a hospital bed watching my blood get sucked from my arm and into a vial for testing. They couldn't draw the blood from my port for testing, so my veins would take the brunt of the abuse for the time being.

Diagnosis: Pneumonia. *So this is what it feels like.*

My oncologist put me on a heavy prescription of antibiotic medication to combat the pneumonia that was now seeping into my lungs. The side effects to these antibiotics actually proved to be quite beneficial. This is going to sound disgusting, but it made my shit soft and runny, almost like soup! *Mmmmmm, poop soup*. How was this a positive thing, you ask? Ever? Soup-like poop meant no constipation, which in turn meant no butt pain! Sorry, but minor victories, right?

The poop soup actually caused a bit of concern for one of my nurses. He was a male nurse, short, stocky and probably had a Napoleon complex. I based this on the account that he was also a major dick! He entered my room and told me that my diarrhea may be an indication that I could have a condition called C. difficile or C. diff, for short. "It's a bacterial infection that causes severe diarrhea," he said. "It's highly contagious." I didn't know how to respond. "You could die from it," he finally said.

Thanks for sugar-coating it. "I think it's just a reaction to the antibiotic," I suggested. He rolled his eyes. *Another patient playing doctor,* he must have been thinking.

"When you go to the bathroom, I want you to go in the bowl I placed over the toilet seat so we can test it," he instructed. Sounded simple enough.

"Poop in the bowl that sits in the bigger bowl. Got it," I said. The time had come to do my business, so I rolled out of my bed, unplugged my monitor from the wall and made my way to the bathroom with my beeping buddy on wheels. I was quite proud of myself for some reason. I can't explain it, but I think it was the fact that for the first time in a long time my butt didn't hurt when I went to the bathroom. The fear of nature calling was no longer a fear. I was victorious . . . sort of. I mean, I could have horrific, life-threatening and extremely contagious diarrhea, but my ass felt great! *Minor victories.*

The nurse returned to my room and I told him what I had accomplished. "It's really runny, man!" I told him. He entered the bathroom, flushed the toilet and stormed out of the funky-smelling room. "That's not C. diff! Not even close!" he exclaimed. He sounded disappointed and almost angry as he huffed like a bratty child on his way out of the room.

"I still have diarrhea AND pneumonia, ya dick," I said under my breath. I couldn't help but laugh. He was upset that I *didn't* have severe enough diarrhea. I just had plain old diarrhea. Not the kind that could kill me. *If it wasn't the kind that could kill me, then what is there to get so excited about? Did I mention I also have cancer? I'll give you diarrhea, pal! Wait, I guess I already did . . . Boom! Mind blown. Toilet bowl, blown! Napoleon complex, one hundred percent!*

New Roommates

This stay in the hospital was proving to be very different than the others. There seemed to be more people my age on the ward this time around. I wasn't sure why, but maybe there is an influx in the summer months of young adults who get cancer? Someone should look into that.

I saw a young Black man about my age walk past my room with his mother in tow. Like clockwork, every hour on the hour, they'd walk by. He was skinny, battered from the chemotherapy. His eyes bulged from his sockets, his cheeks were sunken and his once thick curly hair was now thin and scattered about his head. He was so weak he used his IV pole as a crutch when he lumbered down the hall. His mother walked with him while family members and friends trailed behind. He smiled as he passed my room. He had such a big, bright, beautiful smile. I smiled back. I gave him a reassuring nod of the head. *The secret world of cancer patient communication,* we don't need words to show each other we understand. We just get it.

My roommate was pretty cool too, but he was much older than me. His name was Angelo. He was Italian—I mean, his name was Angelo and when he spoke he sounded exactly like my dad, so it's not like I'm stretching too far on this one. He had thin grey hair and a big nose, which was matched by an even bigger potbelly. He opted to sit in a wheelchair rather than lie in his bed for the day. I think he felt more in control that way. I couldn't blame him. He had more than enough to deal with, especially when his wife showed up. Oh God, his wife was the worst!

An old, bitter Italian woman stuck in the 1950s showed up every day before lunch and just verbally laid into Angelo. She spoke with the familiar Italian "a" between every other word and appeared to be on a mission to give Angelo "a" hard time. He wasn't eating all that much and she couldn't handle it. She was so Italian it hurt. "You have to a eat, Angelo! I'm not going to keep a coming here to watch you a sleep!" she said. He just stayed quiet and nodded his head. He gave me a look. Without any words, I understood his frustration. A look like, "Can you believe this one?" and I'm like "Brother, I feel ya." It was all in the eyes.

I don't think his wife understood how difficult it was to eat for anyone undergoing treatment.

When his wife left for the day, I took my moment to chat with him. "Hey Angelo, sometimes you just don't feel like eating and there is nothing you can do about it."

"Yeah, I'm not worried about it. She's always on my case," he said. We laughed.

I was secretly hoping that one day Angelo would say something like, "Would you just shut up, already? You're killing me here . . . literally!" But he just sat quietly and took it. He needed her and she needed him. It was actually kind of cute. *Barf.* Literally. I puked moments later.

When it came to eating, I was now on a steady diet of Boost-brand meal replacement drinks high in vitamins, protein and . . . crap? Must be crap. I usually opted for the chocolate flavour over strawberry or vanilla. It didn't taste all that bad and it was all I could stomach, so I plugged my nose and drank it down. I was also eating a lot of soups to help me get through . . . oh, and milk. Good old milk. Still the life blood for sure.

Everything was becoming pretty routine: blood work at 4 a.m., breakfast at 8 a.m., blood work and antibiotics at 10 a.m., lunch at noon, blood work and antibiotics at 2 p.m., dinner at 5 p.m. and some more antibiotics for dessert. But you could never get too comfortable in the routine because things could and would change quickly.

It was early in the afternoon, around lunchtime. Not sure. I heard a siren go off. *Was there a fire? A bomb?* A woman's voice blared over the intercom, "Code blue in room 321. Code blue in 321."

"That's right next door," Mom said. Four or five nurses and doctors ran by my room, a streak of white lab coats and blue scrubs. There was so much confusion and chaos. "What's a code blue?" I asked Mom. She shrugged her shoulders and stepped out into the hallway.

"Please stay in your room ma'am," a nurse warned her. Suddenly, I saw a bed on wheels rush past my door, pushed by the same group of doctors and nurses from before. They raced down the hall. A Black woman was running after them crying and yelling, "No. Please God, no!"

It was him. It was my friend who passed by my doorway,

walking laps around the ward, pushing his IV pole. He was under the white sheet. He was the code blue. The screams, squeaky wheels and footsteps faded as they pushed him down the hall, until finally, silence. Now, there was that moment, that moment of breathless and soundless empty space. My senses were numb. I was in shock.

The beeps of my machine faded back in slowly. The sound of sneakers squeaking down the hall echoed off the walls and the smell of hospital food wafted through the air. I looked up at Mom. Fear covered her face as she held my hand. We took a moment and gave each other a knowing look. A look that needed no words. He was gone.

Sometimes it's difficult to talk about death, but for me it had become so commonplace. During treatment, I had become numb to the reality of it all. Cancer doesn't discriminate and it doesn't feel sorry for you. Death is scary. Some make it and some don't. It was overwhelmingly sad, but if I had gotten caught up in the sadness and depth of it all at the time, it would have destroyed me. The only thing I can even imagine that losing a fellow cancer patient would be similar to, is war.

I am deep in the Amazon rainforest. I've been stationed there to take down a deadly assassin who is taking the lives of innocent civilians. I am partnered up with an African soldier who speaks little English. We will speak through hand signals and body language most of the time anyway, so the lack of verbal communication is of little concern to either of us. Maybe he was drafted? *I think to myself. I was drafted too. He didn't want to be here, and I didn't want to be here either, but we* had *to be here. We have been assigned the same task:* To take down the enemy at any cost.

We are ordered to fight, immediately. Before we can say yes or no, there we are, fighting, trying to wrap our heads around the fact that we could die and there is no turning back. We didn't ask for this. We didn't want this. It just happened. So there we are, fighting. Suddenly, my fellow soldier gets hit by a bullet and goes down in a heap. He's hurt. He's hurt bad. I crawl over to him as bullets whizz by. I hold him in my arms and try to stop the bleeding, but the wound is too serious. He takes his dying breaths and it quickly dawns on me that this is for real. He could have been me. I feel horrible. I feel ill. I think about his family, his friends and all the people his death will affect, but I can't stay to help or mourn because I have to move on. I could be next. I keep running as bullets keep zipping by bouncing off the ground beneath my feet. The bullets are now hitting more and more fellow soldiers to my left and right. No time to reach out and save them, I have to keep running. As I run, poisonous snakes from the Amazon jungle bite deep into my skin, injecting me with venom. It's all part of the deal, I think to myself. Wait, what deal? I never asked for this!

I'm dodging more and more bullets as they whiz by my head. There are more and more snakes digging their fangs deep into my skin. I am running as fast as I can but I can't seem to pull away from the enemy. I can't even see the enemy! Suddenly, a bullet ricochets off the top of my helmet and knocks me to the ground. Blackout.

I stay on the ground, motionless, and wait for the bullets to stop. After a moment, the bullets let up and the coast is clear, but I can't know for how long. It's now or never. I get to my feet, shake off the pain, and I keep running. I just keep running.

The deaths of my fellow fighters hits me harder now. Now that I'm further removed from it. I've lost so many people to this disease. Fuck cancer.

Happy Birthday

On August 10th, 2008, after a four-night bout with pneumonia and a disgruntled nurse, I was released from the hospital. I was back in Guelph with a prescription for antibiotics to combat the pneumonia and my butt was feeling a bit better. *Minor victories.* My oncologist gave me specific instructions to take the prescription of pills three times a day for two full weeks. He was very clear about the fact that I had to finish all the medication, regardless of how I was feeling. I repeat, *ALL* of the medication regardless of how I was feeling. The prescription pills I went home with looked vastly different than the ones I was taking in the hospital. I mentioned this to the doctor who filled the prescription, but he chalked it up to the fact that it was just a different brand of medication with the same medicinal properties. I didn't think much of it other than the fact that they weren't as easy to swallow due to their size. They were significantly larger than the ones I took in hospital, but it was nothing a little extra water couldn't help with. *What the hell do I know?* I swallowed them down.

My 26th birthday was two weeks away. Emotionally, I was feeling really low, as my mind was constantly deep in thought, trying to find purpose and meaning in it all. Physically, my body seemed to be breaking down more and more from the side effects of the chemotherapy. Specifically, I had developed a mean case of mouth sores that lined the inside of my cheeks and throat and covered my tongue.

The sores had made eating increasingly difficult, as just the physical act of chewing was now very painful. Certain acidic fruits and salty foods were off limits from now on. The feeling was comparable to squirting lemon juice into a canker sore. Multiple canker sores . . . all at once. The physical pain was becoming too much to bear and all food, even water, was becoming impossibly painful to swallow.

Swallowing my own saliva was one of the most painful experiences of all. The agony had become so intense I couldn't even open my mouth to speak. I had resorted to hand gestures to ask my mom for help, or grunted like a caveman to respond to "yes" or "no" type questions. Something was terribly wrong, and I had a firm belief that this had to do with the antibiotics I was taking. It was one of those gut feelings that I couldn't seem to ignore. I had this sick feeling that, if I voiced my beliefs, it would make me sound crazy for even suggesting it and I'd be labelled a "bad patient." I was sure I needed to stop the antibiotics, but as instructed, I had to finish the prescription to the end no matter how I was feeling.

Crystal, a good friend of mine, told me she was making preparations for a big party at my parents' house to celebrate my upcoming birthday. "I'll put it all together and invite everyone so you don't have to worry about a thing. You cool with that?"

she said excitedly over the phone. The gesture was beautiful, but the timing couldn't have been worse. I knew for a fact my friends had no real sense of just how much pain I was in or how difficult it was to get up off the couch, to speak, to laugh, to be. I didn't want to disappoint them, so I did what I had been doing the entire time. I acted like everything was okay.

"That would be really cool!" I mumbled, holding the pain in as I tried to speak.

"Well, we love you and want to be there for you on your birthday," Crystal continued with excited energy.

"It's on."

I love my friends.

AUGUST 24th, 2008. You can see I have a beard and some fine hair on my head. The beard was a strange phenomenon that even the doctors couldn't really explain. It eventually fell out too . . . but I rocked it while I could! The spots on my face are open sores. They were everywhere.

August 24th, 2008, my 26th birthday had arrived. It was a Sunday afternoon and thirty of my friends had driven down from Toronto to celebrate. My one friend, Don, even came all the way in from Buffalo, New York. *He's crossing the border just for me? That's so insanely nice!* I thought.

Crystal decorated my parents' deck with green, white and red banners to showcase my Italian pride. She also brought over party hats, food and gifts. It was a very PG birthday party with cake, pop and chips . . . kind of like the ones you have when you're five years old.

My friend Dimetre made hot dogs and hamburgers for everyone on my parents' BBQ. The smoke and smell of grilled meat wafted through the warm sticky air. He was sweating like mad in the hot August sun, but kept cooking away with a big smile on his face. I, on the other hand, was freezing cold. I began to salivate from the smell of grilled meat as I took tiny sips of an energy drink, each one stinging as it passed my dry, chapped lips.

Just as I was beginning to think that the timing of all of this was terrible, someone showed up who made all the difference in the world. With her bright smile that lights up any room, Jenny entered the front door. "Happy birthday, Stolfi!" she shouted, holding out both arms triumphantly in the air before giving me a big hug. She told me how much she loved me and that she was thinking about me all the time. Our curious past—of me being an ass-face to her—all seemed to wash away at that moment. She was my friend. Not an ex-girlfriend and not a girl I dated once but Jenny, my really great friend.

"It's time for cake!" Mom called out, as my friends meandered to the kitchen. I sat at the kitchen table with my trusty bottle of strawberry-flavoured Gatorade, not aware of the amazing surprise that was about to be bestowed upon me: my friends made me a Michael Jackson cake. The kicker? MJ's face was replaced by my face! It was unbelievable. A chocolate cake with an image of MJ from the *Thriller* album, where he's holding the little tiger cub, with my face plastered onto his body. It was hilarious and took me away from the pain, the worry and the cancer for what I hoped would be forever. Reality, however, quickly set in.

I was feeling so sick, and my mouth was in so much pain that I couldn't physically eat the cake. My emotions took over and I felt this wave of love mixed with positive energy, mixed with frustration and anger sweep through my body. *Everyone here cares so much about me and they went out of their way to do this very special thing for me, to be with me in my time of need,* I thought to myself.

SIDE NOTE: My fandom for MJ has recently changed amidst the scandal that broke after his passing. I've had a really hard time separating the man from the music. For the sake of this book and when this all went down, I was a huge MJ fan. Like, next level. His music helped me through a lot of difficult times. For that, I'm grateful.

"Make a speech," Don from Buffalo called out.

I was five words in. "Thanks so much for coming . . ." and

then I started crying uncontrollably. *What in the hell is happening?* I couldn't stop crying. Tears streamed out of my eyeballs while I tried to ramble about how grateful I was that everyone was there. The words struggled to leave my mouth in any coherent manner. "It just means a lot to me that everyone would come down . . . and say happy birthday to me." More tears. "I want everyone to stay. Stay! Stay, please. Please, and keep celebrating. Don't feel like you have to go. Stay and have fun, please." Still crying. As much as I tried to will the pain and fear away, it wasn't meant to be. I suddenly felt chills surge through my body. One of the hottest days of the year and I had to move to a couch in another room to lie underneath a blanket. It was getting bad.

"I think it's the antibiotics," I told Crystal.

"You have to keep taking them until the end," she reminded me.

"But I really think they gave me too much."

"You have to finish all of them!" Mom shouted from the kitchen.

I reluctantly agreed and took my antibiotics, forcing the horse-sized pills past the sores and down my throat.

I think it was that moment that it clicked for my friends as to how difficult everything really was. I don't think they were prepared to see me in such a fragile state. They got a wake-up call that I didn't want them to get. I felt bad. I wanted to be strong for them, to ease their worries. The last time a lot of them had seen me, I was fifty pounds heavier with thick curly hair atop my head and a tan that could rival any of the best beach bums in LA. I was dancing on stage with them, performing comedy with them and laughing with them. But I couldn't do any of that with them now. I was dehydrated and hadn't eaten for a couple of days. My mouth sores were burning, and I was an emotional wreck.

It was time for them to go back to Toronto. I would soon follow, as I needed to admit myself back to C-3 for another sleepover. This time, it would prove to be my longest stay yet. Things just kept getting worse. But I repeated my mantra: *One second at a time. One minute at a time. One hour at a time. One day at a time . . .*

The Big House
Keeps Knocking

I was in a different room on the C-wing this time around—a four-plex with three roommates . . . but it was all the same shit in the Big House. My doctors seemed baffled as to why I was reacting so poorly to the chemotherapy. They had warned me in the past about the potential for mouth sores but on this day, they assured me that my mouth sores were the worst they'd ever seen. I was starting to take pride in the fact that I was breaking all these "worsts" for the doctors. *So I was the best at being the worst? Amazing!*

My red and white blood cells were critically low and my oncologist was beginning to worry. Without my white blood cells I couldn't fight the sores ravaging the inside of my mouth or combat any other virus that may be running wild throughout my body. Their solution was to give me blood . . . other people's blood.

Blood transfusions are, well, sort of fucked. I knew the general concept: Someone else's blood goes into my body. Seemed simple enough. But when you're the other body receiving the blood? It's fucked. A clear plastic bag of someone else's blood was strapped to my IV pole and then a needle was inserted into my arm. Over a twenty-minute period, some selfless stranger's blood oozed into my veins. Seeing the dark purple and red liquid hang above my bed as it slowly made its way inside my body was a bit terrifying. I was super grateful for the donors who took the time to give their blood but at the same time, there was just something so strange and scary about the whole process. It's like Frankenstein-type stuff. *What if it's the wrong type of blood!?*

Transfusions are supposed to raise the levels of your red and white blood cells. They are supposed to make you feel better and they are supposed to give you energy, but they did absolutely nothing for me except freak me out a little. My blood counts were at the same level as they were when I came to the hospital and my mouth sores weren't subsiding. The short of it: the blood transfusions didn't seem to have the effect the doctors were hoping for.

The pain in my mouth was so intense that my oncologist recommended I take some painkillers. "It's a self-injected liquid drug, five times more powerful than morphine," he said. "You can control the dosage at the touch of a button." I had heard of this sort of thing from friends of mine who had broken their foot or arm and was actually sort of excited to give it a try. "It makes you super high, man!" a stoner buddy from university once told me. *Five times more powerful than morphine, though?! This should be fun!*

A nurse attached an armband to my right bicep, which was held tight by a piece of Velcro. The armband had a needle in it that poked into my skin, injecting the potent drug on my command into my body. Well, let me just say, this stuff was powerful!

Let the hallucinations begin!

I pushed down on the little red button, triggering the needle to prick my skin, which injected the first dose of painkilling liquid into my arm. I felt a little pinch in my upper right bicep as the magical elixir seeped its way through my body. A few minutes passed without incident. Mom sat at the foot of my bed reading a magazine while talking about something I couldn't seem to focus on. *Maybe pasta? Is she talking about pasta?* I took a little pocket mirror off my food table and looked into my mouth; I would do this routinely to check how the sores were progressing. Upon first inspection it just looked like little red open wounds lining the inside of my cheeks and lips. Then, seemingly out of nowhere, the inside of my mouth was covered in dark red blood, oozing out between my teeth. "Mom, I need a napkin. I'm bleeding!" I called out. She didn't answer. She didn't answer because she wasn't there. I looked back at the mirror and my friend, Jeff, from Timmins, looked over my shoulder. His face was a reflection staring back at me. Lifeless. Pale. I put the mirror down and looked over my shoulder and Jeff was gone. I checked my mouth with my fingers to feel for blood, but there was no blood. I was terrified. I shut my eyes tight for what felt like only a brief moment, but when they opened, it was quiet. *The middle of the night?* I was screaming now because someone had pulled my IV out of my arm! The nurse came rushing into my room. "My IV was ripped out! Someone ripped out my IV!" I called out to her. *I've never seen this nurse before. Who is she?* Her face was disjointed. One eye was much bigger than the other and she had a scar that ran the length of her face. *Who are you?*

"Your IV is still there. All is fine, sweetheart. Go to sleep," she assured me. I looked down at my arm again, and just as quickly as I thought the IV was pulled out, it was back in, but now the plastic tube was disconnected from my machine and stretched over a yellow curtain, which now surrounded my bed. The long, thin, clear tube travelled out the door and into the hallway. I wanted to scratch at the tape that held the tube tightly to my vein. It was itching unbearably, and I couldn't stand it. I feared the pain it would cause if I tore it out of my arm. I began to panic. Then, suddenly, my ears popped and my eyes focused on my IV as it returned to normal, now attached to the monitor and itch-free in the fold of my arm. The beeps of my machine made their familiar noises once again and the fluorescent lights of the hospital hallway shone through the open doorway to my room. I felt drowsy. My eyelids were heavy. Blackout.

I opened my eyes. Morning. Mom was now at the foot of my bed flipping through a magazine and I immediately feared that she was another hallucination. The drugs were taking over my mind. *I'm going fucking crazy!*

I tried to speak but couldn't form full sentences. I started with a few words that ended in mumbled nonsense. I was so confused. My emotions were all over the place. I couldn't organize my thoughts. *What is happening?!* A doctor entered my room. "How are you feeling today? How is the pain?"

"How the fuck do you think I'm feeling!?" I blurted out. *Was that a thought or did I say that out loud?* Mom stood quickly.

"I'm sorry, he's not in a very good mood today," she explained, looking at me like "I should smack you!" *I guess it was out loud.* I didn't care, though. I couldn't control my mind or my emotions. My roommate was fucking pissing me off now too. *Fuck, that guy complains like an entitled kid who wants chocolate for dinner. He's always ringing his damn bell for every little thing and the nurses treat him like shit. I feel like I'm in a zoo!* The nurses yelled at him for trying to go to the washroom. "Poop in your diaper, sir! We can't walk you to the washroom every time you have to go. Just poop in your diaper!" They'd shout. Was I still hallucinating? Nope. This was for real.

This was life on C-3. I needed to get a grip! "Can we lower the dose on the morphine stuff, please? I'd rather take the pain than see things that aren't real," I told the doctor. I was losing control and needed to get it back.

"Sure thing. We'll lower it a few levels and then we can work up the dosage from there if you need it." He patted my foot gently and left the room.

The morphine was lowered and the pain returned but my mind was clearer. My emotions stabilized and the hallucinations stopped. *Minor victories.*

Due to my mood swings and random outbursts, the doctors sent me a psychiatrist to find a diagnosis for me. I knew I was depressed. Of course I was. I didn't need a psychiatrist to confirm this for me. A young guy, close to my age, entered my room and sat casually beside my bed. He had this air of arrogance about him. The way he crossed his legs, looked down at his clipboard and clicked his pen. The way he adjusted his glasses and cleared his throat was just so pretentious. He hadn't even said a single word and my douche radar was detecting a giant one. *Arrogant fuck*. Maybe it was the meds.

"So,"—he paused, taking a deep breath as he finally looked up at me—"how are you feeling?" *This guy was textbook. Solid opener, bro.*

"I feel moody and angry and I'm snapping at people for no reason."

"You're depressed," he said knowingly.

No shit, pal! You go to school for that?!

"I have some drugs that can help with the mood swings--" Before he could continue, I interrupted

"In all honesty, I feel that it's the drugs that are causing the depression. Just take me off the antibiotics for the pneumonia and I think I will be okay."

"Well, I can't prescribe taking you off medication. I can only prescribe you medication for the depression."

No one believed me. No one wanted to listen. They thought I was acting crazy. I had told my friends, my mother and the doctors that the antibiotics were making me react that way, but they all told me to just keep taking them until the prescription finished.

I refused the drugs for the depression from the psychiatrist, dismissing him from my room. I opted to wait to finish taking the antibiotics, although I wanted to throw them in the garbage.

Later that day, my oncologist walked into my room and

looked at me sheepishly. "So, I need to tell you something."

"What is it, Doc?" I asked, as if he was about to deal me another blow.

"It turns out Dr. Forest prescribed a higher dosage of antibiotics than what was originally prescribed."

"What's that?" I inquired, as if I didn't hear it.

"Roughly three times more," he continued. *Son of a bitch! I was right!* "We'll be taking you off the antibiotics at this time and the chemotherapy entirely for a week. This will give your body time to recover a bit and then we can get you out of here. We'll start the treatment again next Wednesday."

FUCKERS!! You fucking fucks! Fuck!

After Major Medical Mistake Number Two by my team, I realized that I had to be more diligent in my treatment. I made a pledge to become more of an advocate for my own care. I had to listen to myself more and trust that what I was feeling was real and justified. I made a vow that, from that day forward, I was going to ask more questions and not just say "yes" to everything. It was time to take control of my health and become a responsible patient. I knew I was taking a step back in order to move forward again but it was a step I had to take. This time I was going to do it right. It was my body and my treatment. It was my cancer and my fight. It was time to go motherfucking gangster on this motherfucking cancer.

With a Little Help
from My Friends

Back home, fresh from my stay on C-3, I took a moment to reflect back on the previous 15 days and nights I had spent in the hospital. I couldn't help but remember the fantastic support and love I received on a daily basis from my friends. During my stay, I had a lot of visitors drop by but none more frequently than my ex-girlfriend, turned new friend, Jenny. Almost every morning, Jenny excitedly entered my room wearing a big blue scarf that appeared to wrap around her entire body. "Hey, Stolfi!" she'd say, smiling brightly.

"Hey, Jenny," I'd say with a weak smile. "Thanks for coming."

"Of course! I literally live down the street so I'm coming to visit you whenever I can," she assured me. As fate had it, her parents' house was a twenty-minute walk from the hospital, which meant I got to see Jenny a lot during my stay. I couldn't have been happier about it. Although I was tired, weak and in a tremendous amount of physical pain, having her there took my mind off the peripherals and allowed me to focus on anything other than being in a hospital bed hooked up to machines.

For the first time in our history together, we were able to become genuine friends. We started to get to know each other as individuals better than ever before. The hospital setting took away any of the pressures that a traditional date at a restaurant could bring. The hospital was a strange place to take a girl for a date, but it worked for her, so it worked for me! *And it wasn't really a date. It wasn't a date! Of course it wasn't a date!* We just got to hang out and talk. I got to see a lot in her that I had missed the first time we dated. She had much more sassiness than what I remembered from university. "Fucking weather, eh, Stolf?" she'd blurt out.

"Ha ha, yeah, it's crazy. I just want to be outside," I'd reply.

"Well, once you're all better, we'll fucking go to a park and feed those punk bastard pigeons or something."

"You're really swearing like a sailor there, eh, Jenny," I'd say.

"Oh shit. Sorry. Too much?" she'd say, then cover her mouth.

"No, no, it's cool. I love it!"

We'd tell gross jokes, share laughs and gossip about what was going on in the world of Hollywood. I was so grateful for her. She was super helpful, always asking if I needed anything. "You want water, Stolfi? I'll get ya water," she'd say before I could answer. She'd leave my room with an empty Styrofoam cup and come back with it full of ice water, equipped with a bendy straw. "I can heat your soup up for ya," she'd say, grabbing the cold bowl from my food tray to give Mom a break from all of my demanding orders. "You just sit. I'll get it," she'd assure her.

"She's great, Daniel," Mom would tell me whenever Jenny was out of the room for a moment.

"I know Mom. I know," I'd reply. I was starting to have a little thing for this Jenny girl but I just brushed the feelings off because, well, I was a complete physical and mental disaster! *Who would want to date* me? *Look at me. I'm 135 pounds, laying on my potential death bed, riddled with cancer, with open sores all over my lips and face!* This was not the time to ask Jenny out on a date. The only place I could take her was Chez C-3. I could see it now: Jenny and I would be eating mashed potatoes while slurping on Boost chocolate-flavoured floats through bendy straws, with the sweet serenade of my roommate shouting, "I need to get my diaper changed! Someone please change my diaper!" How romantic! *It's better that we just be friends,* I rationalized. That way, at least I wouldn't lose her again.

~

My good friend Jeff, the crazy Canuck from Timmins, was also a huge support throughout that stay. We were roommates during university and always had a sibling type of relationship. He was taking architecture at the University of Toronto, so he was in the city and made time to come visit me between classes. Jeff was the kind of guy who wouldn't take no for an answer. He's a guy's guy but has a heart of gold. He would give his right leg to you if you needed it, but he would also punch you in the arm really hard because he thought it was funny.

One day, he made a decision for me that I would have never made for myself. "Let's go outside, Stolfi," he said anxiously, while pacing around my room.

"I'm not interested in moving much, Jeff. I'm in too much pain. Plus, I don't think I'm allowed to," I told him.

"Shut the fuck up. We're going outside."

"Dude, I can hardly walk. I can barely get myself to the bathroom." He was having none of it and he pulled me up by my arms and rolled me off my tiny mattress and onto my feet.

"Okay, fine. But at least unplug me first," I relented.

"Are you saying I can pull the plug on you, Stolfi?" he joked. I laughed. We both have a sick sense of humour.

He lowered me into a wheelchair, which I think he stole from another patient's room, and wheeled me past the nurses' station.

"We're just going to be downstairs for a couple minutes. That okay?" he asked as we rolled on by. The nurses didn't reply, so that counted as a yes to Jeff. He wheeled me to the elevators and we proceeded to the main floor of the hospital. He pushed me through the lobby and then continued to push me through the front doors of the building and outside into the parking lot.

"Jeff, what the fuck are you doing?!" I shouted.

"We're outside, buddy! It's too damn nice out here for you to be lying in that hospital bed." We stopped for a moment and took a look at our surroundings. There was nothing but a giant concrete parking lot packed with visitors and patients getting dropped off via cars, cabs and city buses. It was the chaos of a big city hospital bustling with business. The front doors were as far as we could go. There was nothing that screamed nature about this outdoor excursion. Not one tree could be seen for a few hundred feet, and grass? Forget about it.

"Let's go back inside, Jeff," I told him sternly. "I'm under strict orders not to leave the building."

"Well then, they should do a better job of keeping track of you." No one seemed to notice what we were doing, so he just kept pushing me right across the roadway and through the parking lot. Like a game of *Frogger*, we were dodging cars and people, jumping from lily pad to log trying not to fall in the water.

There I was: my IV pole in hand, the rusty wheels squeaking beside me as we rolled down the sloped parking lot. Each pebble and divot in the pavement rumbled through my body magnified by the hard plastic rims of the wheelchair. *I can see the headlines now*, I thought. *CANCER PATIENT IN WHEELCHAIR GETS PUSHED BY CRAZY NORTHERN CANADIAN INTO ONCOMING TRAFFIC!* We finally came to a rest at a small patch of grass in the veterans' ward. He parked me right where the edge of the grass and the curb met. I placed my bare feet onto the grass, the cool bristles of green felt soothing on the bottom of my naked feet. It was a feeling I hadn't felt in a long time and one that I will never take for granted ever again.

We found some shade under a large oak tree, sat on the lawn and talked. It didn't seem to matter what we talked about or if we even talked at all. I was out of my jail cell, feeling the wind on my face and the sun's warmth tickling my hairless head. There were no nurses to take my blood or give me pills, no doctors to drop in and check up on me, no porter to take me for X-rays and no chaplain to make awkward conversations about death with. I just sat there in calm stillness.

"Thanks, Jeff. I needed this."

In the days that followed, my friend Jordan came by and played his guitar for me out in the courtyard; my friend Jeanette gave me a colouring book and coloured with me; my friends Ryan and Konya stopped by to give me a book to read, *Jonathan Livingston Seagull* (highly recommended), and both of them watched me at one point or another throw up my lunch into the green kidney-shaped basin on my food table.

My friend Sarah, whom I've known since kindergarten, rubbed my swollen feet. She was so caring and warm and gave damn good foot rubs! Rusa, my Second City classmate and good friend always kept my spirits up. When Jenny came by, I'd ask Rusa to leave.

"You're kicking me out for another woman!?" she joked. "Now is not the time to be picking up chicks, Dan! You look like shit."

"Maybe she wants to buy low?" I responded. "Now get out!" She laughed a big hearty laugh and made herself sparse.

My cousin Davide acted as my psychiatrist and gave me all the counselling I needed. I never took one anti-depression drug recommended by the young arrogant hospital douchebag. My friends Shawn, Jessie, Amish and Bobby from my sketch troupe would come by and just make me laugh, giving me energy that I wouldn't have known I had. All of my friends made me laugh. We all needed to laugh. Laughter was and always will be the best medicine.

Without my friends I would be dead. So without my doctors, nurses, mother, friends, family and Jenny . . . I would be dead.

Just thinking about how great my friends and family are makes me appreciate the life I have now and the life I wanted back so badly when I was going through treatment. I don't think I've ever felt like I've thanked them enough for everything they did for me. Maybe they will read this one day. Thank you.

The doctors eventually cleared me to go home from the hospital on Sept 10th, 2008, but not before giving me one more spinal tap and one more round of chemotherapy. I was nine weeks away from completing phase three of my treatment and was out of the Big House for what I hoped would be the last time.

Back Home

tested the bathwater with my hand. I wanted to make sure it wasn't too hot. My skin had become very sensitive to the temperature of water and a couple degrees too hot could feel like I was stepping into a vat of acid. A nice warm bath was what I needed, and it was the first thing I treated myself to when I returned home to my parents' house. I was filthy. I hadn't washed myself in over two weeks and due to the mouth sores, I hadn't been able to brush my teeth in over three. I was an absolute mess, but I was an absolute mess in the comfort of home. I stepped into the tub, turned off the water and lay on my back. The warm and soothing liquid enveloped my body. The sound of the water echoed off the bathroom walls, my subtle movements causing the slightest ripple to sound like a giant wave. I was lying in the basin of a bathtub again, beaten, battered and bruised, just as I did on that one dumb night of drunken buffoonery. This time, however, I was in the comfort of home and this time, I didn't do it to myself. The sun kissed my face as it peeked through the bathroom skylight. I took a clean white face towel and scrubbed the top of my head, gently rubbing the grime and dead skin off my scalp. I looked at the towel expecting to see dirt, but what I saw was a number of tiny black specks comparable to ground pepper scattered around the cloth. Little roots of hair had fully broken free from my scalp and were now clinging to the cloth. *Well, that's the last of it, I guess*, I thought to myself. I lay naked in calm stillness, grateful. I was alive.

Over the next week my mouth sores subsided, and I was slowly able to incorporate solid foods back into my diet. I was in desperate need to gain weight, as I was now 130 pounds "soaking wet." I weighed myself after stepping out of the bath, literally soaking wet, and there it was, the number 130 flashing clear as day on my parents' digitized bathroom scale.

I had now lost 55 pounds and I immediately saw the infomercial running over and over in my head. *A short, overly energetic, fit guy with tight shorts and a pastel blue tank top addresses the camera:* "Do you want to lose ten pounds? Twenty pounds? How about fifty pounds, in just five months!? Well, now you can! With the ultimate cancer and chemotherapy weight loss system . . . *Cancer Cleanse!* Only a couple million bucks' burden on the healthcare system and an absolute emotional and physical roller coaster from hell for you, your family and friends to enjoy!" *He gestures to the camera, thumbs up!* "Get yours today!" *Maybe he even winks with a smile while a sparkle dings off his shiny white teeth.*

~

"Mom, I think we should go to the health store and get some of that weight-gain stuff," I suggested from the living room sofa as Ellen DeGeneres danced away on the television.

"You are not putting that crap into your body, Daniel!" Mom shot back.

"Can we just try it?" I pleaded.

"Fine," she relented. "Let's go." I put on a black Guinness-branded baseball cap a friend had gifted me and we headed out the door. Next stop, the Stone Road Mall, Guelph.

Giant plastic containers full of powder and pills lined the walls of the GNC. A giant man with bulging muscles, wearing a tight black V-neck T-shirt approached us.

"You trying to put on some weight there, squirt?" he asked with a bit of a chuckle.

"How could you tell?" I replied.

"If you want to get those pounds on, I like to use the powders with pure protein and a bit of creatine," he said.

"Creatine? Like Mark Maguire and Sammy Sosa type stuff?"

"Yup!" he continued with a smile.

"Is it okay to take it if I have cancer?" I asked, like the word *cancer* was not an awkward word to just throw around anymore. There was, of course, an awkward silence. Mom, slightly embarrassed, tried to cover for me. "It's just, Daniel is going through treatment right now and he wants to make sure it's safe to take."

"Oh, yeah, sure. Good question." He thought on it for a second. "Maybe the all-natural protein would be better for you. It's made of pure whey protein so it's probably your best bet." *So wait, you're willing to take the plastic protein with creatine, but you wouldn't recommend it to a dude with cancer? Why are* you *taking it!? Could it give you cancer?!* He placed the giant tub in my hands. It felt heavy. My hands were slowly letting it slip out of my grip. To avoid the embarrassment of dropping it, I passed it off to Mom, which, in retrospect, was even more embarrassing than just dropping it.

"Should I ring you up?" he asked.

"Yeah, sure. Thanks," I said as Mom placed the tub on the counter. "Thanks, Mom."

She just shook her head and smiled. "I hope it helps."

~

Although I was now eating more, my blood counts continued to stay low, so the doctors sent me to the hematology clinic for another blood transfusion. This time, they sent me to a special blood transfusion ward located in the basement of the hospital. Fluorescent lights filled the room with a bland sterile glow. Beds on wheels lined the walls as large fridges hummed, keeping bags of blood cool, all categorically organized by blood type. I was assigned a bed and Mom and I waited patiently.

I lay in my bed in the basement hospital room and waited about six hours for my blood. I had to take two bags. Again, someone else's blood going into your body is a very strange concept for me. I wondered who actually donated blood these days? Answer: Heroes, that's who! They must be!

"B negative, right?" the nurse asked from the foot of my bed.

"I hope so," I replied. She didn't find that the least bit

funny. She hooked the bag up to my IV pole, punctured my chest with a needle to access my port and let gravity do the rest. The blood slowly oozed down the long clear tube, eventually finding its way to my chest. My heart was now pumping a beautiful and generous old lady's blood throughout my body.

After the transfusion was complete, the nurse said, "See you next week!"

"I'm pretty sure I'm only in here for this one transfusion," I replied.

SIDE NOTE: I think I must have got my blood from an old woman, because I am so much wiser these days and way more sensitive than ever before! There is a major shortage of blood in the system and it's pretty sad. The people who donate blood save lives. I am truly forever grateful. Unfortunately, I can't donate blood ever again. I've tried. The moment you tell the nurses you had cancer, they just shake their heads "no" with a weird frown on their face, like they just bit into a rotten banana.

"Oh, don't worry, you'll be back. I've seen it a hundred times. They always come back. I'll be seeing a lot of you, I'm sure."

What type of pessimistic bullshit attitude is that? I looked at Mom and said, "Not a chance I'm coming back here." Mom nodded her head in agreement.

The next week, my blood counts were still low. I felt I was undoubtedly heading back to the transfusion wing. I was more upset about having to see that nurse again, to watch her give me that "I told you so," look, than actually having to get the blood transfusion. Luckily, my doctors were on the ball and instead of the blood transfusions (which didn't help my counts much anyway), they injected me with a drug called Eprex. It helped boost my red blood cells. They followed that drug up with another called Neupogen, a self-filled and self-injected needle to my stomach to help boost my white blood cells. These drugs were much more effective than the blood transfusions and as a result, my numbers were on the rise. And that nurse? Well, I never saw her again . . . Boom! *Minor victories.*

Although highly effective in boosting my blood cell counts, these self-injected drugs did come with some major side effects, the worst of which could only be described as bone pain. What is bone pain? It's pain . . . in your bones! Bone pain. *Wait, I can do a better job than that. Here we go . . .* Imagine an electrical charge that shoots through your bones, progressively increasing in intensity over time. It throbs and subsides and then throbs again with impeccable rhythm. These electrical charges occur in your chest, lower back, shins or wherever you have bones, so . . . your entire body head to toe. It was relentless and excruciating and caused me to shout, moan and make guttural sounds that I didn't think I was capable of. Bone pain! That's better.

Oct 9, 2008

Day 199 of 730

I had some severe bone pain in my legs and lower back two nights ago. I haven't been that scared or been in that much pain for that long in a very long time. I'd say it was about 36 hours of intense pain. I hope that never happens again! In other news, I am constipated . . . again. The shit is ripping instead of burning. I think if I can stay somewhat regular and just really focus on the painkillers, creams, fibre, water, sitz baths . . . I sound like an old lady!! (must be the new blood), I should be okay. My blood counts are really low and a fever may be on the horizon again, but I will not let it get me. Be strong. Do what you need to do to make this as easy as possible. No one ever needs to go through this type of pain. It will pass and it will get better again.

HEALTH, HAPPINESSS, FRIENDSHIP, FAMILY, LOVE, HEALING.

There wasn't much I could do to ease the bone pain. I called the specialist at the hospital and he told me to take Tylenol until the pain went away. "Take three if you have to," he said.

"I'm up to five or six but the pain just won't stop," I told him. He didn't have any answers for me. I tried placing ice packs and hot water bottles on my throbbing legs and chest, but after achieving only minor relief, it eventually just burned or froze my skin. I had hoped that I could sleep through the pain but that was proving to be impossible, as the pain only got worse at night. Eventually, due to exhaustion, the very act of fighting off the pain would cause me to pass out. I'm not sure you can call that "sleep." I woke, however, the next morning, pain-free. Like magic, it was gone. But I feared it would return. I got through those 36 hours the same way I was getting through all of it. I would repeat: *One second at a time, one minute at a time, one hour at a time, one day at a time. I am going to get through this. I will beat this.*

Game Changer

Oct 11, 2008

Day 210 of 730

So, I'm having a hard time explaining to people how I'm feeling. People often ask and I respond, "good." Or "much better than last week." These are all genuine and truthful responses, but the fact still remains that I feel like shit, or at least I don't ever feel normal. I haven't felt normal for six months. People who see me and talk to me think I'm doing great because on the outside it may appear all good, but if they knew the physical, emotional and mental pain that I was going through on the inside, they would see a much different person. One day I will respond: "I have a headache that ties me to the sofa, I am weak all over, I have excruciatingly painful hemorrhoids, I have this little disease running through my body called cancer, it's a chore to walk up the stairs, the sun bothers the piss out of me and I still have over 17 months to go! How am I feeling?!" I would never say that. My friends and family are here to support me and

I can't be bitter, but a man can vent, can't he? Keep fighting, work hard, laugh, cry, win, beat this. Leave me alone, cancer. Please ease up.

As time kept creeping forward, I kept slugging away at cancer. I was trying to accept the reality of it all while trying to stay positive. Aside from the physical and mental anguish that I was going through day in and day out, there was one thing that I was really having a hard time dealing with. Every week I would see hundreds of cancer patients at the Sunnybrook Odette Cancer Clinic but I always felt like I stood out like a sore thumb. *Where were the 26-year-olds with my cancer?*

I saw all shapes, colours and sizes of people who were all fighting just like me. The majority, however, were in their later years and I had yet to hear of anyone with my duration and intensity of treatment. I needed to share my journey with someone who could relate to what I was going through, someone who "got my cancer." It was this mutual understanding, this common bond that I was missing and was so desperately in need of. I wouldn't wish cancer on anyone but I was really desperate for some support. *Anyone feel like getting my cancer?*

~

It was around week 25 or 26 at the clinic when the game changer happened. It was a Wednesday. I had switched my in-clinic treatment days to Wednesdays because Mondays were often interrupted by holidays, plus they were extremely busy commuter days on the 401. First day of the workweek meant everyone was eager to cram the highways in hopes to get to work nice and early. Early bird gets the most paperwork done? I don't know. Fridays were just as bad because everyone was leaving work early to get home or to their cottages to relieve the stress of the office nine-to-five. So, I rationalized that Wednesdays seemed the most reasonable days for treatment. It was smack dab in the middle of the week, "hump day," so people could stay at home to do it! Roads must be clear, right? Logic. Boom!

That Wednesday at the clinic was a game-changing day for me. Since beginning this treatment, I had the joy and frustration of meeting someone like Jamie, and I felt the sadness of losing my fallen soldier while in the critical care unit of C-3. In both instances we weren't really in any place to pick each other's brains and open up about our feelings toward our illnesses. We were literally just trying to survive. No time for emotions and feelings and all that fuzzy stuff.

Relating to the length of treatment was not even possible with most patients, as they were typically on four-to-six-month paths. Our personal relationships were especially different as well. I was a 26-year-old comedian trying to sort out my life, hoping to play soccer again, party again, perform on stage again and have sex again! I wasn't living for my kids, or grandkids, or wife. I didn't have kids, grandkids or a wife. I didn't even have a girlfriend! Although we were all fighting the same fight, I felt like I was doing it all on my own.

Then, it finally happened. It was another typical day in the chemotherapy unit at Sunnybrook Hospital. I was getting a briefing on how to fill and self-inject vials of a blood-cell boosting agent, from my primary nurse, Joseph, while I waited to be called in for my infusions. After the tutorial was over, Joseph looked across the room as if his eyes landed on someone familiar and waved.

"Stay here for just a second. There is someone I want you to meet," he told me. A couple of moments later Joseph walked a younger-looking gentleman toward me.

"Daniel Stolfi, I want you to meet Ari. He has leukemia and you are both undergoing the same chemotherapy treatment." It was like heavenly music to my ears! Ari was a couple of years younger than me. It's hard to determine the age of a cancer patient because we all look like, well, shit. He had a full face, swollen from the chemo and pale skin. Fine brown hair crept out from underneath his New York Yankees baseball cap. His eyes were sunken and looked to be in a haze as they were completely glossed over. My heart nearly jumped out of my chest with excitement! I didn't know what to say. My horrible selfish wish had come true, and I was tongue-tied. It was like meeting a celebrity! Like I said, I wouldn't wish cancer on my worst enemy but, you know, he already had it and now I had someone to talk to about it. I played it cool.

"Hey, I'm Dan. You're Ari? Cool. I'm Dan. How are you doing?"

Ari didn't say much. He just sort of looked at me like, *What am I supposed to say to this guy? Is this like a date?* I tried to break the awkward silence.

"You look good, man," I blurted out.

He looked at me with that look that I had given to so many people when they said that to me. *No, I don't look good. Look at me! I'm skinny, bald, tired and feel like shit! I have cancer! I look good to you?!* That look. I shook his hand. It was super soft and lacked any strength . . . *just like mine! We both have super soft hands!!*

"I'll see you around," I said, super cool.

"For sure, bro," he replied. *He said "bro!" I always say bro. It's my word. This is amazing!*

We didn't speak again that day, as the timing just wasn't right yet. Timing. So much of getting through cancer is in the timing. There is this awkward incubation period that happens when you are dealing with cancer. For the first few months you just want it to be over with, so you don't want to get too involved in it and you definitely don't want to build any new "cancer" relationships because it could get messy and painful real quick. You just want to be left alone to sludge through the crap, not to be bothered by "connections" and "life-affirming conversations" or "books you really should read." Barf. Literally. (Thanks for reading this book, though). I, however, was well past that phase when I met Ari but he was still deep in it. I knew he would come around eventually—I mean, we were in this for at least two years, and we would be seeing more of each other for sure. But for now, I took solace in the fact that there was someone else like me. It made all the difference in the world.

The ups and downs of the disease are crazy. One moment you're happy, the next you're depressed. Happy, maybe because you feel like you're making some progress with your blood counts and weight gain or the fact that you had a decent bowel movement in the morning. Depressed because the progress comes at the expense of side effects that cause physical pain, mental sadness, emotional anguish and the fact that you can't do the things you love to do anymore. Watching people play on stage, on screen or on a soccer field was just heart-wrenching for me.

A week had passed. I was home again. I was hopeful that I would see Ari the next day at my appointment, but only time would tell. Late at night, I lay in bed and began to doze off to sleep but my right shin began to ache. These were the first signs of bone pain creeping in again. I tolerated the slight throbs through gritted teeth, but it progressed quickly to the familiar pulsating throbs in rhythmic harmony, intensifying as the hours passed. It was this deep concentrated pain that just shot up my shins and into my knees. I held my legs in the fetal position and moaned in anguish.

My parents are early risers, they'll be up soon, I thought to myself. I kept my weeping and moaning to a low hum throughout the entire night as I didn't want to wake them. *I'll push through until morning.* The sun broke through my window. It was finally 6 a.m. Mom walked past my door. She could hear me cry out in agony. "We have to go to the clinic now," I called out through the door.

"We'll get our things together and go right away," she called back. I had a chemotherapy appointment with my doctor later that day anyway, so he was expecting me. I took some comfort in the fact that maybe I would get some answers about this damn bone pain.

When you have cancer and are deep into treatment, you can pretty much get access to first-class care 24/7. If I wanted an X-ray, I could have it done by noon. A brain scan? Twenty-four hours, tops! How 'bout a shot of poison, any poison I chose? Whenever I damn well pleased. *Minor victories.*

When I arrived at the clinic, I told my oncologist about the pain in my leg and he ordered an ultrasound. Like I said, first class. "We'll have to check your legs for blood clots," he said matter-of-factly.

"Clots? Like those things that can travel into your heart and kill you type clots?"

"Pretty much," he replied. "Clots can be very dangerous," he explained. "The chemotherapy can cause your blood to thicken and that can cause clotting. It usually starts in the legs so the pain you are feeling could be a result of that." *More fantastic news!*

I was back on the ultrasound table, my leg lubed up and ready for action as the specialist worked his magic. Within 12 hours of feeling the initial pain in my leg, it was determined that I did indeed have a clot. They gave me "take-home" needles and vials, filled with a clear liquid blood-thinning agent. I had to fill the needles with the liquid while making sure there were no air bubbles in the tube because that could apparently kill me. I was then supposed to inject the needle into my stomach once a day. Seemed simple enough.

Back home, I lay on my well-worn family-room sofa and waited for the clock to strike 11 a.m. Right after *Ellen* and right before *The Price is Right*, it was time to inject the blood-thinning agent. I couldn't inject the needle myself, as the thought of doing it made me feel faint. I got Mom to do it for me. *Maybe it's not that simple.* There was something about sticking myself with a needle that I just couldn't stomach. Nursing is not for me. Type 1 diabetes is not for me, either. For those of you who have to self-inject every day, I salute you! I filled the needle and flicked out the bubbles from the vial with my thumb and middle finger like they do in the movies. That part was actually kind of fun. I felt like a mad scientist or something. I handed the needle to Mom to do the dirty work.

She was shaking as she held the needle in her hand. "Mom, you gonna be okay?" I asked.

"Don't distract me!" she warned, as she brought the needle down toward my stomach.

"Don't mess this up, Mom."

"This is just as hard for me as it is for you," she continued.

"Okay, just do it."

"I'm trying. Just shut up!" The sharp prick of the needle pierced into my flesh, Mom's hands still shaking as she pressed her thumb down on the plastic plunger. The sting of pain was intense. I breathed in deeply and exhaled slowly as she pulled the needle out. "It feels like wasps are plunging their butts into my body," I told her.

"I'm sorry, I'm sorry," Mom said, as she dropped the empty needle into a yellow disposal box. (The box was given to us by the hospital for any of the medical equipment waste). After 20 or 30 seconds, the pain subsided and I began the 24-hour countdown to the next injection. Just another needle to add to the list of needles I was getting injected with. I was getting poked and prodded every day, and it was taking its toll.

The blood thinner helped with the clots, but it did *not* help with the bone pain. The bone pain kept coming back every three weeks, like clockwork, shooting through my shins, lower back and up through my sternum. My appetite was still touch and go, my mouth sores were coming and going and the pain in my ass would not go away.

My days were now as follows:

1. Wake up at 8 a.m. and go to the bathroom to kick off my day of excruciating butt pain.
2. Try to eat some fruit and cereal for breakfast and take some chemotherapy pills.
3. Lie on the couch and watch *Regis and Kelly* (it was still Regis's show at the time).
4. Watch Ellen dance and then get my 11 a.m. blood thinner injection and chemo pills.
5. Lie back down on the couch for *The Price is Right* or a little reality show called *Restaurant Makeover.*
    5a) Try to eat some lunch.
    5b) If I could handle it, go for a walk to the mailbox some 200 metres up the street.
6. Maybe squeeze in some *Dr. Oz* before nap time, then dinner, pills, TV, pills, bed by 9:30 p.m.
7. Excruciating bone pain through the night.
8. Repeat the next day. This was my new normal. *I wonder if Ari is going through the same shit?*

~

Ari and I not only had our chemotherapy treatments on the same day now but at around the same time too! Not sure how it all happened, but it did, and I was (and still am) so grateful for that. Back at Sunnybrook, I saw him approach me with a little dark-haired lady by his side. *Must be his mom.* I sat in the waiting room with my mom . . . a little dark-haired lady.

"Is anyone sitting here?" he asked. Ari's voice was slightly raspy, similar to mine—a side effect to the drugs we were both on.

"It's all yours, man," I replied. We looked at each other and had a silent moment of understanding; *we were tired of all of this.* We had both been through hell and we didn't know if we were both experiencing the exact same hell or just a unique brand of hell that we must continue to claim as our own.

"I'll give you guys some time together," Mom said. "I'll go for a walk."

It was like we were on a second date. The second date started out a lot like the first: we sat in awkward silence for a while, bobbing our heads, trying to stay cool. Then, with very little discussion, we quickly realized that we were going through a very similar form of hell! He started to finish my sentences and I finished his! He started out by saying, "So does it hurt when you. . ." and I'd say, "Take a shit?" We would then both say, "Yeah!" and laugh about it.

"Dude, I want my hair back," he said.

"Me too, man. I had this majestic 'fro, bro."

"Fuck off. Really?" he asked. I took out my cellphone and

pulled up an old headshot from my acting days. In the photo I wore a Michael Jackson *Thriller* jacket. I had this cheeky little smirk on my face, while I patted my 'fro with my hand. He couldn't stop laughing.

Photo Credit: Chris Frampton

"Check *my* hair out!" he said. The picture he showed me was of him and his boys before a night out at the club. He had a coif of black hair spiked up like the guys on *Jersey Shore*.

"Pimpin', bro," I said.

"I want my body back," he went on.

"Me too. I miss playing soccer."

"Hockey for me, man," he said.

The banter continued for a while until we got into the meat

and potatoes of what we were both wondering but too nervous to bring up. We instantly felt like we could say anything to each other, and no questions were off limits. I mean, we made it this far, so why not?

He started to say, "Have you been able to . . ."

I finished, "Jerk off?"

"Yeah!"

"Nope."

"Me neither, man!"

We laughed. I really loved the fact that we could laugh at what we were going through. I was initially worried about making cracks and jokes about it because it's such a sensitive issue and we were, for lack of a better term, sort of maybe dying? Logic suggested that we shouldn't have been joking about this, but we gave each other permission to laugh and that made all the difference. We were going through the exact same thing, only I was experiencing everything four months ahead of him. I knew he was in for a long haul and that it wouldn't get any easier any time soon, but I reassured him that he just needed to take things as they came . . . and if he was constipated to not push too hard!!

"Enjoy the ups and grin and bear it through the downs. It's a wild ride," I told him.

"Don't I know it," he confirmed. Ari and I would continue to chat until one of us was called in by a nurse to administer our chemotherapy for the week.

We joked week to week about who would get called first. He always seemed to win. *Must be alphabetical or something.*

Hanging with Ari every week was also great because his mother and my mother could chat about what their "babies" were going through, and I think that gave them peace of mind and a camaraderie that they had also been so desperately looking for. Meeting Ari was a game changer. I had a new soldier on the force, but this time we were going to beat this thing together.

Making My Will

"Hey, Ma!" I called out from my well-worked-in white couch. "I should maybe think about getting a will made up, yeah?"

"No," she replied calmly. And that was as far as we would get on that issue.

The God Ultimatum

"**G**od, kill me right now or make this easier. I can't do this anymore." I'm not a religious man, but I was getting desperate.

Oct 12, 2008

Day: 202 of 730

Had Adrian's christening today. This was not a good day. Everything is taking its toll and I need it to end.

What an interesting time it was for my parents. First-time grandparents, their eldest son was engaged, and me? Well, I had cancer. Life is always easiest for the baby of the family.

My nephew's baptism was coming up and I wanted to look good for him and for my family. My hair was completely gone, including my eyebrows, armpit hair and, yes, down there too. There were a few strands poking around haphazardly here and there, but who's counting? I was pale, gaunt and weighed 135 pounds. All I knew for sure was I looked and felt horrible.

I was determined to dress the part for the baptism, so I coaxed Mom to accompany me to the mall to purchase a dress shirt and belt. I saw a purple—yes, purple—dress shirt that screamed Italian Guido at Le Château Men. Yes, Le Château . . . Men. Never heard of it? You're lucky. Le Château carried the latest club-going, peacock-strutting, slim-fitted clothing only a metrosexual male could ask for. The extra small "Euro cut" dress shirt fit like a glove over my new slender frame that the "Cancer Diet Cleanse" had provided me.

"I used to be a large," I told the young blonde girl assisting me at the store. She didn't really seem to care that I used to be a large, but why should she? If anything, she probably thought I was bragging because I used to be overweight or something. You know the people. The ones who just try to casually bring it up in conversation that they used to be bigger but, *oh, look at me now, look at how skinny I am. Now say congratulations immediately and then I'll be all humble and shy about it.* But I was not being that person on that day. I was being the person who was like: *Ask me why I am so skinny now and then when I tell you it's because I have cancer, you're going to feel really awkward for asking me why I am so skinny now.* That's actually way worse! I was officially jaded.

She didn't ask why I was so skinny. She was smarter than that. I purchased the shirt and belt and was on my way. *I am going to look good for this thing,* I'd repeat in my head. I went to bed that night determined to show up the next day rocking it for my sister, my newborn nephew and the close to 60 family members who would be there to celebrate the occasion. I was going to show them that I was stronger than cancer.

It was the next morning. My room seemed brighter than most mornings. I could hear the voices of a large crowd of people downstairs . . . *I slept in! No one woke me up!* It sounded like everyone had been there for a while as they discussed the spread of food that was out for lunch. *Lunch!? What time is it??*

Lunch before church is a traditional Italian thing to do when there are big life milestones. We invited everyone over to the house for cured meats, cheeses, olives, fruit and sweets to welcome them and . . . I don't really know . . . to eat? *I think it's really just to eat. No one wants to be hungry in church, it's boring enough already. Why make it painful too?*

I figured Mom thought it would be best that I got some rest, so she let me sleep in. I got up quickly and snuck down the hallway to avoid being seen by my family milling about downstairs in the very open-concept front foyer of the house. I managed to sneak into my parents' bathroom with a towel wrapped around my waist. I just wanted to take a nice, peaceful shit.

I plunked myself down on the white porcelain bowl. Push, push, easy does it now, push, PAIN! I looked into the toilet and the water was red with blood. *What happened? Why does it look like this? It hasn't been like this since the night of the hemorrhoids six months ago! I thought I was past this!* My brain began to panic. I got up, flushed the toilet and headed for the shower. *I'm okay. I'm going to be okay. I'm going to be there for my nephew no matter what. It's just a bit of blood. I must have pushed too hard.*

I stepped out of the shower and made my way back to my bedroom. The guests had moved to the dining room and their laughter and banter trailed off to mumbled tones. I opened my closet and reached for my brand-new, extra small, purple dress shirt. *I am going to do this no matter how much pain I'm in. I am going to be there for my nephew!*

I notched up my belt to the last hole and was now fully dressed, ready to go. I proceeded slowly down the stairs, each step coming with a sting of pain to my backside. "Hello, everyone!" I said to my sister's in-laws with a fake smile on my face. I gritted my teeth in an attempt to mask my discomfort. They looked at me with these painted-on smiles, as if they'd seen a ghost. They were frozen like deer caught in the headlights of a Mack truck, trying not to make any sudden movements. I quickly made my way to the family room and sat down on my couch. They began to move again, everyone now enjoying the food and espresso. I couldn't eat or drink any of it. Things that were once so appealing to me were now completely uninteresting. I had no appetite, and my mouth was still full of sores. Everyone sounded so happy and I felt so sad. My butt was killing me and I was alone in the family room separated from the party. Suddenly, a wave of emotion came over me and I began to cry. I couldn't control it. I felt pathetic, weak and alone. I wiped my tears away, put on a smile and swallowed the excruciating pain ringing out from my backside, but it was all too much. I eventually caved. Mom entered the room and sat on the couch across from me.

"How are you feeling this morning?" she asked.

"Please go without me," I told her. "I'm really not feeling well."

She looked at me knowingly and didn't push for me to do anything I didn't feel I could. We had accepted the fact that this came with the territory. My whole family had accepted it. They didn't say anything to make me feel bad. They just left and told me to rest. Sometimes I wondered if they were thinking I could just suck it up and jump off the stupid couch and be there, but there was no way to explain or describe how impossible that was. Sucking it up was what I was doing. If I didn't suck it up, I would have been crying on the floor, calling for help, begging for all of it to be over. I would have been in my bed sulking under the covers, never having put on that stupid purple shirt and walked down the stairs. Sucking it up was letting them go without me.

The house was now empty, and I returned upstairs to my room with the intention to lay down in my bed until the pain in my butt passed. On my way to my bed, I crossed in front of my bedroom mirror. Out of the corner of my eye, I saw my reflection. This hit me hard. There I was, in my brand-new, ridiculous purple dress shirt with my new dumb belt cinched to the last dumb notch, holding up my stupid baggy black trousers. I had been stripped of everything I once had. My hair was non-existent, my face was swollen from the chemotherapy, my body was skinnier than I could have ever imagined and the pain in my ass was relentless. Tears began to stream down my face again. Uncontrollable tears. Anger and rage began to pulsate through my body as my reflection stared back at me, pathetic and alone. I threw myself down on my bed and cried for what felt like hours. I was at my breaking point. I looked up at the ceiling and shouted, "God, I'm going to make a deal with you! You either kill me now and make this stop . . . or keep me alive and make this stop. Either way, you have got to make this stop now! I can't take it anymore!"

The pain didn't stop, and God didn't kill me. This God guy was not much help sitting up on his cushion of soft clouds. *God clearly does not have hemorrhoids.*

Turned out I just had to get through the day, like every other day. *One second at a time, one minute at a time, one hour at a time, one day at a time . . .*

After crying for another hour and feeling incredibly sorry for myself, I decided to accept the pain and get out of bed. I reached for my cell phone and called Dad. "Can you come pick me up and drive me to the hall for dinner? I think I'm feeling better now." Without hesitation, he drove to the house and brought me to the hall. The ride to the hall was quite comforting. Dad didn't try to solve the problem. He just told me he understood what I was going through. He isn't much of a talker but he's a great listener. I wasn't saying much, and the silence was nice. Calm. Comforting.

The hall was located in a small grey-brick plaza on the outskirts of town. My cousins, aunts, uncles and friends of the family all sat at tables as the buffet was being prepped and food passed around. It was a bit overwhelming, but nothing like the 300-person weddings I had become accustomed to, growing up in a large Italian family. I was in pain, but I had a smile on my face. *Always put on a brave face.* I sat at one of the empty seats and managed to eat some pasta. I tried to make small talk with my family and be pleasant, but something felt off. Everyone was looking at me funny. It dawned on me that this was one of the first times my extended family was actually seeing me in this condition. They hadn't seen me actually progress to this level.

It was like not seeing a clean-cut, freshly shaven friend for a year and then, boom, *they have a beard and are covered in tattoos! If you were with said friend during his beard-growing and tattoo-getting days, it would be like,* "Yeah, this is my bearded and tattooed friend, Mike. He's great!" *but if you weren't with him during that time, you'd be like,* "Mike, what the fuck happened to you?" It was a major reality check for everyone. Me included. I posed for a few photos, made more conversation with family and tried to stomach the cake. My mind took this time to get real with myself . . . Real talk. I took a deep breath.

I am tired of being sick, I am tired of feeling sorry for myself and I am tired of getting beat up by this disease and this treatment. I am going to beat this thing no matter what. I know that I will have to continue to take my bumps and bruises along the way, but I am determined to get through this. I am getting through this. I released my breath. Calm.

I got a ride home with my cousin Davide, my personal therapist from my stays in the hospital. A saint! The whole way home we kept saying how cancer was "a pain in the ass, no pun intended." Eventually, we started saying, "It's a pain in the ass . . . pun intended." We laughed, which only caused my ass to hurt more. Not sure if you've ever noticed this before but the next time you laugh, pay close attention to your sphincter. It tightens right up on each "Ha," which is fine and dandy if you don't have a torn butthole . . . Just saying.

Oct 24, 2008

Day 214 of 730

Seven months! This journey has been scary, painful, sad, stressful, all suffering, a learning experience. A lesson in life and it isn't even close to being over. I have a lot of fight left to go. Over the last seven months I have been beat down by the beast of disease that is cancer. I have been knocked down every day, as if to serve as a reminder that life isn't easy. It isn't fair and life is difficult. Everyone will face their Goliaths in their lifetime, some later and some earlier than others. I have battled the physical pains in the past and have won. I broke my arm, my collarbone, my leg, my nose, dislocated both shoulders, another collarbone . . . a thumb. I've been concussed, stapled and sewn up. Now I face a physical, mental and emotional giant that no one should ever have to face. Every day is painful, and every day is difficult. I am scared of what tomorrow may bring or even sometimes what the next hour will bring. Headaches, stomach aches, nausea, vomiting, weakness, bone pain, ringing in my ears, mouth sores, chest pain, pain in my ass, dry eyes, lips, skin, loss of appetite, my beautiful hair. Depression. I've spent over 40 days and nights in a hospital bed. I've had five blood transfusions. I could be sterile. I've had over 30 rounds of chemotherapy with over 70 to come. I've taken more pills in the first week of treatment than I had in my entire 25 years of existence. I've been poked with needles more times than I can count, but I will keep fighting. I will win. I won't give up and I will dominate. With the love and support of my family and friends, anything is possible. I will dance again. And I will knock this motherfucker out!

At Adrian's baptism. From left to right:
My sister-in-law Maria, brother Andrew, me "smiling",
Mom, Adrian, Dad, sister Nadia and brother-in-law Sav.

Let's All Have a Look-See

November. Whenever November hits, I start to think about Christmas and the new year. I couldn't believe I was on my way to a new year! This seemed so out of reach to me when this all started and now it was so close I could taste it. Before I could get too far ahead of myself, I had to remember to stay present. *Always stay present.* I needed to take care of some of the nagging issues my body was consistently dealing with that didn't want to go away. The biggest nagging issue of all was in my butt. I asked my oncologist to set up an appointment with a butt doctor so we could finally get to the bottom of my butt pain. Pun intended! I took the trip to Sunnybrook Hospital in the mint green four-door manual transmission shit sedan, with Mom at the wheel, crawling along the familiar 401.

The large glass sliding doors opened automatically as we entered the Odette Cancer Clinic. I pushed down on a pump to dispense hand sanitizer into my palm. I rubbed the bacteria-killing foam into my soft hands as routinely as I would brush my teeth in the morning. It had all become so routine. Mom and I were led by one of the porters to a room that looked like all the others and I took a seat on the parchment paper–lined table.

"She'll be along shortly," the porter informed me before exiting the room. A few moments later, a doctor, very pregnant, walked into the room. "I'm Dr. Smith. I hear you are having some issues in your backside?" I nodded my head, yes. "Let's have a look-see," she said, adjusting her glasses.

"Mom, can you leave, please?" Mom exited with a giggle. I lay on my side, pants down, exposing my bare butt to Dr. Smith's pregnant belly.

"Just look, please. I can't handle any fingers up there," I warned. She respected my request, snapped on a latex glove and took a peek.

"This is the worst case of anal fissures that I have ever seen! Not to mention the hemorrhoids!" She said, almost excitedly. *Anal fissures* . . . I knew that term from Dr. Oz! Anal fissures are cuts and lesions in the butthole! All those mornings on the couch watching daytime TV were paying off!

"Do you mind if I invite some students in to have a look?" she asked.

"Uh, sure?" I said, a bit hesitant. Within a few seconds, multiple women . . . younger women . . . women my age entered the room! They all took their turns looking at my broken butthole, nodding their heads, taking notes on their clipboards and seeming very intrigued. Mom, just outside the room, was asked to wait farther down the hall, outside of earshot, as Dr. Smith wanted to ask me some personal questions. She closed the curtain around the bed to form an even more private room with all her pupils surrounding her like excited puppies. "Daniel, have you experienced any trauma in the area over the last year?"

"Trauma?" I asked. "Well, yeah. I mean, I told you about all the rock-hard shits I've been taking, haven't I? Feels like I'm getting a fist up the butt every time I go to the washroom. Feels like I'm shitting broken pieces of glass. Feels like I'm pooping a sword sideways. Trauma? Yeah, sure, 'trauma' is a good word for it."

"No, Daniel. Like real trauma . . . sexual," she clarified.

"You serious?" I asked. She nodded yes. "No," I said, calmly. She gave me a look like, *you lying to me, boy?* And then I gave her a look like, *don't give me that look, girl!*

"You can pull your pants back up," she said.

She opened the curtain again and let the students out of the room and Mom back in. I laughed. I had to laugh. I was a 26-year-old man talking about how my butt *wasn't* traumatized sexually to a bunch of women my age while undergoing chemotherapy. Humiliation is a big part of the cancer experience.

She prescribed me a cream to put up there and to take even more stool softeners than I was already taking . . . it didn't work.

Humiliation

I t was Sunday, November 2nd, 2008. I was sleeping. It was a good sleep for once. The morning sunlight broke through the window and nudged me awake. I lay on my back for a few moments. I was contemplating starting the day. It was a day like all the others as far as I could tell. Nothing seemed out of the ordinary and so, like clockwork, I felt the sudden urge to go to the washroom. It was a number two. The fear that I had grown accustomed to during this time swept through me. I knew that this visit to the washroom would be a painful one, just like all the ones before it, but I couldn't sit in bed all day, so I prepared to throw my feet off the side of my bed and make my way to the porcelain bowl from hell. I felt that familiar feeling that comes when you have to pass gas . . . you know the one. But before I could swing my feet out of bed, the gas that was brewing in my bowels came out in more of a solid state then a gaseous one. The solid was indeed a poop and not a fart. For a moment I thought I must have been dreaming. *This can't be happening. Did I just do what I think I did!?*

Too weak to get out of bed and too stunned at the current events that had just unfolded, I called out to my parents, "Mom!

Dad! Help!" They came rushing into my room. I was in tears, so embarrassed and ashamed. "I shit in the bed. I don't know what happened," I said completely traumatized. Without hesitation, as though they had done this before, they wrapped me in my bed sheet to form a giant man-sized diaper and carried me to the washroom. Mom said from behind the bathroom door, "Just leave the poop in the bed sheet and try to get most of it in the toilet," matter-of-factly, like no big deal! They didn't laugh or make me feel stupid. "Just leave the sheet on the floor and I will wash it later," she continued. I think my parents were of the mindset that as long as I was not in the hospital with pneumonia, mouth sores or blood clots, then a little shit in the bed was the least of their worries. "Shitty" things are all relative. I, however, was still emotionally wrecked and embarrassed.

I wiped myself off and took a bath. I sat in the warm water, sad, defeated and frustrated.

Dad went for a walk. Mom waited for me downstairs in the kitchen. I wandered down the steps and sat at the kitchen table to stare at my bowl of mixed fruit. We didn't talk about or acknowledge the recent event that took place. "Mom, can we try to go for a walk today?" I asked, breaking the awkward silence. "It's a nice fall day after all. Let's try to walk around the block." It was about 500 yards. The farthest I could manage at that time.

"Of course," she said.

We began our walk in silence as the morning events replayed in my head over and over again. I couldn't contain it anymore and I began to vent to her about how embarrassed

I was about it. She listened. I eventually asked a question that had been nagging me for the last seven months. "Do you think these damn pains in my ass will ever stop?" Mothers seem to have the inability to lie to their children when they need to be lied to the most. "I hate to be the bearer of bad news, but I don't think hemorrhoids or fissures ever go away. I think you will have to deal with it for the rest of your life," she said. This. Made. Me. So. Angry!

The emotional roller coaster that chemotherapy and fighting cancer will put you on is incomprehensible. I felt so much rage and anger sweep through me. I stormed ahead of her, almost speed-walking now, driven by my sudden burst of energetic rage. She didn't bother to keep up, sensing my disappointment with her. I was a full hundred yards ahead of her when I got home. I waited, stewing and steaming, pacing back and forth, just daring her to walk through the front door. As soon as I heard her footsteps enter the house, I *lost my fucking mind!* I screamed so loud my throat became hoarse. "I can't believe you would say that! Why the fuck are you being so negative?! I need positivity!" I continued to rage as I kicked my blue rubber workout ball clear across the room. I was fuelled by a pent-up anger that had been brewing for months. "You don't know fuck all! You're not a doctor!" I kept going. JUST LOSING IT! Mom was my official verbal punching bag, and I was letting her have it. Never would I physically do anything to harm her but when I got yelling, I got yelling! I have one of the loudest voices on the planet. ON. THE. PLANET! I think the whole block knew how upset I was with her.

She really didn't do anything wrong. She just shared her honest thoughts with me. I couldn't control myself, though, because it wasn't me reacting, it was the illness. Cancer's voice is angry, crazy and mean, and I just wanted my voice to return. I broke down in a heap on the couch, exhausted.

My voice will come back to me. It will take time, but it will come back. It always comes back. I took a deep breath and tried to calm my mind. Mom watched my diaphragm pump in and out dramatically. I rested on the couch until I became still. The anger subsided as Cancer's voice faded away and my voice came back to me. I prepped a needle for my 11 a.m. blood thinner injection. Mom poked me with it. It hurt, but the pain reminded me that I was still alive.

Phase 4: Maintenance – Is This Working?

Nov 27, 2008

Day 248 of 730

Phase three is over! No more drugs like L-asparaginase, Doxorubicin or Vincristine! I guess all the other drugs are the same, but I just get less of them. And no more injections right into my ass! HA HA. I hope it gets easier. January = Gym? I am beating this. I will win.

Love, Courage, Strength.

After ten months of harsh cocktails, it was finally time to lighten the load and begin the maintenance phase of chemotherapy. I had also reached the point in my treatment where I would finally get to know if all this crap I was pumping into my body was even working or not. My oncologist had signed me up for a PET scan, which was kind of a big deal. A PET scan is a much more detailed MRI or CT scan. It highlights any cancerous activity throughout the body and is generally used to determine whether or not a cancer has gone into complete remission. There was only one PET scan machine in all of Ontario or something insane like that. So, in order to get a scan your doctor had to register you under "clinical trial" or something even more insane like that! This was done so that the government could approve the validity of using the only PET scanner in the province on little ol' me. Long story short, my oncologist pulled some strings, chalked me up as a clinical trial patient and ordered me the PET scan. *Shhh, it's a secret.* Thanks, Doc!

I arrived at the hospital, threw on my blue ball gown and got hooked up to an IV, where a dye that contains radioactive tracers was injected into my port. I was then rolled down a hallway on a bed on wheels into another cold room where a large machine sat ominously in the centre. Two specialists hid behind a glass wall. The porter transferred me from the rolling bed to the machine's hard plastic table. I fell into a trance-like state as I waited for the sound and light show to begin. They asked if I wanted to listen to any music as they ran the test. I asked them to play Michael Jackson's 25th anniversary album. Of course I did. As Michael Jackson's "Thriller" played, my body was run through the machine, inch by inch. A series of beeps and bops pulsated throughout the room. The sounds echoed off the walls, mixing with MJ's signature sound. I held my breath upon instruction, exhaled after a few seconds and repeated this process for several minutes. "You're all done, Mr. Stolfi," the voice on the intercom instructed.

"Just another day at the office," I joked as I shuffled out of the room. They gave me a chuckle and the signature thumbs up. I finally got my laugh from the techies! That felt good.

A few weeks later, my results were in. I had a meeting with my oncologist, as he was to present me with the official letter that had all of the PET scan results. These results would determine whether or not the chemo was working and whether or not the cancer was in remission.

"Hello, Daniel, how are you?" Dr. Chang asked as he entered the examination room. I felt my butthole perk up a bit accompanied by a twinge of pain. Mom and I were more nervous than ever.

"Good," we both said in unison, clearly trying to keep it short. *Let's get on with it!*

"Well, instead of me telling you myself, here is the official print out of the PET scan results." He handed me the sheet of paper.

I began to read aloud, "The tumour, which had measured at a total diameter of 15 cm, has been reduced to scar tissue and there are no signs of other lesions or cancerous cells present. Full and complete, comp—complete . . . remission." I could barely spit it out. The air escaped the room. Silence. Time appeared to stop.

Pause. One second. Two seconds. Three seconds.

"YES!!!" I shouted, as I broke down into tears. All the pain and suffering, all the emotions that I had kept locked down deep; the worry, the stress, the anxiety, the "what ifs" and "whys" just disappeared after reading that one word. *Remission.* I was on top of the world for just that one brief moment. I was staring cancer in the face, grabbing it by the throat, and choking the life out of it. My mind began to race: *I did it. I beat cancer! I beat cancer? This is insane!* I felt this overwhelming sense of accomplishment. I was doing it. I was really actually doing it.

The feeling, however, was brief, because it suddenly dawned on me that I was only eight months into treatment with 16 months left to go! I took a deep breath. I shook it off and focused on what still needed to be done . . . roughly 70 rounds of chemo so I could continue to choke the life out of cancer. All I wanted was for it to get easier. I wanted to be able to do some of the things I loved again. I wanted to run again, jump and dance again. I wanted to get on stage again. Most importantly, I wanted to live my life again. Fuck cancer!

ACT III

'Tis the Season

Christmas, 2008. It was my uncle's company Christmas party, which takes place the first week of December every year. It's a tradition that has been going on ever since I can remember. I still vividly remember the haze of cigarette smoke that filled the reception hall in the church basement many years prior. It burned my little nine-year-old eyeballs. Smoking indoors was still legal in the '90s. Now, however, the event would take place in a reception hall at my university. Smoking indoors very much not allowed . . . it causes cancer, you know.

One hundred and fifty people would be in attendance and I was determined to be there. I still looked and felt like crap, but when I arrived, I headed straight to the antipasto bar. It was the first time I was able to eat pain-free and without nausea in the last nine months. There was a huge spread of sundried tomatoes, olives, shrimp, fresh salami, breads, cheeses . . . all my Italian favourites on display to enjoy. My mouth sores had finally faded and it was time to eat as if I'd never eat again. I was even getting some fine baby-type hairs on my head! Little light brown strands were caressing the top of my scalp. I was so proud of my baby brown strands of hair.

"Nice, you're growing your hair," my cousin Paul said with a big smile. This made me very happy.

"Yeah, it's coming in," I said proudly. I wore a suit jacket that was now four sizes too big for me and looked like something the Joker from *Batman* would wear. It draped over my scrawny shoulders like football pads. *But who cares?* I thought. *I'm happy. I'm beating cancer! Vanity is for the weak.*

I said hi to some family members at the event who congratulated me on my recent milestone. Mom had been bragging about it for days on the phone. It was all a little surreal for me.

Normally, at this party, the DJ undoubtedly played a Michael Jackson song, and my cousins would all look at me and say, "Come up and dance!!" Sure enough, I would take them up on their offer and start busting out some Michael Jackson moves: the points, the pops, the crotch grabs, the leg kicks, the sliding and gliding, the popping and locking—and of course, the signature moonwalk. This time, however, when MJ's "Thriller" came on, there would be no dancing. My body was too weak, my legs too sore and my heart just wasn't ready for it. I *will dance again when the time is right.* I bobbed my head to the music for the time being. *Be patient, Dan. You will dance again.* I'll always remember that night as acting like another mile marker on the marathon I was running. I was getting closer to the finish line. Keep running.

~

On Christmas Eve, I got to spend the day getting chemotherapy. Cancer doesn't take breaks for Christmas. Christmas Eve happened to fall on a Wednesday that year, so I stayed the course and "got 'er done," as we Canadians like to say. On the bright side, there was no traffic going to Toronto and it was smooth sailing on the 401. A piece of advice: If you have to drive long distances across the 401, Christmas Eve is the day to do it! We got to the clinic in 45 minutes. Dad's lead foot was real heavy that day. We went into the clinic, got called quickly, and, well, got 'er done.

New Year's Eve, same deal. No traffic and the weather was actually decent, so the drive was quite pleasant. After my treatment on New Year's Eve, I was so tired that by 10 p.m. I was in bed. Mom and Dad stayed up to watch the coverage of the New York City ball drop in Times Square. I fell asleep in 2008 and awoke, the next morning, in 2009. Just last year on that exact same night I was in my Toronto apartment having a wild party with about 40 to 50 of my friends, drinking champagne, smoking weed, dancing and loving life. I was in New York City partying the very next day without a care in the world! I was invincible! I think 2007 was the last full year I would know what it was like to be young, dumb and full of rum.

In 2008, I saw my career, my health, my life and even the economy go from an absolute high to an ultimate low. What did 2009 have in store? Well, it had to be better than 2008! Right? I didn't know. Nothing is ever for certain when it comes to cancer, or life for that matter. *One second at a time, one minute at a time, one hour at a time, one day at a time . . .*

Dec 31, 2008

Day 282 of 730

Last day of 2008. I want to leave this year behind and move on to 2009. Good job getting through this year, though. Pat yourself on the back, good sir. You've been through absolute hell. You are getting through it. Gonna turn the jets on in 2009. Let's make it a good one!

2008 Recap:
Sketch comedy pilot aired!
Acted in three episodes on a TV comedy series
Diagnosed with non-Hodgkin's T-lymphoblastic lymphoma. Shit.
300 days of chemo
10 days of brain radiation
Spent 40 days and nights in a hospital bed
Ingested thousands of pills that I can't pronounce
Gallons of chemotherapy injected into my veins
Poked with hundreds of needles
Taken dozens of X-rays
Received 5 blood transfusions
Endured 15 spinal taps
4 ultrasounds
4 CT scans
2 MRIs
1 PET scan
And a partridge in a pear tree.
Oh, and I lost 50 pounds, my hair, strength and boners . . . Ladies!

Do What You Love

So there I was, almost 10 months in with 14 to go and my new goal was to get all the things I had lost to the disease back again. All the things I used to love to do. All the parts of me I used to love. They were all still there, waiting to be discovered again for the first time.

I started with my biggest passion: the stage. In January, I decided it was time to get back on stage to see if I still had my comedy chops.

I registered myself for an open-mic comedy night to perform five minutes of stand-up comedy in Toronto. Nothing crazy. Just a little taste of what I'd been so desperately missing. Kind of like a crackhead addicted to the sweet rock, but my drug was comedy. This was actually my third attempt at getting stage time. The first time was set for July 2008 but I found myself emailing the coordinator of the event from my hospital bed due to the terrible fever I had. Sadly, I had to cancel. She understood and said we could reschedule. Doing stand-up from the hospital bed would be interesting . . . but impossible. On my second attempt, I got bumped, not because I was too sick, but because there was a fundraiser for cancer (ironically enough) and they had a list of accomplished comedians coming in to do their bits in support of the cure. Why didn't they ask the guy who actually had cancer to do his bit about having cancer? Who knows? I didn't get it, but I waited patiently and took my spot on January 12th, Dad's 55th birthday, to be exact. Hey, it's not like it was his 60th. . .

Jan 10, 2009

Day 292 of 730

I'm doing stand-up on Monday and I will be trying this whole cancer bit that I've been working on for the past ten months. I hope it goes well and at least my friends laugh. Will be nice to see whoever comes either way. I really appreciate all the support I get from my friends and family. They are wonderful. I will keep fighting and beat this beast. I want to be stronger than ever.

Peace and Love.

I only told two people that I would be performing that night. I told Jenny and one of our mutual friends, Nelson. They said they "may" tell some people I'd be doing a set, so I'd have to wait and see if anyone showed. I arrived at the famed Rivoli comedy club in downtown Toronto at about 8 p.m. I made my way through the dimly lit bar to the back room where nightly stand-up comedy was performed. I hadn't been in the space since I performed there with my sketch comedy troupe a couple years back. A high stage sits at the far end of the theatre with cabaret-style seating scattered about the floor and tealight candles placed randomly throughout the room. It had a very beat-poetry-jazz-bar type of feel, as if people resorted to snapping their fingers over clapping when they were digging a performance. In reality, it was one of the toughest rooms in the city for comedy. The patrons there were ruthless. They didn't necessarily heckle, but if you weren't funny, they would definitely let you know it. Silence is a comedian's worst enemy.

I decided to go to the washroom to splash some cold water on my face. The nerves were starting to kick in. As I exited the washroom, I saw a lineup of people trying to get in the front door. Word must have spread to my friends because about 30 of them stood patiently waiting to get in. To put that into perspective, a comic at an open-mic night will usually have no people or maybe two people come out to support them. I had 30 on a moment's notice. My heart filled with so much love, quickly followed by my stomach filling with so much nervousness. Nelson and Jenny must have told more than just a few people . . . liars!

I hadn't been on stage for a long time. I hadn't done stand-up for about two years! So what the fuck was I doing? *Who cares?* I felt alive.

I paced in the back room nervously waiting for my name to be called. "Tough crowd tonight," a comic said, as he returned from his set. I nodded and smiled, swallowing the fear that was pulsating through my body. *What if no one laughs? What if everyone thinks I suck? Who cares?! You are beating motherfucking cancer, so fuck it.* I was shitting my pants . . . figuratively.

The host introduced me. "Ladies and gentlemen, please welcome Daniel Stof-li? Stolfi? Stoph . . . Daniel, to the stage!" *See, no one ever gets my name right!* I laughed it off as I always do, and I began my bit.

"So, who here has acute non-Hodgkin's T-lymphoblastic lymphoma?! Anybody? Just me? Well, this is going to get awkward." The response was instantaneous. The laughter and energy shot through the room like a bolt of electricity. I held back my tears of joy and pushed through. I went into a bit I was working on called, "Cancer Makes You Gangster." It was a bit I wrote while I was in Montreal visiting my sister. The essence of the joke is this: Cancer will beat you up, knock you down and walk all over you and because of that, cancer makes you a gangster. Before I had cancer I'd take life a lot more cautiously but after you've stared death in the face every day, you have a tendency to do things a little more gangster. For example: When I come to a crosswalk, do I wait for the little flashing lights? No. I jaywalk with swagger across the street while flipping the bird to the crossing guard . . . like a gangster!! When I'm at the grocery store, do I just try a grape when no one is looking? No. I eat all the grapes off the vine while flipping the bird to the produce manager . . . like a gangster!! This was all accompanied by Tupac and Snoop Dogg's "2 of Amerika's Most Wanted" blaring over the speakers, of course.

The audience blew up with laughter and I knew at that moment that cancer could be funny. That was my breakthrough moment: If my experience with cancer was presented in a way that was relatable to the audience's emotions and was performed honestly and sincerely, it was okay to laugh. The audience needed permission to laugh, and presenting my cancer experience in this way did exactly that.

Jenny waited for me offstage. She was the first one to greet me after my set. "You still got it!" she said, with a huge smile on her face.

I yelled with my hands pumping in the air, "I still got it!" We hugged . . . *She smells nice.*

Jan 13, 2009

Day 295 of 730

Big night for me last night. I did Amateur Night at The Rivoli. I can't believe how many people came out to support me. I got a good reaction, but I really don't care about that. I had so much fun and if no one laughed it still would have been fun. If people booed, it still would have been fun. I guess just being up there again for me was enough. That's all I want. To have the ability to perform. I want to do it for the rest of my life and cancer is not going to stop me.

It was during that stand-up comedy routine that I decided to fully commit to the creation of a one-person show that would chronicle my experience with cancer. I wasn't even halfway through my treatment but I figured, *if I'm still alive, I might as well write, and if I don't last long enough to perform it, at least it was written.*

~

"Hey Stolfi, I have tickets to the new Second City Main Stage show in Toronto. Wanna come with me?" Jenny asked over the phone. I sat on my white cancer couch and pondered this question for all of one second and then immediately responded with enthusiasm, "Totally!" Then my cancer voice kicked in and I said, "But can we wait until we're closer to the date? I don't know how I'll be feeling that day."

"Totally, Stolfi. Just let me know." It was a no-brainer. I really liked hanging out with Jenny; she was fun and smart and pretty, and she seemed to like hanging out with me too. She made me feel like I was unstoppable, even when I was tired, weak, fed up or depressed. She just had a way of making things better. *Even if I'm feeling sick that day, I'm going!* I thought.

The show took place on a Wednesday and I was scheduled for another spinal tap in Toronto that day, so I figured why not stick around for a comedy show? A little spinal tap and laughter never hurt anybody. Like I said, she made me feel unstoppable, but I knew that I was pushing myself.

The day had arrived and the spinal tap went off as planned. I was a little sore and tired. I made my way to the car and Mom and I proceeded to a small Italian dinner joint on Yonge Street to share some pizza and pasta together. We finished our meal and she dropped me off at the theatre downtown where the Second City comedy show was taking place. The Second City theatre was my old stomping grounds and a beacon for comedy in Toronto. I was beyond excited and the pain I was feeling from my spinal tap seemed to disappear for the moment. "So, can you keep yourself occupied for a couple of hours until the show is over?" I asked Mom anxiously through the car window.

"I'll go to the mall or something," she replied with a worried smile. I was 26 years old, and my mommy was driving me to meet up with a girl. So lame! I also just realized that there were no malls close by for Mom to go to. She's the best. I wonder what she actually did?

Everything went as planned. I arrived at the show on time, saw Jenny's smiling face, and we found our seats together. Sure enough, once the show started, my lower back became increasingly sore from the procedure. The comedians on stage performed some wacky skit, where they were playing ping-pong. The music was blaring, the lights were flashing and the audience was howling with laughter. I wanted to join in on the amusement but my back was in too much pain to focus on the funny. At intermission, I got up and walked around a bit to ease the discomfort. I proceeded to the washrooms upstairs. I was moving very slowly up the stairs, each step reminding me that I just had a giant needle jammed into my spine. Everyone else was hopping up the stairs and shuffling down with ease. *Where's the fire?* I thought. One positive about cancer is that it slows life down for you and you really realize how precious time is and how important it is to soak in your surroundings. Let it simmer. Let it rest. Stay present. Breathe.

As I walked up the stairwell, I took a moment to appreciate all the pictures of the famous comedians who had performed at The Second City in years past. Mike Myers, Jon Candy, Catherine O'Hara and Eugene Levy, just to name a few. I grew up on Eugene Levy. That guy is a legend to me. I always loved his characters and his quirkiness. I find him to be so genuine and subtle in his comedy and he is always able to commit so deeply to his characters and play them with perfection. I took a deep breath in and exhaled. Ah, the smell of urinal cakes.

When I returned from the washroom, just before the intermission was over, I sat down beside Jenny, leaned over to her and said, "I'm going to do my show here." She shot me a look like I was out of my mind. The house lights faded to black and the second act began before she could speak.

Forty minutes later, the show was over and the house lights came up. The audience applauded and Jenny shouted over the ovation, "I want to help you do your show!"

"Cool! That would be awesome!" I shouted back. "Looks like we better get to work!"

As Jenny and I exited the Second City theatre and waited for Mom to return from "the mall," I immediately started to think of my show. *I want to finish what I started those first few days in the hospital when a "friend" told me a show about cancer had been done before "so don't bother." Honestly, fuck her! All I think about, from when I wake up in the morning to my dreams at night and back again, is cancer. It has become my life, my job, my new normal. All of my conversations with people revolve around the topic. For some reason, every other commercial or news story I see on TV has to do with cancer. It's everywhere! I have so much to share, and I need to get it out, not only for me, but for all the others who are going through this shit. Let's do this!*

We dropped Jenny off at her parents' house. "You should ask Ferg to direct," Jenny suggested, as she exited the car. Andrew Ferguson (Ferg) was a good friend and the director of my Toronto Fringe show before I got sick and had to cancel it.

"Of course I'll ask him! That's a no-brainer," I replied.

"So . . ." she continued.

"So, what?"

"Are you going to call him?"

"Right now?"

"No time like the present," she said. I couldn't argue with that logic. So I called Ferg. As soon as he picked up the phone, I told him I was writing a show. Before I said anything further, he said, "Yes! Anything you want, man. I'm in!" *Well, that was easy.*

"He's in," I told Jenny, as I hung up the phone.

"Of course he is," she said with a smile.

The next day, back home, I set a date to perform at The Second City, Toronto, for May 29th, 2009. I figured by that time I should be feeling good enough to perform. *Five months should be plenty of time for a dude taking chemotherapy drugs to write, rehearse, produce and perform a 60-minute one-person show, right?*

I wanted to get on stage so badly. Ferg and Jenny were in shock that I would want to do this show with so little time to prepare, but I can be pretty stubborn. I was hungry to get back out there! Maybe it was the chemo brain?

Writing the show was a challenging process, as to sit down at my computer and complete the simple task of typing was still incredibly difficult. I was in a lot of pain and very weak on most days, the equivalent feeling of being extremely hung over all the time. I was still receiving my maintenance treatment once a week on three-week, intensity-varying cycles, and every 16 weeks I got my lovely spinal tap, which put me out of commission for a few days as well. But, May 29th, 2009, it would be. I was determined to find a way to make it work!

There was a method to my madness. I began to recognize a pattern in my new treatment cycles. I was having a strange allergic reaction to one of the drugs I was taking. I wasn't ultimately sure which one it was, but after some simple math and deductive reasoning, I figured that it was the steroid, Dexamethasone. I took about ten pills of Dexamethasone a day. The side effects were a whole lot of hiccups that lasted for five days, followed by an incredibly itchy rash that broke out all over my scalp and chest. The rash resembled serious acne: red welts with whiteheads. The giant red welts were not only physically unattractive, but painful as all hell. They completely covered my scalp and parts of my face and chest. It was impossible to prevent the side effects but I was able to time out when they started and when they started to subside.

My voice was also affected for the first week of treatments. It would sit in a higher register, giving me a raspy falsetto pitch, limiting me from projecting or doing character voices. If I performed my show on a night where I had any of these side effects going on, I would have to cancel. There was still the bone pain that came up every six weeks or so that was so excruciating it left me bedridden for days at a time. I also had to keep in mind that I would receive spinal taps every 16th week, and if the show fell on that week, it could be disastrous. I would have to navigate my way around all of it, including my weekly chemotherapy procedures, which were still on Wednesdays.

System overload, for fuck sakes!

With all these factors considered, I calculated that I had a small window of opportunity once every three weeks for about five days, which fell between the end of my third week and the beginning of my first week of treatment cycles. It was during these five days that I would be at my optimum performance ability. Optimum being a relative term for a guy on heavy chemotherapy drugs.

Friday, May 29th, 2009, fell right near the middle of my third-week cycle and just before a spinal tap. It was perfect! I had to go for it. Just when I thought I had it sorted out, The Second City sprang this puppy on me: "The only time we have available at The Second City, on a Friday night, for stage time, is 11 p.m." *What the fuck?!*

My bedtime was still clocking in at 10 p.m. and that was if I felt like being a rebel and burning the midnight oil on New Year's Eve. "Yeah, sure. That's fine," I said, like a fucking boss! I was going to have to break curfew just this once. I planned around cancer like a high-performance athlete plans for the Olympics or a woman plans around her period. I finally understood. Okay, maybe that's a stretch . . . but I was doing this!!

Love and Cancer

As the show started to near, my relationship with Jenny grew.

I love you like the moons of Jupiter, her text message read on the screen of my flip phone.

I sat on my white couch and let the warm feelings sink in, as I contemplated what I would write back. *She just means love, like friend love, not* in *love, right?* I thought to myself.

I wrote back, **I love you as much as the ocean is deep.** *That's just friend love stuff, right?*

I was developing a bit of a crush on her, but there was no way she could have wanted anything to do with a cancer patient who was bald, pale, skinny and covered in rashes while having hiccups with an alto soprano voice! So, I was not going to try and think too much about it and just focus on the show. *Ah, fuck it! I liked her too much!* But, I couldn't let her know.

I developed an elaborate scheme to ask her out on a date, but not a real date, because then it would be too obvious that I liked her. It was close to Valentine's Day, but it was not actually Valentine's Day, so she couldn't get confused with what was really going on here, right?

I called her up and acted all cool, almost as cool as when I called her from my apartment in university. "So, to show my appreciation for all the work you're doing on the show and for your birthday"—which was four months ago— "I'd like to use my gift certificate to a pretty nice restaurant here in Guelph . . . on you." *Smooth.* I continued, "We didn't celebrate your birthday, so . . . would you wanna come with me?"

"Of course!" she replied enthusiastically. *That went well.*

Our dinner date that wasn't a date was set. Jenny made the drive down the 401, a highway she was absolutely terrified of because of a rolling-tire near-death incident she encountered once. The long stretch of road shook her to the core whenever she drove on it. She picked me up, pretended that she wasn't completely rattled from the drive, and we headed to the restaurant for our 5:30 p.m. reservation (their earliest available time). I wore my purple Le Château Men's dress shirt, my four-sizes-too-big black suede pants and my black Nike running shoes. A real looker, I was. Jenny wore a black flowing dress with black leggings, her hair was down and she was looking as beautiful and fashionable as ever. *She's way too good for me.*

The restaurant was empty. It was 5:30 p.m. Who in the hell makes a dinner reservation for 5:30 p.m.? Guys with cancer who have to be in bed by 10 p.m. at the absolute latest, that's who! Before ordering, Jenny reached into her bag and pulled out a large manila envelope with my name on it. "What's this?" I asked.

"Oh, it's just a little something that I wanted to give you on your birthday," she said.

"But we're out for *your* birthday!"

"Just open it, Stolfi."

I peeled back the seal of the envelope and reached my hand inside. I pulled out a white piece of 8x10 photo paper. It was a headshot. *But whose?* I turned the paper over and there he was. A black-and-white original headshot of the one and only, Eugene Levy. My comedy legend. He wore his signature black-framed glasses. He rocked his salt-and-pepper hair with his big bushy eyebrows. He was looking at me like, "I got you." My eyes made their way over the image and eventually fell upon a signature. It was signed! "Hi Dan! Wishing you the very best—Eugene Levy." I was speechless.

After a moment, Jenny spoke. "He apparently never does this sort of thing for anyone."

"How did you . . .?" I asked, still in shock.

"I reached out to Dan and Sarah Levy. We went to high school together. I told them your story and they immediately reached out to their dad and Eugene was more than happy to sign it for me."

It was the nicest gift anyone could have gotten me. "Thank you so much! I don't know what to say."

"Don't say anything. You're welcome. Let's eat."

We "indulged" on the prix fixe menu that ended with a delicious chocolate fondue, which we shared. I wanted to tell her that I liked her and that if I came out of this whole cancer thing okay, that we should give it another shot. But I froze up and after paying for the bill (throwing down my gift certificate). I said, "Drive safe, the weather is brutal."

She smiled and said, "I love you like chocolate fondue." I took a breath.

"I love you like chocolate fondue too," I replied. An awkward pause.

"I'm *in* love with you, Stolfi," Jenny clarified. A beat. Then the dumbest thing I've ever said in my life came out of my mouth: "No you're not." *I'm such an idiot! Who says, "No you're not?" when a girl you clearly like A LOT tells you she's in love with you? I do. That's who.* My mind was trying to figure a way out of this terrible hole I just dug.

"What I mean is . . . I like you so much and I am still really sick, so I don't want to hurt you or get too close and then, you know, something shitty happens. Like I die and stuff." *Real smooth, Stolfi.* I was in shock. *She loves me? She's IN love with me?* Being in love and loving someone are two totally different things. *Damn it, I know I am falling for her, but I don't want to commit to love because it will hurt that much more if I don't make it out of this thing.* Then cancer kicked in, and . . . *fuck it.* I kissed her!

Time seemed to stop for a moment. Her warm, soft lips felt familiar and completely new at the same time. It was a nice, soft, gentle kiss that was just the perfect length. I felt warm and calm on the inside, but my heart raced like a jackhammer. I hadn't kissed a girl in forever! I was instantly addicted to her. *I am still so sick, I look like absolute crap, she has seen me in the worst possible conditions I could have ever been in, and she's in love with me?* Jenny is what I like to call, "The One." Without her, I'd be dead. I may have already said this but without her . . . I'd be dead. So to recap, without my mom, my friends, my family, Dr Chang, all the lovely nurses and staff, and of course, Jenny . . . I'd be dead. No doubt.

I didn't tell her I was *in* love with her that night. It was too much for me. I knew I was falling for her, but with everything going on, I couldn't find the strength to open up. We both knew we had to take it slowly.

~

I framed the signed headshot of Eugene Levy and placed it on my parents' fireplace mantel. It officially replaced our family photo, and I would look to it for motivation every day from my white cancer couch.

A lot of visitors thought it was my dad. True story.

My Strength

Exercise has always been a big part of my life. Before I was diagnosed with cancer I was a bit of a gym rat. I'd be at the gym five days a week pretty regularly. I'd play recreational sports at least once a week, consisting of either soccer or basketball, and I was always up for any type of physical activity at a moment's notice. Overall, I was a pretty good athlete, never the best, but always pretty good. If you were the captain of a team, picking players for your squad, you'd pick me pretty high. Like number two or three. Just sayin' . . . for perspective and all.

My New Year's resolution, on top of performing my show, was to get back in the gym. I needed to get my stamina back, as performing a 60-minute one-person show can be physically exhausting. I am a firm believer in pushing myself to do things that are difficult no matter how uncomfortable or daunting they may seem. Why? Probably because I watched too many *Rocky* movies. I learned early on in my life that in order to improve and grow, you need to feel uncomfortable. If it's too comfortable, you begin to accept the status quo and never get better.

In order to get uncomfortable, I started walking up and

down my parents' staircase. One flight, exactly 14 steps, left me breathless. I was so weak and my muscles had become so atrophied that it felt like I was walking on new legs, starting the walking process all over again. It was as if I was a baby again, slowly strengthening my legs to hoist me upright with the hopes of turning walking into running. I used to bench-press 180 pounds, curl 40 pounds, do 150 sit-ups and run for 30 minutes on a treadmill at my gym visits without too much difficulty. *This was all just ten months ago?* This was all just ten months ago! To get back to that place seemed impossible. I was going to have to get really uncomfortable.

I was a long-time member of the YMCA in Guelph, conveniently located a couple blocks away from my parents' home, but when I moved to Toronto, I had found a much smaller gym that was way cheaper and exactly what I needed. It was only $25 a month but I had to sign a one-year contract. When I asked to get out of my contract, because I had recently been diagnosed with cancer, they refused. I had to pay them $150 to opt out of my contract, the remaining months on the one-year deal. *My cancer card is no good here? Jerks.* I had a bit of a crush on the girl who worked at the gym at the time. She signed me up for my membership when I first enrolled and after she refused to let me out of my contract, I officially despised her. Her loss, right?

Now, there I was, ten months later, about to go to the YMCA in Guelph weighing 135 pounds with no hair, pale, weak and frail. I spent my teenage years and early twenties there building my body up to a great state of health only to have it completely ripped from me in a few short weeks.

I decide to set small goals for myself. My first small goal was to actually walk to the gym itself, which was about 750 yards away from the house. I figured, if I could slowly build my way up to completing the walk, I would be in good enough shape to make it through a one-hour show. There was really no logic to this, as a solo show requires so much more energy than walking half a mile, but walking a greater distance than from my bedroom to the washroom was a good place to start.

"I'll go and get the mail today, Ma!" I shouted as I put on my black running shoes. The hill from the driveway to the mailbox looked so daunting. I remember as a kid, running up and down that hill with ease, jumping off the curbs and splashing into puddles of water.

I stepped outside. The bitter cold February air punched me in the face like a swift jab from a seasoned boxer. My nose hairs tingled as they began to freeze. Memories of the day after Valentine's Day came rushing back in. I shook them off. *Not this time.* I walked to the top of my street, grabbed the mail, and returned home again. I threw myself down onto my white couch and rested.

The next day, I walked past the mailbox to the end of the second street and back home again, winded and begging for the couch.

The third day, I pulled my legs all the way to the gym. As soon as I got there, I called Mom from the gym's payphone. "Hey, Mom, I'm here."

"Congratulations! Good for you. I'm so proud," she said.

"Can you come pick me up? I'm not going to work out today and I don't think I can make it home on my own."

"Of course," she said, laughing a little. I was making baby steps and it felt good.

Day Four: I stood at the entrance of the YMCA doors and proceeded to the front desk to reinstate my gym membership. "Okay, just fill out these forms and you'll be all set," the girl said from behind the desk.

"We went to high school together," I told her. She tried to place me, then looked at my form. "Stolfi? Dan? Oh my God, I didn't recognize you!" she said excitedly. "It's the new hairdo!"

"Yeah, wasn't really by choice," I said awkwardly, hoping she could put the pieces together herself. There was an awkward pause. *I think she gets it?*

"Okay, so we'll have to get you to take a new photo."

"Don't you still have my old photo on file? I'd really like to use my old one," I said.

"Sorry, but that's protocol. All new members have to have a current photo taken," she replied.

"Okay, but when my hair grows back can I take another one?" I asked. She looked at me blankly.

"Uh, sure. I guess?" *She doesn't get it.* The camera flashed. "Your card will be available for pickup after your workout."

"Thanks."

I walked slowly past the treadmills, stationary bikes and stair climbers, toward the weight room. Semi-retired people, night-shift workers and unemployed trophy wives blasted their deltoids and quads with reckless abandon. I could feel the gaze of onlookers as I grabbed a one-pound weight from the rack and sat on a black leather workout bench. I pulled the weight up slowly toward my shoulder, "flexing" my bicep. *One. Two. Three.* That was plenty.

I then lay down on a mat on the gym floor and did ten sit-ups. No push-ups. I wasn't ready for push-ups. It was time to go home and rest up.

After two weeks, my strength was slowly coming back, the regulars weren't staring at me as much and I was getting into a bit of a routine. I decided that it was time to take it to another level and attempt to do something I always loved to do at this gym. In the space below the workout gym, a small basketball court sat empty, waiting for my mean skills to dominate the rims. The primary gym space, with all the heavy machines, surrounded the basketball court on an upper level in a *U* shape, creating a very "open-concept" type space. It's a very *"Hey, everyone! Take a look at this guy trying to play basketball downstairs"* type of vibe.

I descended the stairs to the court below and picked up a basketball from one of the racks. The ball felt foreign in my hands. It was heavy and rough to the touch. My skin was baby smooth, removed of any calluses I once had from my frequent gym visits pre-cancer. I lifted the orange ball with black stripes over my head and extended my forearm up and out, flicking my wrist through my fingers. The ball barely escaped my hand before gravity pulled it back down to the wooden gym floor. Something that had once been such a simple routine motion was now completely new and difficult again.

I stood directly beneath the mesh and pushed the ball upwards one more time. The ball travelled a slight distance farther but quickly descended to the floor. A group of kids scurried down the stairs and onto the court with an energy that seemed impossible. A boy with red hair and freckles hurled a basketball from half court toward the basket I was under. The sound of the clang echoed through the gym as the ball bounced off the white steel backboard. I ducked out of the way and covered my head. The ball whizzed by my ear as another boy grabbed the rebound and hurled the ball clear across the gym to the other hoop. *Don't these kids know I'm in the midst of battling cancer?* I checked my surroundings for flying objects . . . the coast was clear. I pushed the ball up toward the rim again. It barely brushed the bottom of the mesh and returned to my hands. Another ball swished through the net and I ducked out of the way. "Swish, baby!" the red-headed boy yelled triumphantly. Kids don't respect their elders these days.

I used basketball as a way to gauge my strength and progression. I figured the farther and farther I could back away from the basket and get the ball up to the rim, the stronger I must have been getting. I dodged the flying balls and focused on the task at hand: *Get the ball in the hoop.* I looked up at the white backboard with the orange square and zoned in on one tiny spot. That spot, where if the ball hits it at the right angle, it would effortlessly fall through the basket. *Use the backboard, Dan. Just like when you were a kid. It doesn't have to be nothing but net. It's worth the same amount if you bank it in. Just make sure you call bank.* I dribbled the ball once, then twice, and hoisted it up over my head. I bent my knees and pushed the ball through my legs and up to my arms with both hands. With the ball at the end of my fingertips, I felt the muscles in my back, shoulders and arms tighten, then release as it left my hands. "Bank!" It ricocheted off the backboard with a subtle pang and fell through the mesh. *My first basket! The crowd goes wild!* I felt vindicated and proud as I looked up at the onlookers on their stationary bikes, thinking, *Did you see that? How awesome was that? And I have cancer!* The crowd was roaring! The generic sounds of feet pounding the treadmills and metal weights clanging in rhythm came slowly back to life. There was no roaring crowd. No one seemed to care. They were all just there, living their lives. *They probably have somewhere important to go later tonight.* As far as they were concerned, I was just a really shitty skinny basketball player with thinning hair. But, for me, the moment that ball went through the hoop was the best feeling in the world and no one was going to take that away from me. *Minor victories.*

~

It all takes time. Every day was different. I made my first basket at the gym but I was still having trouble getting out of bed in the mornings. I could hardly lift a jug of water at the dinner table. Opening a bag of chips was close to impossible. My hands just didn't want to work for me. I was intending to dance my ass off in my show in front of 300 people to let cancer know I still had it and it couldn't stop me from doing what I love. It dawned on me that there was no way I was going to be able to do that if I couldn't even open a bag of chips! I was starting to panic. My mind started to race . . .

I am still breathing heavily after climbing up a flight of stairs. I am lifting one-pound weights at the gym. I can hardly push a basketball into a net. I feel like shit. What am I thinking?! I should just cancel the show.

"I don't think I can do this, guys," I told my family, as we sat around the table for a Sunday night dinner. Everyone was there, my brother, his fiancée, my sister, her husband, my nephew and my parents.

"I can show you some exercises if you're up for it," my brother suggested.

"I'll try anything," I replied. *He's a physiotherapist so he must know what he's talking about.* My brother showed me some strength exercises to slowly work my way back into shape, reminding me, "It won't all come back in one workout, one day, one week. It takes time." He was right. *One second at a time, one minute at a time, one hour at a time, one day at a time . . .*

As for walking to the gym, I had worked up enough strength to walk there AND back. It took me about three months but, damn it, I did it. I had to time my workouts in the same way I had to time out my treatment for the show. It was all based on the rashes, hiccups, spinal taps, bone pain and all that fun stuff. *I can do this. Be patient. It takes time.*

Feb 14, 2009

Day 327 of 730

Valentine's Day. WOW. A year since I first felt those aches in my bones! Fuck you, cancer! I had a better day today. I went to the gym and increased all my weights to about ten pounds. I will stick with this for the next week or so . . . until March. Then kick it up another level. I've come a long way. I remember just the other day looking at myself in the mirror and seeing this skinny, bald, old-looking man and thinking, how will I get out of this? When will I get my body back? Now, slowly but surely, it's coming back. One day at a time. Go to the gym. Work out. Get in shape. I will get it back and it will be glorious. I am making a comeback and it's halftime. I was down 100–10 after the first quarter, and I have cut the lead to 50. I will make my full comeback in the second half. Win, baby, win!

Game Changer – Part II

Things just sort of started going my way . . .

For 14 months straight, I had spent every week of treatment lying down in the back of my parents' clunky, ugly, snot-green Hyundai Elantra, flying down the 401 through rush hour traffic, snow, rain and heat, accompanied by the sweet sounds of Lady Gaga tracks blaring over the radio. "Just Dance" . . . *I'm working on it!!* During that time, the idea of requesting the option to receive treatment in Guelph was talked about but never fully pursued. A good friend of mine, Raj, was entering medical school when I was first diagnosed, and his father worked at the chemotherapy clinic in Guelph. Raj would always ask me, "Why aren't you getting treatment done here? They have the facilities." I never had an answer for him. Whenever I brought it up with my oncologist or the staff at Sunnybrook in Toronto, they sort of looked at me blankly, as if it just wasn't an option.

It was another Wednesday when I arrived at Sunnybrook Hospital for my weekly check-in, blood work and chemotherapy appointment. With Mom by my side, I waited to be called in by my oncologist for our post-treatment meeting. "Daniel Stofli?"

the porter called out. I raised my hand and we made our way to one of the rooms where my oncologist would greet us. The room was empty, so we took a seat. A young doctor, with curly dirty-blond hair entered my room. He had a clipboard in one hand, half-eaten Granny Smith apple in the other. "Hey, we have the same name!" he said as he looked at his clipboard, mouth still full from the apple he was chewing. He reached out to shake my hand. "I'm Dr. Dempson, but call me Danny. Dr. Chang is on vacation, so I will be filling in for the next couple of weeks. Is that cool?"

"Yeah, for sure." *I like this guy. He said, "cool."*

"So, Daniel, what is it that you do for a living?"

"I have a full-time job as a cancer patient. Money isn't great and the food is shit," I joked. He laughed. After a moment I continued, "In all honesty, I'm an actor and comedian."

"Really? I'm a huge fan of comedy," he said. He took a look at my chart and made a curious grunt sound. He looked up from the clipboard and asked, "You live in Guelph?"

"Yup," I said.

"You drive all the way to Toronto every week for your chemotherapy?"

"Yup. Well, my mom drives." She looked on, proud.

"Don't they have a chemotherapy clinic in Guelph?"

"Yeah. My buddy told me they do."

"Oh, they for sure do. I'll look into getting you in for treatment down there. It would probably be a lot easier for you. Why go to the farm and milk a cow when you can drink the milk from home . . . What's the saying? Anyway, you know what I mean." We laughed.

"That would be amazing!" I said excitedly. *He speaks in made-up, almost accurate sayings too!* I officially had a man crush.

Mom and I were so happy. I was happy because Mom is, in my humble opinion, the worst driver of all time! No more life-threatening drives on the 401, or at least not as many! She was happy because I am brutal to drive with, always in her ear about how bad a driver she is. And, get this, parking was $24 a visit! I'd save some time and stress; she'd save some time, stress and money. It was a win, win!

Dr. Danny looked into it, worked his charm, and a few weeks later I was receiving two out of every three weeks of treatment in Guelph. On the third week, I would return to Toronto to have treatment and follow-up meetings with my oncologist, Dr. Chang. On the downside, I had just been introduced to another young patient named Zach, who had the exact same cancer as me and was just starting his treatment. I would now only get to see him and Ari once every three weeks, which was a bummer as we were basically running the chemo unit now like a bunch of old mob bosses who meet in mall food courts to tell stories about what life was like in the good old days. But after the first round of this new schedule, I realized it was the Best. Move. Ever!

The nurses in Guelph were so kind. They got to know me on a first-name basis, unlike the mispronounced "Stofli" I was referred to when I was in Toronto. They were so supportive and friendly. I felt like I was part of a family there. It was a much smaller clinic than the one in Toronto, so they could take the time to know each patient individually. I can't believe I am saying this but I actually looked forward to going into the chemotherapy unit each week. It was madness! I never thought I would have enjoyed it but oddly enough, I was starting to.

I will forever be grateful to Dr. Danny for taking that initiative and having the foresight to adjust my schedule.

It's these minor victories that make all the difference.

NOTE FOR HEALTHCARE PROFESSIONALS: Little things like this can save people's lives. Pay attention to the details of your patients' lives and how these life details fit into their treatment. Don't think about how their treatment can fit into the system. You can make a huge difference. Just a note. Not an order . . . but sort of an order!

Let's Make a Show

In order to create a one-person show, I figured I should probably go see one first. So I'd never seen a one-person show before. Sue me. I flipped open my cell phone and called Jenny from my white couch. "Hey, Jenny!"

"Hey, Stolfi!" she said, excitedly. "What's up? Everything okay?"

"Yeah, I'm great. I just realized that I've never actually seen a one-person show before." There was a brief pause from Jenny on the other end before she responded.

"Really?! Oh, you should see one before you do your show."

"I know. That's why I'm calling. Do you know of any solo shows playing in Toronto that we could go see?" I asked.

Jenny, the theatre whizz, quickly responded, "Yeah, there is this one playing at the Factory Theatre main space. The guy doing it is supposed to be really good. 'The master of the one-man shows,' it says."

"Sweet, let's book it," I told her.

"Deal." And just like that, it was on.

We arrived at the theatre and took our seats in the cozy black box–style space. The lights faded to black and the "epic" was under way. A middle-aged actor, strangely dressed like the recently deceased Heath Ledger's Joker, from *Batman*, walked out on stage. He acted very smug and arrogant. He drank a full can of Coke, crushed it underneath his foot and then knocked it into the audience with a cane. He talked about his failed career as an actor and showed the audience a bunch of high-tech, very glossy videos from his past. I leaned over to Jenny. "What in the hell is this shit?"

"I'm sorry. They said he was the master."

"Master? Master of jerking himself off on stage, maybe . . ." I whispered. We laughed. We left the theatre after the show and ranted on and on about how self-indulgent and boring the show was. I took what I didn't want my show to be from this "master class performance," and decided to trust my instincts of what I felt a one-person show should be. But with not much to go on and time running out, I started to panic. The show was a few months away and all I had were a couple of stand-up jokes about cancer, which I only performed once in front of a live audience. I didn't have the flashy technical videos the master of one-person shows had, but I also knew I didn't want them. I just wanted to tell my story, my way.

"Cancer makes you gangster," I said to Jenny as we left the theatre.

"Totally," she said.

"I'm going to build the show around that bit."

"Go for it, Stolfi. Whatever you do will be magic," she said with a smile. *Can't argue that logic!*

On the drive back to Guelph, all I could think about was

my show that wasn't even a show yet. I had to trust my instincts and put actual "pen to paper," or, I guess, type to screen? *Whatever. Fuck it. I have cancer!!* Cancer makes you gangster.

With this mindset in place, I began to write. The first draft of the script was really just a mix of character monologues, each character representing an attribute that I lost to cancer: My Hair was played by an old Italian barber. My Strength was played by a tough no-nonsense gym teacher. My Appetite was played by a club-going Guido who still lived in his parents' basement. My Sex Drive was played by the smooth-talking ladies' man, Bruise Portego. Cancer was a character that I would struggle with for a bit. Who is Cancer? What does he look like as a person? What does he sound like? That would have to be answered later. For the moment, I had to figure out how to mesh the performance pieces, music, stand-up comedy and personal journal entries together as the script really had no cohesive shape. It was just a bunch of little skits, one after the other. The most difficult part was finding a way to piece the material together in some sort of structure that told a whole story. It wasn't until my director, Ferg, got his hands on the script that the fine-tuning began. It was magic. It all just rolled really well and felt effortless. We found ways to bridge the story gaps through musical transitions and dialogue tweaks. This would give the show a more familiar story-like structure, with a clear beginning, middle and end to each act.

We sat in his Toronto apartment, wracking our brains about one major element and missing piece, which was arguably the most important part of any show. "How are we going to end this thing?" Andrew asked, as he paced the length of his living room.

"Well, I have to live of course," I joked.

"Yeah, Stolfi. You live. Come on, think!"

"I got it! It's obvious. Cancer and I have to have a dance-off!" I shouted.

"Of course that's the move," Andrew confirmed. "But you want to play Cancer?"

"Well, yeah. I sort of have to, don't I?" I reasoned.

"Sure, but who is he to you?" he challenged.

"Maybe Cancer is a mean rough and tough guy who is just a dick?" I suggested.

"Nah, I think we go the other way," Ferg challenged again.

"Okay, so maybe he's a nasally douchebag. He listens to country music, which I hate, and he's that guy at work who's such a loser but part of you feels bad for him because he is such a loser, but then you realize he's a loser 'cause he's a dick!?"

"Perfect!" Ferg exclaimed. "Let's take the audience on a rollercoaster ride of emotions by letting them into your head to feel what it's like to have cancer, and then we flip it to something funny," he went on. We both agreed that if we could make the audience laugh, cry and maybe even puke at the same time, the show would be a success! We pretty much wanted the audience to experience the emotions of cancer without actually having to go through it.

"What do you want to call it?" Ferg asked.

"How about, 'Cancer Can't Dance,'" I responded. "You know, 'cause I have a dance-off with cancer and all."

Ferg thought on this for a second and then responded, "I think you should add, 'Like This' to the end. You know, 'cause cancer can't dance . . . like this!"

"You mean, like this?" I got up off the couch, did my signature MJ spin, stopped on a dime and threw my hands over my head.

"Exactly!" Ferg exclaimed as we both laughed.

"'Cancer Can't Dance Like This'. I love it!" I said as I made my way back to the couch, a little dizzy now.

Then, Ferg hit me with a major question, a question that if I didn't have the right answer to, there would really be no point in doing the show. "You need to ask yourself, why? Why are you writing this show? Why do you want to share this story?"

Wow. That's a doozy. I took a second and then laid it out for him. "Honestly, I want people to know what I didn't know before I was diagnosed. I was so ignorant to the whole disease and many other diseases, for that matter. I feel that there is a certain injustice being done, if all people aren't educated on the most horrific disease in the world, a disease that kills millions of people every year. A disease that can actually be treated if found early or prevented altogether in a lot of cases. I feel that if I inform people on what it is really like to go through cancer: the chemotherapy, the pain, the radiation, the spinal taps, the hair loss, the drugs, the loss of appetite, the physical, mental and emotional toll it takes, all of it . . . people will feel more empowered and inspired to live their lives to the fullest. I want people to leave the theatre thankful for what they have and appreciate the little things. The minor victories. Put the little problems into perspective. Maybe they will think about life a little differently when a good thing turns bad or bad thing turns worse. I want to keep dancing—dance in the face of any adversity. Laugh. I want people to *laugh* in the face of adversity. I want to remind people to keep pushing for whatever it is they want, no matter how high the odds are stacked up against them. I really want to express that we can't let moments in our lives, or outside forces that are beyond our control, dictate who we are. I want people to know that giving up is not an option. Keep fighting, no matter how hard you're getting hit. And if it's your last fight, go out swinging." There was a brief pause.

"Good answer," Ferg replied. "Let's do this."

March 13, 2009

Day 354 of 730

Almost 12 months down! Twelve to go! I'm looking and feeling better. I still have a long way to go and when I beat this I will shout it from the rooftops! I just want to perform again, doing what I want and saying what I want. I don't know if people understand how much it means to me to be able to perform again. I want to have fun. That's all. Have fun with no pressure. Enjoy it while you can and love every second of it. Do what you can but don't overdo it. Jenny is going to let me cut her hair! She's donating it for me! She's unreal!!

Showtime

May 15, 2009

Day 417 of 730

Two weeks to the show! Things are going well. I feel like I have the energy. I need to stay well-rested before the show and be ready to rock it hard. Gotta get the lines down 100%, especially the opening! I have a meeting with my radiologist on Wednesday and we will discuss follow-up radiation treatments. This is fucked. Cancer never takes a break. Seems never-ending. I want to beat this thing and be done with it. Almost 14 months down with ten to go!

May 29th, 2009. Opening night. It's on!

I was sixteen months into my treatment. Three hundred and thirty people flooded the Second City main space in Toronto at 11 p.m. on a Friday night. The venue oversold tickets and was breaking fire regulations just to squeeze in the last few patrons. The theatre had difficulty getting more than 200 people on Saturday nights, let alone turning people away at the door on a Friday . . . at 11 p.m.! This was a good sign. My bedtime was currently set for 9:30 p.m. but the adrenalin carried me well past that. As I paced nervously in the backstage greenroom, I had all this familiar nervous energy, an energy I had missed for so long. It was warm and inviting but scary as all hell. It's an energy that reminds you why you do what you do but always makes you want to run and then question why you do what you do!

The lights went dark and the sound of a few hundred people, talking in unison, quickly came to a quiet whisper and then, finally, silence.

It was time to share my story.

I called out the first lines of the show from the darkness, "Hey, Ma! Where is it? I can't find it anywhere! In the basement!? What's it doing in the basement?!" The lights came up and I stepped onstage in a tacky purple jacket, giant curly wig, Italian club-going sunglasses and white cotton headband. Tucked in the breast pocket of my black collared shirt, right beside my heart, was a set of black-framed glasses with a piece of white tape in the middle. This was Cancer. *I will save you for later,* I thought to myself.

The audience applauded wildly. Some friends and familiar faces stood, clapping proudly, showing their love and support. I took a photograph in my mind, now burned in my brain forever. *They are all here,* I thought. *The ones who saved my life, I took note: Mom, Dad, my brother, sister, cousins, aunts and uncles. Jenny, Jenny's family, Ferg, Ari, Zach, Dr. Chang, Nurse Joseph, Stefan, Steve, Ni, Matt, Nelson, Raj, Davide. They are all here! Jeff "the crazy man from the North," Sarah "the foot rubber," Rusa "the get-out-of-my-room-Jenny's-coming friend," Crystal "the party planner," Dimetre "the BBQ king," Chudz "my friend and lighting legend." I see you! The Morganettes from my Captain Morgan crew, and my sketch comedy troupe: Jessie, Shawn, Amish, Bobby.* I took a moment to let it soak in and then I took another moment to hold back the tears that were welling up inside me. I turned to face the "director's chair" (a main set piece for the show) and there, on the back of the chair, in bold white letters was my name, D. STOLFI. Ferg, decided to surprise me by adding my name to the back of the chair, which he donated for the show. With my back to the audience and my name staring back at me, I couldn't help but get even more choked up than I already was. I fought back the tears.

The show must go on. I pushed through. Brace. Breathe.

It all started to click. My stage manager, Shawn, was knocking the cues out of the park and I was hitting the punchlines with voracity. We took the audience from uproarious laughter to complete stillness in an instant. I shared real moments from my personal journal, the lights dimming on point with precision and perfection. There was an energy in the room that can't be explained, that can't be matched. The show kept pushing on and everything felt familiar again. The little pause between laughter, the timing between jokes. I could feel the exact moment I needed to deliver the next line to get the best laugh. I was on point. I'd been on stage for just a few minutes and it felt like I'd never left.

As the show pushed on, I could feel the adrenalin carrying me forward and before I knew it, I was a full hour into the show, and it was time for my final dance-off with Cancer. I was completely exhausted and my legs were shaking, ready to buckle. The music kicked in and that infamous Michael Jackson "Billie Jean" backbeat hit as familiar as ever. My pelvis started to thrust, the music in control now. My right hand was on my belt, left hand pointed down and behind as I swept away the red-and-black Thriller jacket I was now wearing just as MJ would, both hands having to leave their positions momentarily. I looked up, kicked out my right leg, slapped my knee and glided backwards across the stage, as if floating on air. The beat changed, I tensed any muscle in my body that was strong enough to go along for the ride, in what could only be described as "the best robot dancing machine of all time" (my words, thank you very much). I threw in a couple more crotch grabs because, *fuck it, why not?* I spun, stopped and stared at the black-framed, white-taped glasses in my breast pocket. I plucked them out and placed them on the stage floor in front of me . . . *this is my cancer.* It was time. I jumped as high as my thin legs would take me and stomped down, both feet crashing to the stage, breaking the plastic frame in half, crushing Cancer and killing it for good. The music and the lights snapped to . . .

Blackout.

We sat in darkness. One. Two. Three.

The lights went back up to full.

We sat in the light. One, two . . . Brace. Breathe.

The audience jumped out of their seats, applauding and howling loudly. *They must all be drunk*, I thought. I bowed and waved to the crowed. "Thank you!" I yelled, but I couldn't hear the sound of my own voice. The roar of the crowed was deafening. The applause wouldn't stop. Calls for an encore were shouted out, "Encore! Encore!" I exited stage left and entered again, bowing and thanking everyone for being there. The beautiful noise from the audience drowned out my voice once again. I was sure I should have been in a puddle of tears or at least in a heap on the stage floor due to exhaustion, but I had more energy than ever before. For the first time in 14 months, I didn't feel sick, I didn't feel like I had cancer. I felt alive. I felt normal. Sixty minutes I will never forget. Sixty minutes I will cherish forever. I made them laugh. I made them laugh from the gut. They cried, oh they were crying, and like I said, some of them were drinking and maybe, just maybe, they drank so much that they puked later that night. Mission accomplished.

Blackout.

Finding Support

It was June of 2009. I was testing out some material from my show at an open-mic comedy night in Toronto. I had been reworking some stuff about Lance Armstrong. This was pre Lance scandal. The joke was about him setting the bar way too high for other cancer survivors. I mean, the guy won seven Tour de Frances for fuck sakes and that was after a whack load of chemo and getting his ball removed. That's insane! Turns out he was cheating, but for a guy with only one nut, it's pretty ballsy.

The bit went off without a hitch. The audience laughed and applauded, congratulating me as I walked off the stage. One audience member, a tall woman with brown hair, maybe a couple years my senior, pulled me aside and said, "Hi, I'm Leslie. I'm a cancer survivor." Two things went through my head. One: *Awesome, someone my age who had cancer!* Two: *Oh shit . . . what did I say to offend the cancer survivor in the audience?* She went on, "That was an awesome set!"

"Thanks!" I replied, relieved that she wasn't about to punch me in the face.

"Are you still in treatment?" she asked.

"Yeah, still got about ten months to go."

"Ten months?! Holy shit! What kind of cancer do you have?" I was getting used to this reaction. From the conversations that I had with other cancer patients, it became very clear to me that most treatment protocols ranged from three to eight months. Two years was almost unheard of.

"Yeah, I know," I replied. "Lymphoma. But it's just the protocol I'm on. Two years total. It's crazy."

"Tell me about it." She went on, "I had thyroid cancer." She pointed to the middle of her neck, revealing a discoloured scar about four inches long.

"Nice!" I said, like it was the coolest thing I had ever seen.

"Thanks," she said, proud. She then went on, "Have you ever heard of Young Adult Cancer Canada?"

"No, I don't think so."

"It's an organization that helps young adults between 18 and 39 who are going through cancer or have gone through it."

"Like a support group?" I asked, hesitantly.

"Yeah, sort of. But way cooler. They send cancer survivors and patients on retreats. You should check it out." I was skeptical, but also intrigued. This was an opportunity to meet other people who were fighting a similar fight, a group of people who understood what I was going through. The programs the hospital recommended were more tailored toward older patients and usually consisted of fifty-to seventy-year-old women in the throes of battling breast cancer, so it was hard for me to relate. I still had Ari and Zach to chat with every few weeks but figured it couldn't hurt to check it out.

"Send me the info," I told her. "I'll take a look." I gave her my contact.

"Great," she said. "I'll email you tomorrow."

"Cool. Thanks." And with that, a few weeks later, I signed up for a cancer retreat with Young Adult Cancer Canada. It was a fully paid getaway in northern Quebec at a camp sanctuary in the middle of the woods for young adult cancer survivors. I was allowed to bring one supporter and it couldn't be a parent, not that I wanted to bring Mom anyway. I was planning on going solo but thought maybe Jenny would want to join me. We had been dating now for a few months, so the only logical thing to do was to ask her to come along with me on a four-day retreat with cancer patients at a camp in the middle of butt-fuck nowhere. *Way to keep knocking these dates out of the park, Stolfi!* Lucky for me, without hesitating, she said yes. We were on our way!

There were about 30 cancer survivors, patients, and supporters in total. Some spoke only French, some only English. Some brought supporters, some didn't; most were women, and by most, I mean all but two (me and a handsome young man from Africa). We took a large yellow school bus deep into the hills of the Quebec countryside just north of Montreal.

It was an old campsite for children. Log cabins sat next to a huge lake in the middle of a lush green forest. There was a large main cabin where we would eat, have our meetings, do crafts and take part in discussion circles. It was like being at a youth sleep-away camp, but for adults . . . who had cancer. We weren't allowed to bunk with our supporters as they didn't want to promote "hanky-panky," so I was roomed up with Pascal, my male counterpart from Africa, who was in Canada on a student visa. Pascal didn't speak English but understood French, so we chatted a bit, but nothing in great depth. *"Comment ça va?"* I asked. *"Ça va bien,"* he replied. That was about it.

I'll be honest, I wanted to leave as soon as I arrived! It was very intimidating and scary as all hell. My mind raced; *What if my hemorrhoids flare up or I get a fever? What if my treatment is different then everyone else's? How will they react to me? How will they respond? This is stupid. I want to go!* It turned out I wasn't alone in my feelings. I later found out that everyone wanted to run. No one wanted to face their fears in front of a group of strangers. Yes, we all had something in common. Yes, we all had cancer. Yes, we were all struggling with our age, our place in life, our physical well-being, our relationships, our jobs, our mortality, our sex life! But we didn't want to share all that shit with strangers. *This is insane! I want to leave!* But we were stuck there. So there was nowhere else to go. We all had to grin and bear it.

As soon as we checked in to our cabins, we gathered in the meeting hall and sat in a giant circle. We were briefly introduced to the supporters and nurses of the program and the owners of the camp. A lovely older couple welcomed us with open arms. "My name's Don and this is my wife and partner, Nola." They were clearly a hippie couple of the '60s with their laid-back attitude, long grey hair and welcoming presence. "I make a mean salad dressing. Everyone loves my special salad dressing," Don went on. The salad dressing was awful. It was basically garlic and vegetable oil. So much garlic it would ward off the mightiest of vampires. Sorry, Don, I love you, but everyone has been lying to you for years! Your dressing is bad.

As we sat in this giant circle, in the rustic log cabin, we were asked to share our stories with one another, one at a time, until everyone had spoken. One of the counsellors explained the rules to the group, "We'd like you to be as open and as honest as you like. Start with your name, your age, your diagnosis and then a brief description of what you are going through and what you hope to get out of this experience." We all shifted a bit in our chairs awkwardly. Sensing our discomfort, she went on, "But rest assured, all your stories and whatever is said here today, will stay confidential. We are here to support each other. This is a safe space." So with that, we began.

To stay true to the confidentiality of my fellow peers, I won't share any of their stories with you. But I will say this: hearing others speak of their experiences and the range of difficulties and challenges each faced was incredibly eye-opening, awe-inspiring and absolutely terrifying at the same time. Some of us were just starting out in treatment, there to receive any advice on what to expect. Some of us were there to share that they had lost hope and the doctors had given them just months to live. Some were long-time survivors, sharing their stories of life after cancer. Many tears were shed. Many tissue boxes were destroyed. I was sitting in a circle of incredible people with incredible energy and strength. This was the strongest group of women I had ever met . . . and of course there was my bunk buddy Pascal, too. We stuck out like sore thumbs, but we were safe.

After our first session of sharing our stories, one of the counsellors mentioned that there would be a talent show at the end of the retreat. "Something fun." Each person was to share one of their talents with the group. It could be anything. I leaned over to Jenny and said, "I should do a bit from the show . . . see how it plays."

"One hundred percent," she replied.

I was nervous but when else can you have a group of 30 cancer patients, survivors and supporters all in one room listening to your cracks on cancer? I had done the show in Toronto to a very supportive crowed, mostly made up of friends and family. They call this a "soft" audience in the business. My metrics for how good the show was, was based on people who already knew me and my sense of humour. If my routine worked at the talent show, however, it would offer true validation that what I was expressing and how I was expressing it was warranted. And these were the people that my show was made for. So, *let's give them a show!*

I did my "cancer makes you gangster" bit. Jenny ran the sound cues on a small CD player from the left edge of the stage. Yes, I instinctively brought a CD with the show tunes on it. Random, I know.

There was an English-to-French interpreter in the audience translating my bit for the non-English speakers. I stood at one end of the stage, called out my signature line, "Now I jaywalk like this!" Jenny pressed play on the 1990s-style boom box and the music played as I walked across the stage, flipping the bird to the audience as a big fuck you to cancer! There wasn't even time to breathe as, in unison, my cancer gangsters all stood up and began to applaud wildly. Even the ones who weren't as physically able as the rest jumped to their feet. They applauded and cried with appreciation. "I'm going to keep it gangster from now on!" one of the girls said. "That was the best!" another chimed in. One shouted, "I'm laughing so hard I might pee!" I was so happy. I was able to give them hope, but more importantly remove their fears and anxieties for a brief moment. We left the retreat reenergized, with a new zest for life. All of us gave each other hope, courage and inspiration. We gave each other ownership of the disease. I would never trade those four days for anything in the world. I came back invigorated and ready to take on the rest of my treatment with a new sense of purpose. We were a team now. I had my people in my corner. There was no stopping me and my gangster squad!

I became close friends with all those beautiful people and kept close contact with a number of them over the years that followed. We all stayed connected for quite some time following our treatments.

Unfortunately, the harsh reality of cancer has since taken a few of these wonderful souls from this earth far too soon. As the years went on, post-treatment, we lost six incredible people from that circle. The pain I felt for all of them stays with me to this day. They will always have a special place in my heart. They helped me in ways I could have never imagined, and I am forever grateful for my time at that retreat with them.

The Show Must Go On

O nce returning from the retreat, I felt compelled to continue to share my story through my show. Initially, I had the intention of performing my show once only at The Second City for my close friends and family. After that, the plan was to finish treatment, return to the stage with my sketch comedy troupe and continue the grind of acting. But the trip to the retreat left me inspired to do more. I decided to bring the show to my hometown of Guelph at the biggest venue in the city called the River Run Centre. My family thought I was a bit crazy, or suffering from chemo brain, to even try taking on such a big space. I was still undergoing treatment but I didn't care. I didn't know what my future held and I guess we never do. So I did it anyway. We sold out the 700-seat theatre to an amazing response. Gangster.

The show then took off from there and we started getting offers from different health organizations to use the show as an opportunity to fundraise for cancer research. I was all for it. It was an opportunity to do what I love, inspire others and raise some money for a good cause at the same time. A triple win!

My most memorable experience occurred when we were

offered to do the show at the Bluma Appel Theatre in the heart of Toronto. It was an 800-seat theatre space reserved for some of the hottest acts in town. Comedians like Russell Brand and my boy Eugene Levy had graced this stage, and now Daniel Amedeo Camillo Stolfi, a cancer-surviving comedian from Guelph was going to tear it the fuck up! This would be my biggest show and it is still the biggest space I've ever played to date. But I didn't do it alone. I couldn't. That would be impossible. Jenny and Ferg were with me every step of the way. My stage manager, Shawn Murphy (Murph), and lighting designer, Michael Chudnovsky (Chudz), were also with me from start to finish. It was a team effort, and in the end, we helped raise $35,000 for Sunnybrook Hospital in one night! We also left a big impression on the comedy community, one large enough to garner the Canadian Comedy Award for Best Solo Show. All the accolades and charitable donations aside, the biggest honour from doing that show came after I stepped off stage and got to interact with the audience waiting in the lobby of the theatre. "That was amazing!" one woman called out as she shook my hand. "So proud of you, Daniel," a friend whispered in my ear. Strangers were actually asking for autographs! One man even told me how he could relate to the part about impotence. I didn't have the heart to tell him that my erections were back, so I just nodded and smiled and said things like, "Yeah, it's hard . . . pun intended."

As I was chatting with some audience members, something caught my eye through the throngs of people. I saw this light pink object bobbing up and down within the crowd, heading directly toward me. As the pink object got closer, I saw that it was a girl wearing a pink headscarf. She had tears streaming down her face. I was immediately terrified. *I must have offended her with my bit about the Weekend to End Breast Cancer. But I mean, come on! The weekend? How are you gonna end cancer over the weekend?! Regardless, here it comes, my first verbal beat down from a cancer survivor.* She was so emotional she couldn't speak. A woman standing next to her, also in tears, began to speak for her. "My sister is very emotional right now," she sputtered out.

"I'm so sorry," I said, slightly terrified. There was a beat. A beat that was long enough for me to think of all the nasty things she was about to say to me. I began thinking of all the apologies that I would have to try and spew out to fix it. She finally spoke. "Don't apologize. My sister wanted me to tell you that you took the words right out of her mouth, tonight." She continued to whimper and laugh at the same time. "I should apologize to you for being so emotional." I didn't know what to say.

"Thank you. Thank you," was all I could say.

"Her name is Miranda, and she thinks you are just amazing and so inspiring." I looked at Miranda and she looked back at me, nodded her head, then cried some more. She continued, "Miranda is dying." Full stop. *Shit.* Time stood still. *This just got very real.* My heart ached. My knees became weak. Then . . . "This was exactly what she needed! You gave her hope. You gave me hope."

Wow. No words were coming. I didn't know what to say. I just reached out and hugged her. I then hugged Miranda and she wept in my arms. "Thank you for being here," I told her.

"Thank you for sharing your story," she whimpered.

It was an incredible moment and I will never forget it. It was the real reason for doing the show. It gave people hope and that was the best feeling in the world.

A few months after my performance at the Bluma Appel Theatre, I received a Facebook friend invitation from Miranda's husband. I didn't know who he was until he sent me a personal message, explaining that Miranda was his wife and that she was in the hospital. Apparently, she was asking about me. Her husband wrote: *Miranda said she'd love it if you could visit. It would mean the world to her. I also think it would help lift her spirits as things aren't going so well right now."*

I asked him which hospital she was staying at and assured him that I would visit her as soon as I could. As fate would have it, she was at Sunnybrook Hospital, on C-3. I hadn't been there since I had left it for the last time in 2009. It had been about two years and there I was, wandering the halls again, the familiar sights, smells and sounds of that eerie space. I entered Miranda's room. She was lying in her bed, her sister and husband flanking her side while seated in their chairs. "Ladies, yeeaaahhhh!" I called out in a loud whisper. Her face lit up. "You have a private room! Lucky," I went on sarcastically. She laughed.

"Thanks for being here!" she said, her voice hoarse and muted. Her husband shot up from his chair and reached out to shake my hand. "Thanks for coming, Daniel. Means a lot." The phone rang, interrupting our very brief encounter.

"You should take that," her sister said. Miranda reached

over and picked up the phone.

"Hello. Yeah. I'll sign them when you bring them. Let's just stick to what we agreed on. Yeah, that's fine." She hung up the phone, frustrated. "Dealing with lawyers," she said matter-of-fact. Silence. *This is heavy.* She was literally on her deathbed working out the details of her will. She was preparing for the inevitable. I couldn't believe that she requested to see me during her last days. I didn't quite know how to be in that moment. Before I could speak, Miranda's sister spoke. "Thanks for coming, Daniel. Miranda is not going to make it." Miranda didn't flinch. She had come to terms with all of it. I was in awe at how well she was dealing with it. How brave she was being.

"Miranda wanted to tell you a story." She then turned to Miranda. "Go ahead, tell him." Miranda coughed subtly and shifted her way up to a seated position in her bed. "After we saw your show, we went out to a bar. I normally would have been in bed at that time, but I said, fuck it! I'm a gangster! And we danced all night. I hadn't danced like that since I got diagnosed. It was the greatest night of my life since all of this. Thank you for giving me and my sister that."

I felt this overwhelming sense of emotion. I felt pride, joy, pain, pride, awe and sadness all mixed into one giant cocktail of something I've never felt before. "Wow. That's incredible. You're so very welcome. Dance like no one's watching, right?" We chatted for a bit longer and then it was time to go. Miranda needed her rest.

Miranda passed away a few days later. Her husband wrote me to break the news. He asked if I would like to go to the funeral, but it was too much for me. I couldn't bring myself to go and politely declined. I wanted to remember Miranda and those moments we shared when she was with us. I still think about her to this day. I think she's dancing her heart out in a country bar somewhere. Unlike me, she loved country music. But hey, whatever makes your feet move and your heart groove, I say, go for it.

New Year. Same Deal.

New Year's Eve had arrived . . . again. Just one year ago, I was ringing in the New Year fast asleep, tired and beaten from the day's chemotherapy treatments. I was determined to ring in this New Year, 2010, awake and with a bang! But cancer doesn't take a break for special occasions. My parents decided to attend a New Year's dinner and dance celebration at some random hall that did this sort of thing year after year, catering to the generation that no longer wanted to go to house parties but still wanted to go out and dance.

I asked Jenny if she wanted to spend New Year's Eve with me, in Guelph, at my parents' house. "We have the house to ourselves and we can dress up all fancy and order pizza while we watch the countdown," I suggested.

"I love it!" she exclaimed.

"I'll wear a suit!"

I figured I'd be able to fit into one of my old suits, as I had been packing back on some of the pounds.

"I'll wear the new dress I just got!" Jenny said excitedly.

My parents were all set to leave the house just as soon as Jenny arrived. There was a knock at the front door. I walked toward the door, but Mom whizzed by me and beat me to it. "You look beautiful!" Mom told Jenny as she greeted her.

"Thank you. And you look lovely as well," Jenny returned the compliment.

"Thank you. Thank you." Mom spun as Dad rolled his eyes. "Okay, we will leave you two for the night and see you in the new year!" They left the house excitedly and closed the door. This was one of their first nights out together in a long time.

"Nice suit, Stolfi! You look great!" Jenny said with a big beaming smile.

"Thanks, Jenny. Still fits . . . sort of." The suit jacket didn't fit the same in the shoulders or chest. It was bigger, baggier now. "You look great too!"

We sat in the living room for a while and played cards. I removed my jacket and took a seat on my cancer couch. I felt warm. "Did my parents crank up the heat in here?" I asked Jenny, now feeling even more flushed.

"I don't know. I feel fine. Are you okay?" Jenny asked.

"Yeah. I'm fine. Just feeling funny."

"Do you want to eat anything? We can order pizza," Jenny suggested.

"I'm feeling really funky." I was beginning to sweat now. "I think I should check my temperature." Jenny popped up from the couch and bee-lined it for the cupboard where my parents kept all my cancer paraphernalia. Chemo pills, mouth-sore rinse, hemorrhoid creams and, of course, a thermometer. Jenny checked my temperature: 38.8. A fever.

"Dr. Chang said that anything over thirty-eight, I need to get myself to emergency," I said disappointedly. I was slightly terrified but couldn't show it.

"We're not playing with a few decimal points here, Stolfi. Let's go!" Jenny instructed. I grabbed my wallet, Jenny grabbed her purse and we jumped in her car and drove to Guelph General Hospital.

We arrived at the hospital around 9 p.m. I leaned over to Jenny and said, "I hope we can be back home before midnight."

Jenny looked at me like I was crazy. "Who cares about New Year's! I only care about you!"

"Fair point." We put on our pale blue masks, tucked the elastic bands behind our ears and sat in the emergency waiting room . . . and waited. We were called into a room around 10 p.m. The doctor working the night shift was very kind. He hooked me up to an IV with a bag of saline solution and handed me a couple pills of Tylenol while Jenny sat by my side holding my hand.

"Anything over thirty-eight you should come in. You made the right call," the doctor assured me. "Fevers can be life-threatening for cancer patients."

"Well, that's fun," I said sarcastically. He laughed.

"You should be fine, but better to be safe than sorry."

He could tell I was getting anxious to get out of there as the clock ticked closer to midnight and my temperature slowly ticked lower. "You think we'll get out of here before midnight?" I asked.

"I don't think so. But I'll tell ya what I'll do. I'll dim the lights and close the door and you can ring in the New Year together." The lights dimmed, the door closed and Jenny and I sat in silence as the large analog clock on the wall ticked closer to midnight.

We started the countdown: "Ten. Nine. Eight. Seven. Six. Five. Four. Three. Two. One! Happy New Year!" we whisper-shouted. We lowered our fancy surgical masks and kissed.

"Happy New Year, Stolfi!"

"Happy New Year, Jenny!"

We put our masks back up and waited for the saline solution to slowly drip through.

Last Treatments

It was March 17th, 2010. My second-last chemotherapy treatment. This treatment would occur in Guelph. They had this interesting tradition in Guelph, and I've heard at other hospitals as well, where patients get to ring a bell to signify their completion of treatment. After the last bit of yellow liquid ran through the plastic tube sticking out of my chest, I got up from my chemo chair and I rang the shit out of that bell! The nurses made a toast in my honour with non-alcoholic Jell-O shots to congratulate my victory. They even got me a card, which they all signed. I was beyond grateful. They were so supportive in Guelph. Guelph General Hospital had become a second home for me. The staff was like family. I got to hang out with them almost every week. I got to know about their lives, and they got to know about mine. They were supporters of my show and my art. They all came to my show in Guelph and were the first to reserve 20 tickets front-row centre. There was a deep love there and it was actually really hard to say goodbye. I missed them. I still do. Yes, they were poking me with needles and administering me with heavy amounts of chemotherapy, but it was my new normal for so long and I was starting to oddly enjoy the routine. I felt safe there. But it was time to say goodbye.

~

My chemotherapy treatment officially ended exactly two years after it first began. March 24th, 2010 was day 730 of 730. I was back in Toronto two years to the day from when it all started. I thought for sure there would be some sort of special send-off like there was in Guelph. I thought for sure there would be some sort of recognition for raising money for the hospital, as little as it was, and a couple tears shed by the nursing staff for the time we spent together over the last two years. Sadly, there was no tickertape parade. No bell to ring. No Jell-O shots. *Why should there be? I was just another patient, like all the others. Suck it up buttercup.*

My name was called out: "Daniel Stoppi." A short Filipino nurse waved me over. I made my way through the familiar doors into the familiar room and sat in the familiar pink puffy chair to get my last dose of familiar chemotherapy. "Today's my last day," I told the nurse with a smile.

"Oh, that's nice," she said. "Address and telepone still the same?"

"Yes," I replied. Then, she stuck the needle into my port and the chemo began to drip into my heart. An hour later, she returned, ripped the bandage off my chest, took out the needle and bid me farewell. *Just another day at the office.*

I was done. That was it.

I was OK with the fact that there wasn't a big to-do. I was

just happy to finally be done. The reality of it all hit me pretty hard in that moment. I went through the entire chemotherapy process thinking that when it was all said and done something magical would happen, like the skies would open up and someone would give me some sort of medal of honour or something ridiculous like that. However, I quickly realized that no one was going to give me anything. Life goes on. But it didn't matter that I didn't "get anything," because I got something even better anyway. Something I had been wanting every second, every minute, every hour and every day, for two full years. I got my fucking life back. I got my LIFE back! I get my life back? What does that even mean? I get to go back to work? I get to go back to the gym? I get to go back to a new relationship? Back to stressing out about work, the gym and my new relationship!? What is life, anyway? Cancer really puts things into perspective, and for me, it taught me three things about life. Ever since I walked out of those hospital doors for the last time life was, and will forever be, about three things: health, family and friends. Without those three things, you have nothing. If you ever find yourself without one of them, you'll need the other two to carry you through. Take care of those things. Cherish them. Don't ever take them for granted.

~

Although I was done my treatment, I didn't feel like I was fully ready to celebrate my demolishment of cancer. I was in this grey area, not really happy and not really sad, just grey. There was still one thing left to be done. The shackles had to come off. I had to get the damn port out of my chest. The little plastic device inside my body was a constant reminder that cancer and I were still going at it. He still had his claws in me. So until I took it out, it wasn't quite over for me. I asked Dr. Chang if I could get it removed as soon as possible, and the following week, I was scheduled to have it taken out.

I lay on a hospital bed surrounded by a blue curtain in some area of the hospital that I'm sure I had been in before. I was fully awake and had a front-row seat of the procedure. "We just need to freeze the area first," the surgeon explained. "It's a lot easier to take out than it is to put in." A sexual innuendo or two went through my mind but I opted not to make a joke. I watched him cut me open with a razor-sharp scalpel, stick his blue latex-gloved finger into my chest, remove some silver wire clamps and pull the device out of the blood-soaked hole in my chest. I barely almost fainted. *Minor victories.*

"Can I keep it?" I asked.

"Uh, sure. Why not?" he said, casually. He instructed one of his assistants to clean it up and put it in a clear plastic cup with some saline solution in it. He handed the cup to me and I took a moment to examine the floating object inside. A white plastic ball, about the size of a pinball, with a thin blue tube extending from either end hung weightless in the saline solution. That was it. *This thing helped save my life,* I thought. *This will be my medal of honour.*

I left the hospital with Mom. We drove back to Guelph in silence, reflecting. I sat on my parents' deck with my medal propped up on the patio table. I looked out at the sun setting over the giant cedar trees in my parents' backyard. The warm rays tickled my face. I was at peace. Then, this overwhelming sense of accomplishment came over me. All of a sudden, this little plastic ball started to hold so much more meaning. I was overcome with this feeling of pride and joy, met by a flood of *did I really do it? Is it really over? Yes! Fuck. Yes!* I stood up, walked into the house, hugged Mom and shouted, "We did it! We did it!" She wrapped her arms around me, and we hugged as I began to cry. Mom held me and said, "Yes Daniel, you did."

It was finally over.

From Mom

Daniel asked me to write a chapter to share my experience as his mother and main caregiver during his battle with cancer. I had a front-row seat so I saw it all. I have many blessings in my life but the greatest blessings by far are my three children, Nadia, Andrew and Daniel. When Daniel was born I remember feeling that my family was complete. I had three beautiful, healthy children. I thought the rest would be easy. I just had to raise them, love them and keep them safe and happy until they left home to live their own lives.

When Daniel was diagnosed with the biggest threat imaginable, Amedeo and I went into support mode for Daniel. Yes, I became Daniel's main caregiver during his two years of treatment. And I am immensely grateful that I was able to do it.

It is said that it takes a village to raise a child. It is also true that it took a village to bring Daniel back to health. His sister, Nadia, lived in Montreal at the time. She was pregnant with her first child, our first grandchild. She made the trip by train as often as she could to be with her brother. "I just want my brother back!" she once shared with me. Our son Andrew was engaged to be married. He lived in Guelph and would visit often. He was confident that Daniel would do well with the treatment and be well again. At least that is what he told me. Daniel was in his second year of treatment when he was best man for Andrew's wedding. Amedeo was still working. Like me, he put on a good front emotionally, drove when I couldn't, and came to appointments whenever he could.

I had known that Daniel had made some good friends but I had not known what wonderful, authentic human beings they were. Jenny, Jessie, Crystal, Rusa, Shawn, Ryan, Jonah, Jeff and Sarah, to name a few, were there for him. They came to visit and spent time with him. Sometimes they would show up at the Odette Clinic when they knew he was coming in for treatment. Jenny visited him often. She made the drive from Toronto to Guelph. She had a way of lifting his spirits.

My family and Amedeo's family went into support mode too. They visited, they called, they prayed. We know they did everything in their power to help us and we are immensely grateful. Like us they feared that they would lose one of their own.

Sometimes, to be honest, I came away from my supporters deflated. I know that everyone meant well. But any time I heard a comment that made me see the horror of the situation, comments that reminded me that we could lose Daniel, I felt disheartened and weakened. My oldest and dearest friend suggested I contact Hospice. She had always given me good advice, so I didn't even bother to find out what kind of facility Hospice was. I trusted her advice and I needed support, so I called and made an appointment. I hadn't realized that Hospice was an end-of-life facility until the lovely lady who was to be my counsellor shared that she had lost her adult daughter to cancer ten years earlier. I cut the meeting short. I did not make another appointment. I needed supports that would nurture my hope, not fuel my fears.

The chemotherapy was brutal. My son was skin and bones, his face pasty white, his eyes stark and empty, his head bald, his voice weak. We had watched our baby grow into a beautiful young man ready to live life to the fullest and in a few short weeks he was felled. He had lost 50 pounds and aged 50 years. Watching Daniel transform from a confident, strong, handsome young man of 25 to an emaciated humbled old man in a few short weeks was heart-wrenching. But I could not let it show! I had to hold my tears in check. I had to stay strong for him so that his resolve to beat this beast would not weaken. I thought of Terry Fox who had fought hard and lost his life to cancer. From time to time we would learn that cancer patients we had met at the Odette Clinic had lost their lives to cancer. When the fear of losing our son tried to take over, I remembered his doctor's words, "You have an aggressive cancer, but it responds well to treatment. It is curable." *Curable* was the word I repeated over and over to myself when things got challenging.

Daniel was officially declared cancer-free in March 2010. He had follow-up appointments with his oncologist at three months, then six months and then annually for the next ten years. I went with him to his appointments. I held my breath each time, hopeful that everything was normal. We knew the survival markers, two years, five years, ten years. After ten years the oncologist did not want to see him anymore. It was what we had been hoping for but also sad; we were saying good-bye to a good friend.

It took some time for Daniel to get back to normalcy. He did it one step at a time. It took time for me to stop holding my breath and be less fearful and be fully present in life. I had to work at it and take it one step at a time too. I'm still working at it. But that's me. The reality is that when someone you love hurts, you hurt. That pain is magnified when it's your child that's hurting. It's a trauma that takes time to get over. There were times when Daniel wanted to give up because it was so hard on him. He had to really fight hard. I am so grateful that he chose to fight and stay with us.

Not everyone who faces cancer is as fortunate as we were. We were fortunate that Daniel's cancer was treatable. We are fortunate that we had an amazing highly skilled team of medical professionals to treat him. We are fortunate that Daniel had the courage and will to keep going. We are fortunate that he is still with us today. I pray for those families who have lost a loved one to this awful disease. Each individual and each cancer is different. What is common to all cancer diagnoses is the sheer terror it metes out.

For All the Cancer Gangsters

So I beat cancer . . . Now what?

So I beat cancer! Congratulations! Now what the fuck do I do? It's incredible to think that when all is said and done, the nausea, the vomiting, the hair loss, the weight loss, the weight gain, the near brushes with death, the headaches, the money spent, the sleepless nights, the mood swings, the hot flashes, the "why me's," the awkward conversations with friends and family, the frustration, the fear, the fights with my mother, the highs, the lows, the laughs, the tears, all of it . . . What in the hell does it all mean? I went through all that . . . so now what?

A lot of my cancer survivor friends, who I had met and grown closer to over my treatment, all faced the same sort of dilemma. "We're still young and we've been given this weird second chance at life where we can either go back to the banking job we had or succumb to this weird pressure to do something epic . . . like cure cancer!" Some people felt really compelled to get involved in charities, others felt compelled to travel the world and some just wanted to go back to their life . . . the way it was. At the end of the day, there is no right answer as to how you re-inject yourself into the world.

A word of advice: Don't feel any pressure to do anything. Do whatever your heart tells you to do. There is something beautiful about cancer, though. It can always put your "problems" into perspective. The missed job opportunity is suddenly not that big of a deal. The sore lower back is probably just constipation. The barber messed up your haircut? Big deal! You have hair!

Somewhere along the way, however, two, three, four years down the road, that ability to put things into perspective started to slip for me and I found myself practicing old habits. I started to question if I could or should do this or that. I started to wonder, *What will people think if I do this or that?* I was sweating the little things again. But then the cancer gangster in me smacked me in the face and shouted, "Who gives a fuck about what people think! You had motherfucking cancer!!" So, with that, do what you love. Do what makes you happy. Cancer is, in some ways, a gift. I never thought in my wildest dreams that I would ever say that! Cancer is the greatest teacher you could ever have. I don't wish cancer on anyone, but if you are going through it right now, as you are reading this book, try to embrace it. Try to own it. Once you take ownership of your cancer, you will find a way to live with it, endure it, get stronger as a result of it and if you are fortunate enough to get through it, live a long and rewarding life after it.

Keep it gangster. Always.

Epilogue

With the intention of only ever performing my show once, since its debut, I have performed *Cancer Can't Dance Like This* more than 50 times across Canada. The show has helped raise over $100,000 for cancer research and other life-saving initiatives. In October of 2011, my team and I won the Canadian Comedy Award for Best One-Person Show. The show has also been performed off-Broadway in New York City and in multiple cities across the US. I became a member of the Playwright's Guild of Canada and found an amazing supportive agent who reignited my acting career. I continued to date the lovely Jenny De Lucia, until July 7th, 2012, when I proposed to her in Central Park, in New York City. We married on September 21st, 2013, and we are happy. So fucking happy! We also inherited the beautiful emerald green Hyundai Elantra from my parents, called it "Baby Girl," and then drove it into the ground! I play recreational league soccer again and have helped win five men's league Division B championships! I work out three times a week and if you asked me to run 5K tomorrow or hold my breath and swim the length of a swimming pool, underwater, I could. I have a new life. A new normal. A normal that still comes with the ups and downs life will throw your way. My hair isn't as thick as it once was but it's there, curly again, on top of my head where it belongs. My memory's not as sharp, my vision's a little weaker, and my butt is still a bit of a pain in the, well, butt. But I love my butt. Life goes on:

~

On January 30th, 2015, *Cancer Can't Dance Like This* had its final curtain call, to a sold-out theatre of 330 people in downtown Toronto at The Great Hall, five and a half years since its premiere.

Shortly after that show, I decided that there was one last thing I needed to do.

I returned to the fertility clinic where I had been keeping my sperm frozen for the last seven years. "I'd like to check my counts, to see if my sperm came back on its own," I told the same blond receptionist, cleavage still busting out of her top. *She's still rocking the same low-cut top, eh? Good for her.*

She sent me to the familiar room but this time the leather chair was covered in parchment paper, so this time, I took a seat. My parents weren't in the parking lot and the clinic only had DVDs now. I pushed play. *Inferno 3* was the movie of choice. No jail, no security guards, no incredible plotline this time . . . just straight to business. I did what I had to do, and I handed my plastic cup to the nurse. Three days later I got the phone call as I sat at the dinner table with Jenny and my family, which had now grown to 12.

"This is Dr. Stern from the fertility clinic. You called regarding your recent deposit?"

"Yes, I did," I replied anxiously.

"Very healthy counts," she continued. "All is normal with roughly 35 million moving and active sperm. That's really good. Congratulations! Bye now."

A shot of adrenalin surged throughout my body.

"I'm back, baby! I'm back!" I shouted. I popped a bottle of champagne with Jenny, Mom, Dad, my brother, sister, sister-in-law, brother-in-law, niece and three nephews to celebrate. We laughed about it because we are weird, but happy and grateful.

~

I am now over ten years out of treatment. My last annual follow-up was March 24th, 2018, exactly ten years to the day since I started my treatment. I no longer have to go to the Sunnybrook Odette Cancer Clinic to see my oncologist. I am no longer considered a cancer patient. I am officially cured. I celebrated this by creating a ten-year anniversary follow-up production of *Cancer Can't Dance Like This* and performed it to a sold-out crowd in Toronto on May 30th, 2019, exactly ten years and one day from the original show. Jenny and I live in Toronto and have been happily married for seven years now. We got a dog and named him Pacino!! I write these words during the global pandemic of 2020. Life is crazy. The world is crazy. It's what you make of it that makes all the difference. I still carry cancer around with me every day. There is still not a day that goes by that I don't think about it. I don't think about it in a negative way, though. I think about cancer when I'm experiencing all the little things in life that we can easily take for granted. When I'm sitting in my backyard, with the warm sun shining on my face, I think about all the sunny days I had to stay inside because the sun felt like acid on my skin, and I think, *damn . . . this is living!* When I shave my beard and I have to clean up the tiny hairs on the bathroom sink that are starting to go grey, I think about how lucky I am to be getting old enough to witness my hair starting to go grey! I use cancer as a source of inspiration to keep fighting, not an excuse to give up. Thank you, cancer, for giving me more than just my life back. Thanks for making me stronger and teaching me about what truly matters in life . . . but seriously, fuck cancer!

~

Oh . . . and on January 17th, 2021, day 4683 of 730, at 1:55 a.m., Jenny and I welcomed our daughter Etta Rose into this wild and wonderful world. I guess my boys can swim! I guess she'll be considered a "Quaranteener" or "Corona Baby," or whatever clever generational tag some social media influencer comes up with. Either way, we love her madly. She has curly hair!!

I hope she gets to read this book one day. Maybe when she's really mad at me for not letting her go on a date or something, I'll say, "Read this! Look what me and your mother had to go through to bring you into this world!"

To your health, family and friends.

Thanks for reading this book.

Me and my best friend, Jenny, on our wedding day, Sept 21, 2013.
Photo credit: Renaissance Photography

My last day of chemo in Guelph, March 17, 2010.

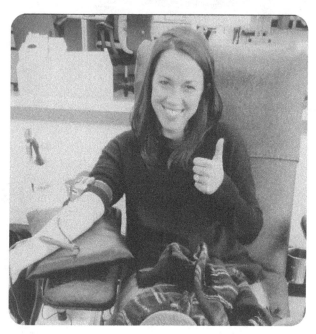

My lovely wife, Jenny, giving blood. She's A+ I'm B- . . .
so we are way off! But she's saving someone's life.

Opening night of *Cancer Can't Dance Like This* at
The Second City Toronto, May 29, 2009. Me playing My Hair,
Capo Capelli, The Italian barber. (I'm wearing a wig.)

Cancer Can't Dance Like This – 10-Year Anniversary Special, May 30, 2019.
Photo credit: Jessie Gabe

Acknowledgements

There are a number of people I'd like to acknowledge, for without them, this book would not be possible.

My wife and partner, Jennifer De Lucia, for encouraging me to publish this book, always encouraging me to go for it and for being the best partner in life. My mother, Elsa, for editing my shit grammar, saving my life and reading this memoir six times! My father, Amedeo, for always keeping things light and supporting me in whatever I do. My siblings: Andrew, Nadia, Maria, Savaria and The Kids for their support and encouragement. Nadia, thanks for doing a pass on this as well!!

The De Lucia Family: Bill, Mamma Jo, Billy, Laura, Becky, Roque, Emmy, Matt and all the kids (they keep coming). Thank you for always supporting me and Jenny in all of our artistic endeavours.

The Crew: Jenny De Lucia for crushing it with me at every show!! Andrew Ferguson for your direction, asking why and for always pushing me to do better. Michael Chudnovsky, the best lighting designer a guy could ask for. Shawn Murphy for hitting cues! Gerrard Suyao for the amazing sound design. Jon Nelson for being a super fan and coming to almost every show!

Breanne TeBoekerst for the sick digs. Deanna Palazzo Dalzell, for locking down The Second City and being an OG.

My mentors, family and friends: Alan Filewod, Cathy Sullivan, Zal Press, Dr. Matthew Cheung, Gian Cavallo, Patrick Yang, Jeff Guillemette, Casey Dutfield, Kendall Anderson, Katie Anderson, Dave McConnell and Sarah Mac. Carly Wahl, for being my book buddy and pushing me to keep writing. Rusa Jeremic, Dimetre Alexiou, Crystal Koskinen, Dean Buchanan, Don Gervasi, Niheer Ravaliya, Rajeev Billing, Stefan Tochev, Elena Tochev, Steve Kirkwood, Matt Hodgson, Heather Marshall, Jon Corbin, Kevin Morris, Reva Nelson, Scotty Adams, Ryan and Konya Kayet for being such huge supporters throughout my journey and beyond. Ari Goren and Zach Spalla for being my cancer clinic chemo buddies and beacons of hope! Jessie Gabe, for always being there and the sweet testimonial! Amish Patel and Bobby Umar. Shawn Ahmed, for always checking in on me on Wednesdays. Beth and Jonah for being Beth and Jonah. Amanda Baine, Lindsay Banack and Christina Doyle for the title feedback and constant support. Dominic Smith for providing your invaluable feedback and for being a fan of Jordin Sparks. Shane C, for giving me hope to get back out on the pitch. Davide Di Renzo, for the chats in hospital and giving me a place to live in Toronto! Dario Di Renzo, for the Thursday afternoon lunches and Raptors games. I cherish our conversations. Emily Klama and my whole crew of agents at The ART Agency. Mario Tassone for saying "yes" to this book and being the best publicist ever!

The Canadian Cancer Society, Sue Robson and Lymphoma

Canada. Geoff Eaton and Karine Chalifour at Young Adult Cancer Canada for introducing me to the most amazing community of survivors and for "getting it." The Breast Cancer Foundation. Tyler and Caitlin at Apt. Vince and Bruna Barzotti and Barzotti Woodworking for loving me and sponsoring the show! The nurses of Oncology and my team at Sunnybrook Hospital. The entire team at Tellwell! All of my friends and supporters who came to all my shows over the years! I can't thank you enough! And last but not least, all of my aunts, uncles and cousins who make up my giant, supportive and loving Italian famiglia.

To the friends that I have lost to this disease, you will be missed. Thank you for your inspiration. Thank you for sharing your stories. Alston, Dawn, Wei Fun, Pascal, Rutunga Nadine, Marie Claire, Anne Marie, Balinda, Miranda, Jasmin and Emmanuel. Love you all. Keep it gangster up there and save some space on the dance floor for me.

About the Author

Daniel Stolfi is an award-winning actor, writer, comedian and producer from Toronto, Canada. He is a graduate of the University of Guelph Theatre program, the Second City Conservatory program and studied comedy in New York City at the Upright Citizens Brigade. For the stage, Daniel has written and produced four original plays. Most notably, his Canadian Comedy Award–winning one-person show, *Cancer Can't Dance Like This*, which toured across the country, playing in almost every major city in Canada, while raising over $100,000 for cancer-related charities. In 2019, Daniel wrote and produced a revamped version of *Cancer Can't Dance Like This* to celebrate the ten-year anniversary production at The Great Hall in Toronto.

Daniel has performed on stages all over North America and can be seen in award-winning television shows and films on networks such as: CBC, Netflix, Amazon, USA Network and BBC America.

Daniel currently resides in Toronto and lives with his wonderful wife and producing partner Jennifer De Lucia, their super-cute dog, Pacino Stolfi, and the love of their lives, Etta Rose Stolfi.

This is Daniel's first book.

CPSIA information can be obtained
at www.ICGtesting.com
Printed in the USA
BVHW071409300122
627213BV00002B/10

9 780228 863274